THE GREAT ESCAPE

"Annabelle is a superb travel writer. This book is deeply researched, and brought wonderfully to life through her telling of Britain's 400 years of holiday history, through the earliest rail holidays to package holidays on the Med. It's nostalgic, inspiring and also extremely endearing; a real heartwarming portrait of Britain and our love of time off. I couldn't put it down."
Cathy Adams, *The Times* travel desk

"Behind *The Great Escape*'s whimsical look at the Brits' love affair with the holiday is the true insider voice of Annabelle Thorpe. She has her finger on the pulse of past, present and future travel."
Jane Anderson, Travel Editor at *Prima* magazine

"From (just about) no tourism to overtourism, Thorpe reports on the rise of holidaymaking in the country that invented it. This is a concise, incisive analysis of how we have adapted to use our leisure time as technology – from trains to jet planes and the internet – has advanced and opened up the globe. How we spend our time off tells us a lot about who we are – and Thorpe understands that."
Tom Chesshyre, author of *Slow Trains Around Britain*

"Full of fascinating titbits and with prose like velvet, *The Great Escape* reads like a 300-page holiday."
Ben Aitken, author of *Sh*tty Breaks*

"An engaging, perceptive and thought-provoking exploration of the evolution of the British holiday, covering everything from spa breaks and seaside resorts to climate change and overtourism. Deftly blending history, interviews and personal stories, Annabelle Thorpe writes with charm and style about how, where and why we travel."
Shafik Meghji, author of *Small Earthquakes*

"Annabelle Thorpe uses her considerable experience as a travel journalist to cast a perceptive and often witty eye over the past 400 years of how the Brits have holidayed, both at home and abroad. The result is an engaging, entertaining, enlightening and insightful social history."
Mary Novakovich, author of *My Family and Other Animals*

THE GREAT ESCAPE

BRITAIN'S 400-YEAR LOVE AFFAIR WITH HOLIDAYS

Annabelle Thorpe

First published in Great Britain in 2026 by
DK RED, an imprint of
Dorling Kindersley Limited
20 Vauxhall Bridge Road,
London SW1V 2SA

The authorized representative in the EEA is
Dorling Kindersley Verlag GmbH. Arnulfstr. 124,
80636 Munich, Germany

Copyright © 2026 Dorling Kindersley Limited
A Penguin Random House Company
10 9 8 7 6 5 4 3 2 1
001–351605–May/2026

Text copyright © Annabelle Thorpe 2026
Annabelle Thorpe has asserted her right to be identified
as the author of this work.

All rights reserved.

No part of this publication may be reproduced, stored in or
introduced into a retrieval system, or transmitted, in any form, or
by any means (electronic, mechanical, photocopying, recording,
or otherwise), without the prior written permission of the
copyright owner.

DK values and supports copyright. Thank you for respecting
intellectual property laws by not reproducing, scanning or
distributing any part of this publication by any means without
permission. By purchasing an authorized edition, you are
supporting writers and artists and enabling DK to continue
to publish books that inform and inspire readers.
No part of this publication may be used or reproduced in
any manner for the purpose of training artificial intelligence
technologies or systems. In accordance with Article 4(3)
of the DSM Directive 2019/790, DK expressly reserves this work
from the text and data mining exception.

A CIP catalogue record for this book
is available from the British Library.
ISBN: 978-0-2417-6416-9

Printed and bound in the United Kingdom

www.dk.com

For my Dad, who always knew
the value of a good holiday

Contents

Introduction	**9**
Waddling to the Waters	**15**
A Grand Adventure	**33**
The Search for the Picturesque	**49**
Beside the Seaside	**65**
The Wings of the Wind	**79**
A Place to Stay	**95**
The Great Outdoors	**109**
Wakes Weeks	**123**
Good Morning Campers!	**137**
The Rush to the Med	**151**
Cruise Control	**167**
Holidays on Screen	**183**
The New Wave	**197**
Passports Down	**211**
Where Next?	**225**
Acknowledgements	**239**
Notes	**243**
Bibliography	**265**
Index	**269**

Introduction

June 2025, Sussex

As I write this, the great British summer has finally arrived. The mercury is touching 30°C, all anyone can talk about is how impossible it is to sleep, and the early-evening air is already tinged with June's signature scent of barbecues and mown grass. Tonight, the rain will sweep in and the temperatures will fall, but no one will mind; this is holiday season, the brief heatwave a glimpse of what awaits us in Mallorca, or Santorini, or wherever we've chosen for this year's getaway. Plans are afoot, cat-sitters booked, shops full of tropical-print swimwear, deeply impractical sparkly sandals and floppy straw hats that will get crumpled in transit and never actually worn. Conversation in offices and pubs (and hairdressers, naturally) is all about when and where and how long for, and whether we plan to do nothing or everything, all day long.

Few things unite us as a nation, increasingly so these days, but holidays are one. We didn't need a pandemic to prove how important they are to us Brits, but it served as a reminder, all the same. What was once a luxury for the wealthy few has become an essential part of our lives; whether a family holiday to Spain, a spa weekend with the girls, a long-haul adventure with temples and tuk-tuks or a few days rambling through the

British countryside. Instagram and TikTok flicker and roll with endless images of foreign sunsets and faraway adventures, bios on dating apps are littered with lists of countries and bucket list ticks. The internet is crammed with infinite travel sites; booking engines, villa rentals, reviews, recommendations and thousands of blogs and travel pages written by those keen to share their adventures with the world.

And I'm one of them. If such a thing as the explorer gene exists, I'm pretty sure I have it; even as a little girl, I was always inexhaustibly curious for what was round the next corner, across the field, on the other side of the hill. I remember my dad's tales of military service in Myanmar (then Burma) and Singapore after the war, how extraordinary and adventurous it sounded; family holidays to Corfu and Croatia (then Yugoslavia) that stamped themselves in my mind. As a teen, I loved films set overseas: *Out of Africa*, *Shirley Valentine*, *Roman Holiday* – all of them exotic, exciting places I was desperate to visit. But it was a holiday to Turkey with my sister Deborah, the year after university, that really lit the touchpaper; one week that we stretched into two, then a whole summer – and a realisation that this beautiful, extraordinary country I was getting to know was just one of a whole world full I could explore.

It didn't happen immediately. But after many months of sending ideas and pestering editors, I got my first travel commission for the *Daily Mail*. Fast-forward twenty-five years, and I've spent those two-and-a-half decades crisscrossing the world in search of stories. I've driven through deserts and across Asian cities, crossed China and the US by train, stayed in five-star palaces and basic B&Bs, and talked to hotel magnates, campsite owners, safari guides, winemakers, concierges and everyone in between. My travels have been rather like stitching together a huge, global quilt; countries and cultures slowly patchworked to form a tapestry of the myriad ways we take our holidays, and the huge and diverse impact the tourism industry has.

Since the pandemic, I have found myself wondering more and more about how this love affair with holidays began. How, in the great sweep of history, did we go from a society that did little but eat, work and sleep, to one where holidays and leisure time are prized above almost all else? Did someone just wake up one morning and say, "What ho! How about a day out to Brighthelmstone?" (as Brighton was once known). Who decided that stepping away from our everyday lives would be good for us? Were seaside towns really the first tourist resorts? Where did cruise ships come from, and who gave us glamping? Most importantly, what is the point of a pier?

Perhaps at this point I should have done the obvious thing: Googled for answers and gone on about my business. Instead, I thought it might make an interesting book. And so I've spent the last eight months researching, reading, travelling and interviewing, to uncover a story of seismic social change across four centuries. The story of our love affair with holidays is stitched through every great development of the last 400 years, from the first Turnpike Trusts, which built the early road network, to the coming of the railways, through medical discoveries and scientific inventions that propelled us forwards and out into the world. And it's shown me that exploration and discovery are an innate part of what it is to be human; right back to the time when "holiday" was yet to be invented as a word and "holydays" – a celebration of a saint's birthday – were the working man's only chance to lay down his tools and indulge in a glass of mead or three.

It's a story that's taken me from the gargantuan peaks of Glencoe to the sunny shores of Torquay, along Edwardian cycle routes and Victorian railway lines, to archives and museums and galleries, where passionate local historians have shared letters and articles, pictures and stories that open up their corner of the past. And although I've dipped my toe into foreign waters on a couple of occasions, this is a story that is quintessentially British, filled with unique characters – from the Reverend William Gilpin, who wrote the first British guidebook, to Martha Gunn, Brighton's redoubtable Queen of the Dippers.

Because while holidays are a universal pleasure – at least in our privileged, Western corner of the world – there are few places where the desire to get away, shrug off the everyday and slow the pace is felt more keenly than in the UK. Where many Americans have two weeks' paid holiday a year, we have four (at least). While many Europeans have a second home they return to year after year – fortunate to be able to experience the warm Mediterranean climate without leaving their country – we flock to airports and ferry terminals, piling into cars and coaches in our millions. Why is this need stitched into our very bones? Perhaps it's the climate, perhaps it's that we're an island people, perhaps – however much we don't care to admit it – one of the legacies of Empire is a familiarity with the far corners of the world, through family and (often deeply problematic) business connections that reach back generations.

Finding an answer to that question – the root of our deep-seated love, and need, for holidays – was one of the starting points for this book, although it quickly became clear I would be exploring not one, but three strands of social behaviour. Holidays are very different from "time off". Neither is the same as "travelling". Anything that allows us to step away from the everyday and experience something different can be classed as a holiday – even a week off work spent at home can come under that definition. But in reality, each of the three offers something very different, as evidenced by the endless articles and books (many with a strong tinge of snobbery) about why being a "tourist" is very different from being a "traveller".

It's a difference I'm aware of in my own life: a week with Mark, my husband, lying by a pool in Turkey, is a holiday. Heading to my sister Caroline's house, for a few days in the beautiful Monmouthshire countryside, is time off, while a solo trip driving through Oman, or crossing China by train, is "travelling". All three offer similar rewards – a change of scene, the ability to step away from the pressures of everyday life – but the first two bring the chance for relaxation and an opportunity to recharge, while the last is about stimulation, discovery and the thrill of an adventure into the unknown (one of my all-time favourite feelings). And so, alongside an exploration of what makes our holidays so precious, *The Great Escape* has also become a celebration of our desire to explore, to immerse ourselves in new experiences, to move beyond that which we know and discover a version of the world that is entirely different to our own – and the power of both "holidays" and "travelling" to change who we are and what we want from our lives.

It's also a story without an ending. As well as looking back, I wanted to explore what the future holds for our holidays, at a time when climate change and overtourism are causing us to ask real questions about how we'll travel in the future. Do our habits need to change? Perhaps more importantly, *will they?* In the years to come, will we be sunning ourselves on the Scandinavian coast, jetting off to the Spanish costas in January and taking virtual holidays in the Metaverse? Because one thing's for certain – no one is giving up their holidays any time soon. They are our joy, our sanity, our most cherished moments, our time with those we love. They have become an integral part of who we are and how we live our lives.

And this is how it happened.

1
Waddling to the Waters
Bath and Buxton

"Oh! Who can ever be tired of Bath?"[1]
Jane Austen

Tricky things, beginnings. According to Julie Andrews, whose wisdom – whether channelled as Mary Poppins, Maria Von Trapp or Lady Whistledown herself – is usually beyond question, starting at the very beginning is a very good place to start. On this occasion, however, I'm not sure she's right. That's the problem with history – when exactly does it begin? And if you're exploring one particular aspect – say, for example, holidays – how do you decide when *that* starts? History has an unhelpful tendency to throw up a load of facts that point to something beginning at a particular time and then, just when you've written it all down, an unexpected twist of fate pops up to prove that what you believed had begun in the 17th century also happened in 1569, and quite possibly the 14th century too, and maybe even during the Dark Ages, mostly because they were Dark, and therefore no one can be quite sure what happened, if anything happened at all. So, I'm going to stick my flag in the sand and say that the story of holidays begins in 1562. Yes, the Romans had their annual week of Saturnalia, when banks closed and servants were given time off, and the kind of drunken debauchery went on that would make a 1990s 18–30 holiday in Ibiza look like a whist drive in Eastbourne. And yes, possibly there was a wet Wednesday in 1487 when two monks on a pilgrimage went a bit heavy on the mead and inadvertently invented the concept of "duvet days", while lying in a heap in Malmesbury Abbey. But for the sake of this book, the story of holidays begins with William Turner, physician and Dean of Wells Cathedral, who published the snappily titled *A Booke of the natures & properties as well of the Bathes in England* in 1562.

It's worth pausing here (early, I realise) to note that while holidays didn't exist, "time off" was very much a part of life, although no one would have defined it that way. The vast majority of the population were agricultural workers, who lurched between back-breakingly long hours in the fields and periods with no work, when how to put food on the table was of far greater concern than the opportunity it offered to put your feet up and relax. The wealthy elite might clatter between their country estates and London mansions in rickety carriages – if they could face the treacherous state of the few byways that existed – but while this offered a change of scene, since none of them worked anyway, there was nothing really to take time off from.

What there was, in no small number, were "high days and holydays" – a phrase we still use now, albeit with the "y" swapped for an "i", thanks to our more secular world. "High days" were important dates in the Church calendar – including Christmas Day and Easter Sunday – that were observed as strict religious occasions, while "holydays" were annual feast days, ceremonies or festivals that usually had a religious component, but also often stretched into several days of mead-drinking, dancing and general hair-letting-down.

"Holydays" such as Lammas (1 August), when bread baked from the new wheat crop was taken to every church to be blessed, or Michaelmas Day (29 September), celebrated to encourage protection from St Michael through the colder, dark seasons, were dotted throughout the year, offering working people a chance to shrug off their shackles, for at least a few days. In the North, most communities celebrated the "Wakes", a week of feasting to mark the village church's patron saint, along with a rushbearing ceremony, when the old rushes that covered the church floor were replaced with fresh ones.

But while time off was a well-established rite, the idea of a *holiday* was yet to exist, and it's fair to assume that the Reverend William Turner had little idea of what would begin to develop from the assertions contained in his book. Turner believed that more than 60 of the Elizabethan era's favourite ailments could be cured – or at least soothed – by bathing and drinking the natural mineral waters that rose up from iron-rich "chalybeate" springs around the country.[2] At a time when medical treatments ranged from blood-letting and leeches to foul-tasting herbal brews and poultices, the thought of improving one's health by a quick bath and a glass or two of the iron-rich waters must have been a welcome alternative to the considerably less comfortable cures for common problems such as gout, rheumatism and digestive issues. Unwittingly, Turner had set down the first step in the development of what we would consider to be a holiday: a reason to travel and a place to visit that offered benefits and experiences not found at home.

Although there was nothing new about "taking the waters" – the Romans had been great spa-goers, when both Bath (Aquae Sulis) and Buxton (Aquae Arnemetiae) became famous for the curative powers of their hot chalybeate springs – the practice had fallen out of favour by the early 16th century. "In medieval times, the extraordinary health benefits of the water were often seen as some kind of miracle," says Fay Donegan, from the Buxton Crescent Experience (BCE), a 21st-century reimagining of the city's health-focused heyday. "But during the reign of Henry VIII, it came to be seen as unholy, and all the wells were closed down." Quite why Henry VIII took against such a harmless habit isn't clear, although, since the law was imposed in 1537,[3] in the early days of the dissolution of the monasteries, it's likely a fear of conniving Catholics plotting his demise while taking a communal soak was partly the cause.

It wasn't until twelve years after Turner's first book appeared that Elizabeth I visited Bath[4] and discovered that a spa treatment or two was just the thing after a busy day of dodging assassination attempts and juggling an endless line of suitors. She declared the spring should reopen, with its extraordinary healing powers available to all those who could afford it (i.e., her). Further north, Mary Queen of Scots visited St Ann's Well in Buxton nine times between 1573 and 1584[5] to take "the cure" for her rheumatism, and doubtless would have continued if Elizabeth hadn't decided to have her beheaded in 1587. While history has failed to record them as the originators of the "spa holiday", Liz and Mary's wellness getaways formed the blueprint for a type of holiday that is currently one of the hottest trends in 21st-century travel.

"There's a huge focus on health right now," says Stella Photi, who owns Wellbeing Escapes, a tour operator specialising in spa and wellness holidays. "I think the pandemic was a big wake-up call for a lot of people; it used to be a spa holiday was just about pampering, now it's much more about what real health benefits it can bring. The buzzword is 'healthspan' rather than 'lifespan' – how to maintain a better quality of life into your 80s and 90s. Meditation, cognitive therapies – even things like cryotherapy and red-light saunas – they're becoming quite standard even at mainstream spa resorts."

I think about this as I step into the warm waters of the small rooftop pool at the Buxton Crescent Spa, looking out towards the same lush hills the royal party would have clattered across in a deeply uncomfortable horse and carriage. I suspect back then, when life expectancy was usually between 35–40 years,[6] a visit to a spa was *all* about lifespan, for the lucky few who actually made it to Bath or Buxton. My journey – although dull – was smooth and comfortable; from the sunny south coast of England to Buxton's rural beauty in four-and-a-half hours. Four hundred and fifty years ago, roads barely existed; journeys were made on horseback or in cramped, airless carriages that were so unstable and dangerous that passengers often made a will before clambering on board.[7] A trip from London to Bath took three days,[7] while reaching Buxton from the south was all but unthinkable for anyone but hardened soldiers and the most determined travelling salesmen. For anyone but royal parties and the very wealthiest landowners, leaving one's home to stay somewhere different was a concept that simply didn't exist. Travel for pleasure was yet to be invented.

Even so, the fascination with the healing powers of spa waters saw dozens of chalybeate springs discovered over the following decades, with new settlements built around them. Harrogate's chalybeate spring had been discovered back in 1571, but it was another 45 years before Tunbridge Wells was established in 1606, with Epsom in 1618 and Scarborough in 1626.[8] Wales had Llandrindod Wells and Trefriw Wells. Scottish spa goers travelled to Strathpeffer, Moffat and the Bridge of Allan. The Civil War put a brake on things for ten years, but when Charles II was restored to the throne in 1660, a new era of innovation began. Scientists discovered everything from bacteria to the binary system, Isaac Newton popped up with his first reflecting telescope and pocket-watches and an early forerunner of the three-piece suit were adopted by every discerning fashionista.

By the 18th century, the London season – a five-month whirl of debutante balls and social gatherings, held between January and July, when parliament was sitting and all the wealthy families were in their palatial city residences – began to take shape, coffee houses sprung up, offering communal spaces for writers, thinkers and philosophers to debate and swap ideas, and a general cooling of overseas hostilities meant travel to Europe was starting to become a possibility. As the first travellers began to return home, new ideas about the health-giving properties of spa waters, picked up in places like Vichy in France and Baden-Baden in Germany, began to filter out into Georgian society.

In many ways, what truly kick-started the spa craze was the printed word. London's first newspaper was published in 1702[9] and, over the coming decades, dozens of printing presses would begin producing leaflets and pamphlets in provincial towns and cities. Spas could advertise their services and physicians wrote of miracle cures, while articles appeared detailing the glittering society that had begun to descend on Bath, the elegant colonnades lined with shops and galleries in Tunbridge Wells and Epsom's bustling Assembly Rooms. Suddenly, there was somewhere to travel *to*, somewhere different to *be*, with neither the strict social rules that governed the London court or the dull familiarity of rural life. The very thing we take for granted in our holidays – the sense of freedom, the chance to step away from the everyday – was slowly unfurling as a human desire, albeit masked by the focus on health as the primary reason for making the long trek from home.

By the beginning of the 18th century, one town stood head and shoulders above the others as *the* spa destination to visit. Bath – which had, for a while, become rather racy and raucous – was changed forever by the arrival of one man, Beau (originally Richard) Nash. Rather like a Regency-era Gatsby, Nash was both charismatic and enigmatic, renowned for leading an indulgently wealthy lifestyle without having come from money, and charming enough to become the city's unofficial Master of Ceremonies without stopping to ask if anyone actually wanted one.[10] Under his influence, Bath became the most fashionable, forward-thinking place in the country, with the City Corporation persuaded to build new roads, a pump room and theatre, along with installing street lighting and creating a night watch. Duels and sword-carrying were out, as was pig-racing, bull-baiting and, most disappointing of all, the popular spectacle of swallowing burning-hot "frumenty" – a thick, wheat porridge.[11] Nash laid out a strict set of rules, including "gentlemen of fashion never appearing before ladies in gowns and caps", and that "all repeaters of Lies and Scandal be shun'd by all company."[12] Bathing in the buff was also outlawed, replaced by long, plain gowns for women and "calecons" for men – short trunks tied at the waist, which had an unfortunate tendency to slide down the wearer's legs at inopportune moments.

Before long, taking the waters in Bath was only a small part of a packed daily social agenda, satirised in many of Jane Austen's novels, most notably in 1818's *Northanger Abbey*.

> Every morning now bought its regular duties ... shops were to be visited, some new part of Town to be visited, and the Pump Room to be attended, where they paraded up and down for an hour, looking at everyone and speaking to no-one.[13]

For most, morning baths (with waters changed daily) would be followed by correspondence and a visit to a coffee house. Breakfast might come with lectures or a concert, before the day's first visit to church, where gossiping in the back rows was far more of an attraction than any idea of actual prayer. At noon, the promenading began, the streets a sea of bonnets and parasols, doors to the milliners and bookshops clicking open and shut, the air thick with conversation and flirtations. Dinner was taken early, before a second bath, then evening prayers and promenade, with tea at the Assembly House before an evening of theatre, entertaining, gambling and dancing. The wealthiest visitors would rent an entire house for their stay, while those on a more modest income would take private rooms in a "lodging house" and have their meals delivered, creating the model for Airbnb and Deliveroo to step into 300 years later.

It's not hard to imagine what Bath must have been like in its heyday – mostly because much of the architecture looks exactly the same. When I visit, the wide streets are swathed in early spring sunshine and flanked with Georgian townhouses and Regency mansions so pristine, so golden-hued, that it feels almost like walking onto a film set. Many of the original buildings remain; the Cross Bath, the Hetling Pump Room, the Hot Bath – all overlooked by the rooftop pool at the modern, glass-fronted Thermae Bath Spa. The town is already busy with tourists and school groups chattering noisily, phones held up to take pictures as they weave through the centuries-old alleyways. Over a million visitors came to see the Roman Baths and Pump Room in 2023[14] and it feels more like an open-air living museum rather than a 21st-century city – albeit a highly sanitised version of what Regency visitors would have had to endure.

"18th-century Bath would have been a very smelly place," says Theresa Jenkins of The Gainsborough Bath Spa. "People didn't really take baths for personal cleanliness in that era, so the air would have been anything but fresh. Sheep and horses would have been standing around in the street – people would have been given pomades to hold to their noses while they bathed to keep away the stench." The waters themselves – which had a strong, sulphurous odour – would have done little to improve the atmosphere, particularly when ingested, which could have a disastrous effect on the digestive system, with little opportunity to deal with this kind of mortifying incident in private. However picturesque Bath is made to look in Jane Austen movie adaptations and bodice-ripping TV series, filth, stench and grime would have been an integral part of Nash's oh-so-elegant city.

Not that it would have bothered most visitors at the time. The Georgians had a rumbustious attitude to cleanliness (or lack thereof) and physical hygiene, not least due to the amount of health issues most people struggled with. The average life expectancy was 40 years and the whirl of unfamiliar foods, wines and products introduced to Britain during the Restoration also brought with them a whole range of uncomfortable, undiagnosable and usually downright unpleasant health concerns. A new treaty with Portugal and Madeira brought gallons of wine into the country, often transported in lead-lined casks that leeched into the alcohol.[15] The agricultural revolution meant diets became far more meat-heavy, while better carriages – and roads – meant people walked far less.

Some diseases almost became a badge of honour; no poet or essayist could be taken seriously unless they suffered with gout, a form of inflammatory arthritis, often affecting the feet.[16] "Gouty persons," said one of Bath's leading doctors, George Cheyne, "are people of good natural parts, large feeders and long-lived."[17] (What we would call bon viveurs now.) Noisily misbehaving bodies became a popular feature of fiction and poems, with flatulence and digestive issues often referred to in unapologetically frank language. Health was becoming a national obsession, and so it was inevitable that the seemingly miraculous powers of drinking, douching and even inhaling the vapours of the iron-rich waters would draw more and more visitors to the fashionable spa towns.

By 1715, more than 8,000 people arrived in Bath for the autumn season,[18] staying for anything from two weeks to two months. Almost all would either have been from the aristocracy – the very richest families, dukes and earls, whose wealth had been handed down through generations of hereditary peerages, often alongside considerable political power – or the gentry; also landowners, but without the gilded titles and ancestral links. Belonging to the gentry wasn't a guarantee of having pots of money or general fat-cattery, but it did mean an appearance of both should be upheld as far as possible, even if that meant relying on cash-rich relatives or friends.

What had begun as a short period of relocation, specifically to treat health issues, was slowly transforming – in Bath at least – into something we would recognise as not a million miles away from the modern concept of a holiday. Much of the town was given over to the pursuit of pleasure – whether shopping for the latest fashions shipped down from London couturiers, gossiping along the promenade or whirling around the ballroom in the arms of a thrillingly unsuitable suitor. Although the phrase "conspicuous leisure" wasn't coined until 1899, when the sociologist Thorstein Veblen wrote a stinging treatise about the tendency of the wealthy American elite to engage in all kinds of high-profile but basically pointless activities, from promenading and social engagements to polo-playing and fox hunting, to show the lack of necessity for work in their lives, one of its earliest incarnations was quite possibly among the social frippery of Bath's social scene.[19] And it wasn't just Bath; in 1724, Daniel Defoe wrote of Tunbridge Wells' visitors: "some drink, some do not. Company and Diversion is, in short, the main business of the Place."[20]

What Defoe was talking about – the frivolous nature of the entertainments, the pursuit of pleasure for pleasure's sake (or "conspicuous leisure" as Veblen called it) – had rarely been seen out of London, or the gilded ballrooms of country estates, and the change in location brought with it a more relaxed and carefree feeling, particularly for female visitors. A trip to Bath could be an education – quite literally, thanks to the "circulating libraries" which offered customers the opportunity to rent books for an annual or quarterly fee, along with a whole range of goods, from hats and perfumes to tobacco and tea. Publishers with links to circulating libraries were twice as likely to publish books by female authors, who often had to struggle against a common belief that writing was an unsuitable job for a woman – after all, what could they say that would possibly be of interest? Female authors were often published anonymously, or as "A Lady", although the upside of such anonymity was the freedom to be happily indiscreet about the liaisons and forbidden relationships that often took place in spa resorts – not unlike the holiday romances of today.

"Bath offered women more freedom than they would have had elsewhere," says Theresa Jenkins. "Sociability was the essence of the place; they could go to a female coffee shop, talk to each other while taking the waters; it was a chance for more closeted women to share stories and experiences about everything from childcare and medicine to health cures and marriage difficulties." What those Regency women were experiencing – stepping away from strict social rules, the chance to escape the monotony of country house life and make new friends (and even the occasional dalliance) – is little different from what draws the hundreds of thousands of women who visit the city now. "Bath is a small city and a safe one," says Jenkins, "and because so many visitors are women, many of the attractions are designed for them. Mums and daughters come, groups of girlfriends, brides-to-be on their hen weekends – it's a relaxed space for them to enjoy."

Judging from the packed streets when I visit in early spring, I'm not sure how relaxing a trip to Bath would be when the tourist season really gets going. The opening of the Thermae Bath Spa in 2006 – at an estimated (there are no official figures) £40 million[21] –

was a massive boost to the city, reviving the spa tradition that had faded in the 1950s, when the NHS declared that bathing in *any* kind of warm water was equally as beneficial as mineralised spa waters. It took 30 years to reopen the spa facilities that now help to bring in around six million visitors a year.[22] But such extraordinary numbers come at a cost; the city grapples with infrastructure problems in the summer months – lack of parking, congested streets – and the Thermae Spa itself receives mixed reviews for overcrowding and lack of space. Just as it became something of a victim of its own success by the late 18th century, when the town's popularity and promise of easy money saw respectable physicians joined by all manner of apothecaries, conmen and quacks, Bath's rich history has made it fall victim to that very 21st-century malady: overtourism – and all the problems that accompany it.

When I arrive in Buxton, late on a sunny March afternoon, the contrast with Bath is striking. The elegant Georgian sweep of the Buxton Crescent – housing one of the first purpose-built hotels in the country, alongside two sets of "lodging rooms", when it originally opened in 1789 – dominates the lower part of the town, with the vast dome of the original, octagonal stable block (once the largest unsupported dome in the world) just behind it. The streets are almost empty, the jade-green lawns of The Slopes – the man-made hill rising in front of the Crescent – silent apart from a solitary dogwalker. The air is fresh and crisp, and there's a stillness, a quietness, that feels the polar opposite of Bath's restless hustle.

"Buxton wouldn't be the place it is today – all this wonderful architecture, all the visitors that come – without the spa water," says Fay Donegan, when I join her for a tour of the Buxton Crescent Experience. "Our water has two very unusual qualities; it's a constant 27.5 degrees all year round and when it comes out of the ground, it's 5,000 years old. It's incredibly pure and very mineral-rich, and it's at the heart of everything the town became."

Where Buxton differs from Bath is that it never put pleasure before health in quite the same way. When the fifth Duke of Devonshire – whose principal residence was the grandiose Chatsworth Estate, 15 miles away – set about creating a resort to rival Bath's primacy, he was determined to retain a focus on the health-giving properties of the town's unique spring waters, albeit with plenty of diversions to keep wealthy visitors occupied.[23] Set 350 metres above sea level, Buxton suffered far less of the stench and poor air quality that affected Bath, while the waters themselves were odour-free and pleasant to drink. "A visit to Buxton was about more than just bathing and drinking," says Donegan. "Physicians would prescribe how long people needed to come for, how much they should drink, how often they should bathe. But it was quite holistic; after bathing, people would go promenading on The Slopes, which was specifically designed with different paths having different levels of steepness to provide gentle exercise."

Convinced by the seemingly miraculous powers of the mineralised waters and the continuing enthusiasm for visiting spa towns, the duke decided to replicate Bath's famous Crescent as the centrepiece of the new Buxton. Finally completed in 1789, after nine years of construction and a budget of £120,000 (£30 million in today's money),[24] his gamble paid off, with wealthy visitors willing to spend £150 (around £30,000) for a month's stay in town.[25] I get an idea of how it might have felt to arrive in the town in the late 18th century, thanks to the BCE's virtual reality balloon ride, which sweeps me over the hills and deposits me in front of the Crescent, just in time for a glittering ball. It's a fun way to imagine how Buxton might have looked (despite a little light nausea) and when I step back into the 21st century and look up at the pristine frontage, it's hard to believe such an extraordinary building lay derelict for decades, finally reopening as a hotel in 2020 after 17 years of work and a budget that leapt from £32 to £70 million.[26] Barely ten minutes after checking in, I'm soaking in the warm waters in the small rooftop pool and trying to ignore the stony looks from the couple on the other side, clearly disappointed at having their romantic tryst interrupted.

At dinner, the tables around me are filled with young couples, a trio of women and an extended family, some British, others chatting in languages I can't quite catch: Dutch, possibly, and German. It strikes me that spas have undergone a major democratisation in the last 30 years; from the days when health clubs like Champneys were the only proper spas, through the craze in the late 90s and 00s for five-star hotels to add on expensive treatment rooms and Turkish hammams, to now, when an afternoon at a day spa has become a classic girls' trip, whether for birthdays or hen weekends or just for an excuse for a gossip and a get-together over several bottles of prosecco and a mani-pedi on the side. But while there's been an explosion in the "pampering" style of spa, there's also increasingly a return to serious health-focused travel, with in-resort doctors prescribing medications and health routines in exactly the way Regency physicians did in Bath and Buxton.

"People who have wealth are starting to invest in their health rather than, say, buying an expensive sports car," says Stella Photi of Wellbeing Escapes. "Many spa resorts have moved beyond being places to just go and relax. Now, you arrive and they do a raft of blood tests that define your specific biology and then tailor treatments and medication accordingly. They'll talk about your deficiencies and symptoms and create a cocktail of vitamins and minerals, along with state-of-the-art treatments like red-light therapy, that helps your mitochondria – the ability of cells to produce energy."

I think of my chat with Stella the following morning, when I pay a visit to the virtual apothecary at the BCE; an animated figure who comes to life to diagnose and prescribe for a specific ailment; in my case bitters, bleeding and purging for gout. It's both fascinating and depressing to realise that cutting-edge medical treatments and trends – from biohacking to cognitive health – are being unrolled at spa resorts to an exclusive coterie of the super-rich, just as the Regency era's new-fangled spa remedies were only available to royalty and country landowners. The only way the poor would have experienced the baths was emptying and cleaning them, or bringing trays of spiced hot chocolate to drink while the rich customers soaked in the sulphurous depths.[27]

"Back then, the city was not without its darker side," says Theresa Jenkins. "Many women would come to Bath from surrounding villages in search of work, and their lives could be ruined by the behaviour of some of the visitors. There are reports of attacks on working-class women and girls, but no one was ever found guilty. They looked after their own."

There were occasional initiatives to make the restorative powers of the waters available to more than just the aristocracy; the Duke of Devonshire installed one "charity bath" in Buxton,[28] while Bellott's Hospital in Bath offered refuge for poorer people who had come to take the waters for medicinal reasons.[29] Ironically, however, it wasn't an influx of the poor that changed the social make-up of the spa resorts, but the new growing middle class of businessmen and merchants that had developed by the beginning of the 19th century, drawn in far more by the tales of glamorous entertainment and glittering balls than daily baths and water cures. "One would think the English were ducks," the famous essayist Horace Walpole quite possibly wrote (although possibly not). "They are forever waddling to the waters."[30]

And as more people came, so the pleasures on offer became glitzier and more impressive; Bath began putting on four or five "gala" nights in the Sydney Gardens each season, with illuminations that would rival Blackpool a century later. According to the *Bath Guide*, published in 1811, the event's "brilliance, taste and elegance cannot be excelled: about five thousand lamps are lighted on the occasion, with a pompous display of fireworks. Three to four thousand persons of the first fashion and consequence assemble at Sydney Garden on Gala Night."[31]

Food also became a big part of a stay; Bath's two weekly markets sold fresh milk, butter and cheese along with Lansdown mutton – known as the sweetest in Europe – fish from the river Severn, game and woodcock and port wine for £1 for a dozen bottles. Pastry chefs arrived from London to create the kind of desserts that could undo all the health-giving properties of the water in just a spoonful or two, and private and public tables would be laden with the kind of gourmet delicacies – pâtés and mousses, rich sauces and unctuous stews – usually only seen in the capital's wealthiest dining rooms.[32]

Somehow, over a century, Bath had shifted from being a place of health and restoration to a hubbub of leisure and pleasure, its tight social restrictions slowly unravelling in the wake of Nash's death in 1761. When Jane Austen arrived in 1801, she was less than impressed, writing to her sister that, "the first view of Bath does not answer my expectations . . . the appearance was all vapour, smoke, shadow and confusion."[33] Many visitors to other spa towns were becoming similarly underwhelmed. "We seem to be surrounded," wrote the poet Anna Seward during a visit to Harrogate in 1796, "by commonplaces . . . and men of any age and class scarce indeed."[34] Austen lived in Bath for five years, and although she barely wrote during that period, she later admitted that Bath "extended her experience and enriched her understanding of contemporary society".[35]

Bath's transition from the exclusive preserve of the super-rich to a destination frequented by members of the gentry and even, horror of horrors, the professional middle classes, sets the template for the development of destinations and holiday resorts through the coming centuries. Wealth and confidence are the two main factors that go hand in hand with exploration and discovery, but as human nature is innately aspirational *and* curious, inevitably others from less gilded backgrounds will follow in the footsteps of the wealthy elite. Then comes development, growth, a "vulgarisation" of a previously exclusive playground (according to the first wave of moneyed travellers), and either the rich move on to enjoy their conspicuous leisure somewhere new, or carve out niches and neighbourhoods that are so exorbitantly expensive, no one else can afford them.

But even if spas had had their day (for the wealthiest classes at least), what they offered – an escape from everyday life, to shake up the country-house torpor and shrug off the restrictions of London – wasn't something that could just be put back in the box. Life had changed; new turnpike roads were making the country more accessible and talk was growing about the opportunities of travelling abroad, of seeing the great cities of Rome and Florence and Paris, all in one extraordinary trip. A new "Romanticism" was on the rise, with a focus on the countryside and the restorative powers of the natural world that made the crowded streets of Bath and Buxton, Harrogate and Tunbridge Wells, feel increasingly out of step.[36] Those who did still visit Bath were just as likely to journey out of the town into the countryside as take the waters in the town itself.

At the same time, the printing presses were churning out leaflets and pamphlets on a whole new form of health tourism; sea-bathing, with fledgling towns such as Brighthelmstone and Scarborough starting to be mentioned as places to indulge in the new fashion for dipping, dunking and drinking the briny waters. The spa era might be drawing to a close, but it had tapped into something in the human psyche that hadn't been reached before; a delight in the possibility of escaping the norm and the freedoms such change might bring – as the diarist and writer Fanny Burney noted in the autumn of 1788, on returning to her home after spending time at Cheltenham spa.

> And thus ends the Cheltenham episode. May I not justly call it so, different as it is to all the mode of life I have hitherto lived here? ... Melancholy, most melancholy, was the return to Windsor: ease, leisure, elegant society and interesting communication were now to give place to arrogant manners, contentious disputation and arbitrary ignorance.[37]

Life – albeit for a privileged few – was beginning to expand beyond the familiar, the notion of spending time somewhere other than your home slowly taking shape, along with the sense that a change of location might also offer a sense of liberation, particularly for women. What began as a health cure quickly became the earliest incarnation of what we would now think of as a holiday; the very first jewel-slippered, grime-encrusted, mineral-water soaked steps along a road that would eventually redefine the human experience forever.

2

A Grand Adventure

London and Devon

"I am in Rome! Whence this excess of joy? What has befallen me?"[1]
Henry Matthews

Almost 30 years ago, on the morning of 1 May, 1997, as the country was dragging itself out of bed and trying to decide whether to vote before or after work, I was setting off down the Camden Road with my then boyfriend, Rob, for a two-month rail trip across Europe. We didn't know, then, as we biffed our rucksacks through the commuters at Camden Tube, that we were about to miss one of the most dramatic elections of the 20th century. Tony Blair swept to power after 18 years of Conservative rule, Cherie appeared on the doorstep in her dressing gown and the whole "Cool Britannia" era – immortalised in a *Vanity Fair* cover two months earlier, with Patsy Kensit and Liam Gallagher wrapped in Union Jack bedsheets – went, appropriately enough, Supernova. Meanwhile, we found ourselves on a beach in Turkey, the first stop on a trip that would take in Athens, Florence, Venice and Nice, and then on to Spain before heading across the Straits of Gibraltar to Morocco.

What I also didn't know then, not being particularly well-read in history at that point, was that our trip was following a trend far older than the vogue for Interrailing and backpacking that had become so popular over the last decade. In recent years, "The Grand Tour" has become a well-known phrase, appropriated by TV executives for everything from motoring to travel shows, while *Bridgerton* – Netflix's unintentionally hilarious reinterpretation of aristocratic Georgian life as a female-empowered sexathon with truly terrible frocks – includes the story of Colin Bridgerton, who returns from his year-long Grand Tour with new opinions, a bagful of souvenirs and considerably better trousers.

Bridgerton isn't renowned for its historical accuracy, but by the first decades of the 18th century, the Grand Tour *was* starting to become a rite of passage for young men from the wealthiest circles.[2] As with the rise of the spa towns, the concept of travelling to the continent had taken some time to catch on; a slow realisation that the countries of Europe could be visited for other reasons besides attempting to ransack the cities, nick all the great paintings or overthrow their monarchies. For several hundred years, Britain's relationship with its continental neighbours had been characterised by a string of conflicts and wars with everyone from the Dutch and the Spanish to the Austrians and the French. Things on the home front had been little better, with the discord of the Civil War only ending with the Restoration of Charles II in 1660 (which created its own "holyday" – Oak Apple Day – on 29 May to commemorate him settling back onto the throne). Small wonder, then, that nipping across the Channel wasn't high on anyone's to-do list, apart from a minuscule number of travellers – most notably, the architect Inigo Jones, who travelled to Italy in 1613–14 with his patron, Thomas Howard, the 14th Earl of Arundel.[3]

Their visits to cities such as Rome, Venice and Naples introduced Jones to both Italian Renaissance and classical Roman design, resulting in a style of architecture never before seen in Britain. His work is best seen today at the Queen's House in Greenwich, which he designed in 1616 as the first "classical" building (in a style derived from ancient Greek and Roman architecture) in the country.[4] Although his work was much praised – and his tour much discussed among those wealthy enough to follow in his footsteps – instability in Europe and at home meant it wasn't until over half a century later that the phrase "The Grand Tour" came into being, used by travel writer and Catholic priest Richard Lassels in his guidebook, *The Voyage of Italy*, published in 1670.[5] Even then, conflicts rumbled on, and only after the latest instalment in the Anglo-French Wars came to an end in 1713 did continental travel start to become more of a realistic possibility.

In many ways, the changes that enabled the boom in British spa towns were also an integral part of the new allure of Europe. Newly established Turnpike Trusts – which collected tolls from travellers to maintain and improve new byways – were springing up across the country, with new roads meaning more carriages, a busier schedule of journeys and a far better chance of reaching a destination with all your limbs still intact. The same information revolution that delivered the doctor's pamphlets, health leaflets and reports on the giddy goings-on in Bath and Tunbridge Wells also produced newspapers, books and magazines, with different types of literature – including travel – found on the shelves in bookshops and stationers; by 1760 the capital had four daily papers and six evening papers, published three times a week.[6]

By the early 1720s, a trip to Europe – a "Grand Tour" – was almost an obligatory part of a wealthy young gentleman's formal education. The numbers travelling were tiny by today's standards – in the 18th century, around 300 families held half the cultivable land in England[7] and the vast majority of those setting out on a Grand Tour belonged to that class. And while more forward-thinking parents might allow sisters to accompany their brothers – and there were some financially independent women who undertook a Grand Tour under their own steam – most ladies of the time had to make do with hearing about the fashions in Paris and the treasures of Rome through correspondence and dinner-party anecdotes – if they were considered worthy of hearing about them at all.

Trips could last anything from a few months to two years, with costs stretching into tens of thousands of pounds, not least for the gilt-framed artworks, sculptures and various exotic souvenirs shipped back to country houses across the land. The most cautious, or perhaps most realistic, parents often paid for a tutor or cicerone to travel with their son,[8] responsible for shielding them from the murkier corners of the continent's glittering cities. It was a tough job, as – like most teenage boys then and now – loose morals, fast women and the chance to fritter away someone else's money in a casino were pretty much the main reasons most wanted to go.

But for many aristocratic families, the additional cost was a worthwhile investment. The Grand Tour would broaden the minds of their young, wayward sons, open them up to the continent's extraordinary art and architecture and instil a greater understanding of the world beyond Britain. More prosaically, it was also an ideal way to give them something to do between leaving school and getting married (many travellers were aged between 17–22),[9] whisking them away from the seedy bars and swinging brothels offered by London's less salubrious neighbourhoods – even if many ended up in even more licentious quarters of Venice. And there was little concern about how being away for such an extended period of time might impact a career or the possibility of getting a job. Paid labour was the preserve of the much-sneered-at middle classes. A true gentleman never worked.

"Those very wealthy young men were the social influencers of their time," says Dr Shona Goodall, a clinical psychologist specialising in health and wellbeing. "They came back with their stories and paintings and souvenirs, which encouraged others to go. And much of what they would have experienced on their tours is no different from young people who take a gap year today. Travel at that age is about developing 'you' as a personality, widening your perspectives – a chance to really learn about the world, and your place in it."

What would have been different was the journey itself. While the Turnpike Trusts were slowly reducing the element of Russian Roulette involved in most journeys along Britain's ragged byways, things tended to get a little dicier after leaving Dover. Most travellers reached Calais via the mail-carrying packet ship that rolled and tossed its way across the Channel, while others chartered private boats. Crossings were notoriously stomach-churning, and those who opted for the packet ship could only disembark by clambering into a rowing boat, which would then travel near enough to the shore for passengers to climb out and wade onto dry land. Falling in was not uncommon, with many travellers setting foot on foreign soil for the first time in soggy socks, damp britches and a less-than-cheery mood. Some opted for the shorter crossing to Dieppe, or from Southampton to Le Havre or Cherbourg, but Calais was known to have good inns where one could dry off and enjoy a first encounter with such indescribable oddities as garlic and baguettes.[10] It may have only been 40-odd miles between Dover and Calais, but the change in culture was immediately noticeable: "The moment we disembarked at Calais we seemed to be in a New World," wrote the historian and writer Edward Nares in 1785. "We looked back with amazement at Dover Castle, scarcely capable of persuading ourselves that England could really be at so small a distance."[11]

From Calais, most followed the same straightforward route to Paris: through Boulogne, Abbeville, Amiens and Chantilly by carriage,[12] with plenty of strange and unexpected sights along the way – vineyards, barefooted monks, and ravening wolves hurtling out of the forests and howling at the coaches. It's extraordinary to think of those travellers arriving in Paris, marvelling at many of the sights that still draw crowds in their millions today. The Eiffel Tower was yet to rise, but the galleries of the Louvre and Tuileries Gardens, Notre-Dame and Les Invalides were all on the visitor's sightseeing list, along with – just as today – plenty of time to shop.

Paris was the epicentre of European style, with many businesses geared to the English visitors who seemed to carry both bottomless wallets and an unshakeable belief that *anything* bought in Paris must be the very height of chic. There were visits to ateliers for the latest fashions, ornate snuff boxes and tapestries packed into luggage, porcelain, mirrors, clocks and cabinetwork carefully selected to be shipped home. "We are the whipped cream of Europe," said the author

Voltaire, somewhat sniffily, in 1735.[13] The city's shopkeepers trousered the cash and happily agreed. Even more "serious" visitors found themselves falling prey to Parisian charms, as Horace Walpole noted in February 1766: "I am robust and well, am become très French, never dine but sup, sit up all night and lie abed all day. In short, heartily enjoy the holidays I have given myself from Parliament."[14]

Once enough money had been spent, enough balls attended, churches admired and dinners eaten, the long and difficult journey to Italy began to unfold. Most headed south to Lyons, where an unusual choice awaited them at the foot of the Cenis mountain pass to Turin. Too narrow for carriages, tourists could make the journey over the mountains in three days by mule or five days carried in sedan chairs.[15] Predictably, many opted for the considerably more comfortable option, and were carried along the pass by sturdy, muscly (and presumably extremely tolerant) locals who became known as the "chair men of Mont Cenis" – famous for quite literally carrying wealthy Englishmen from one country to another.[16] Once the crossing had been endured, a return to the more normal levels of sumptuous comfort was on offer at the British consulates in Turin or Milan, where staff muttered irritably into their diaries about the number of viscounts, earls and dukes they were expected to entertain. ("The town swarms with English," noted James, 1st Earl Waldegrave, the British envoy in Paris, in 1732. "I had near upon a dozen newcomers dine with me yesterday, and shall have near as many more today."[17])

What came next represents a fork in the road – not just in the journey, but in the evolution of how we define our holidays. Young men of a more studious disposition (most likely those with cicerones) headed to Florence and Rome, where great works of Renaissance art and extraordinary classical ruins awaited them, along with the chance to widen their understanding of both ancient and contemporary culture. Those looking for less cerebral pleasures headed to Venice, renowned as the party capital not just of Italy, but the whole continent. Here, among the cat's cradle of dimly lit streets and alleyways, lay the blueprint for every kind of cocktail-fuelled, money-blowing, inappropriate-liaison-filled holiday (and who hasn't had one of those?) in the future, from 18–30s holidays to Vegas gamble-fests and lost weekends in Ibiza. Mask-wearing was commonplace, ladies were known to carry daggers or pistols to deal with any overly demanding lovers[18] and Carnival – a whirl of balls, parties, gambling and music – went on for six months. Venice wasn't *a* holiday. It was *the* holiday.

"Travelling and holidays are two different things," says chartered psychologist Audrey Tang. "Travelling is about broadening the mind, experiencing new places, opening ourselves up to different cultures and ways of thinking. A holiday is a chance to shed the pressures of everyday life, shake off your normal persona and discover who you are without all the expectations of other people and the society we belong to. The more we've been suppressed by the rules and etiquette of society, the more we want to escape."

For young men who had only ever known the restrictive social mores of British society, the drinking dens and debauchery of Venice were considerably more attractive than Roman ruins and Florentine art galleries. Like Bath, where social pleasures had slowly become a more integral part of a visit than the spa waters themselves, experiencing the sexual and social freedoms of Venice, and (to a lesser degree) Europe as a whole, often became the primary aim of a Grand Tour.

If Venice was the first real foreign holiday destination, then it was also the Grand Tour that gave birth to the concept of 'souvenirs', although Georgian travellers tended to splash out on more than a bottle of undrinkable limoncello and a Hot Priests calendar (yes, this actually exists). If the hangovers permitted, a trip to Canaletto's studio in Venice was a must-do, with dozens of paintings of the Grand Canal and Giudecca later hung in drawing rooms across the country, along with marble statues, ancient urns, rococo furniture and an endless array of trinkets that could be packed into the vast amounts of luggage that grew steadily larger as the trip progressed.

And if young men wanted a more personal memento of their time spent indulging in Venice's hedonistic whirl, there was one woman to whom they paid a visit. Rosalba Carriera was one of the city's most famous artists; self-taught and renowned for a rococo style that contrasted with the more conventional style of portraiture at the time.[19] In Rome, Pompeo Batoni painted his subjects in striking, confident poses – chest out, horse to hand, knee bent against the kind of antique Roman statuary a man always keeps in his drawing room.[20] By contrast, a portrait by Carriera could mean the 8th Duke of Westmorland ended up looking like the sixth member of Duran Duran; decked out in flamboyant Carnival costume, with an edgy, androgynous look that was heightened by her use of pale, pastel hues. Works by both artists would have been shipped back to England and it's fair to assume that, once unwrapped, Batoni's works would have been met with a warmer reception by those funding their wayward sons' trips than Carriera's camp-as-Christmas portraits.

Most stately homes in the UK have some mementos from the Grand Tour. Guides did a roaring trade introducing their wealthy guests to local artisans and furniture makers, with paintings being particularly highly prized. Canny artists such as Canaletto made a fortune, churning out countless pictures of Venice for visitors to take home, while dealers in antiquities made the most of the British upper classes' entire lack of scruples about scooping up ancient relics and carting them off home, although some may not have been quite as old (and the paintings not quite as authentic) as the gullible purchasers were led to believe. "We English . . . are apt to think that we can purchase the best works of the great masters," wrote Phillip Francis in *Hints to Travellers* in 1772, "there cannot be a grosser mistake. The Italians are too cunning to suffer the market to be removed out of Italy."[21]

Nowhere matches Sir John Soane's House for Grand Tour treasures; a small but quite extraordinary museum housed in a three-storey townhouse overlooking Lincoln's Inn Fields in London. Once the home of one of the Georgian era's most renowned architects, the house has been kept exactly as it was when Soane was alive – preserved as a museum at his request,[22] but with no information panels, so as not to detract from its feel of a private residence. It's been described as akin to stepping inside someone's mind, and when I visit on a chilly February morning, it seems the perfect description. Every room, hall and corridor is crammed with works of art (100 in the tiny lobby alone), brought back from Soane's own Grand Tour and subsequent shopping sprees at London's auction houses. The main living room blazes with walls painted a deep shade of scarlet known as Pompeii Red, thought to be inspired by a fragment of wall plaster Soane pocketed while visiting the ruins.[23] Beyond, narrow passageways wind past walls crammed with carved panels, fragments of plasterwork and cinerary vases, opening into a double-height gallery, presided over by a full-size cast of the Apollo Belvedere and a bust of Soane himself.

"Soane was very conscious of his immense good fortune at being able to take a Grand Tour, thanks to his scholarship from the Royal Academy," says Sue Palmer, archivist at the museum. "He was Professor of Architecture at the RA and knew many of his students would never be able to afford a similar journey. Even if they could, the Napoleonic Wars made travel all but impossible for several years. He knew how important it was to see things in three dimensions, and wanted his students to understand the intricacies and beauty of European architecture, so he bought widely from auction houses and created a kind of virtual Grand Tour for those who would never be able to do one in reality."

Soane's house offers a vivid insight into the fascination with continental Europe, but what it couldn't reproduce for the students who came to wonder at its riches was the experience of seeing such extraordinary works of art in their original setting. For this, there was nowhere better than Rome, which became so popular that bars and hotels began to change their names in order to lure in as many of the new breed of British visitors, with their deep, money-filled pockets, as possible. Caffé degli Inglesi on Piazza di Spagna was often the first port of call,[24] a hub for expats, as well as art dealers and guides, while one of the city's most famous inns, Lo Scudi di Francia, also situated on the piazza, changed its name in 1740 to La Villa de Londra.[25] In time, the whole area became known as the British ghetto, with English dishes such as bacon and cabbage, boiled mutton and bread puddings appearing on menus as a vastly preferable option to peculiar delicacies such as pasta and artichokes (doubtless to the horror of Roman diners on adjacent tables).

Of all the cities on the Grand Tour, Rome is – for me at least – the one where it's easiest to imagine how those early travellers felt, not least because so much of what was so extraordinary then remains entirely unchanged today. What is different are the numbers who flood into the city; in 2024, over 22 million visitors[26] came to take their selfies in front of the Colosseum, sip aperitivos in the Piazza Navona and eat overpriced gelato on the Spanish Steps – the exact spot where Grand Tour travellers would have congregated centuries before. On my last visit to Rome in 2023, I sat in a cafe in a small piazza behind the Pantheon and tried to spot people who looked like actual Romans in between the tourists. I estimated a ratio of roughly one in ten – one being the slim, well-dressed, sunglasses-wearing men and women radiating irritation, the other nine being those jabbing each other with selfie sticks or trawling along behind flag-waving tour guides.

But although we think overtourism was invented in the 21st century, those who undertook a Grand Tour often believed themselves to be experiencing something similar, although the numbers they considered remarkable seem piffling by today's standards. "From the cold weather and English in this place, I have sometimes fancied myself in England," wrote Frederick Frankland MP in 1739. "It is reckoned we shall be about eighty in Rome."[27] Quite what they would have made of the overwhelming crowds experienced by Gen Z backpackers on their 21st-century tours through Europe is hard to imagine.

"We chose Amsterdam, Berlin, Prague, Florence and Genoa, and Florence was definitely the place where we experienced over-tourism," says Lily Allenden, who set off in the summer of 2023 for a post-A-level, multi-week rail trip across Europe with two girlfriends. "The crowds of people, combined with temperatures – it was just too much. We rarely went out during the day, walking around was just really overstimulating." For Allenden's generation, the guidebooks used since the earliest days of the Grand Tourers, right through to the backpacking era of the 1980s and 90s, have been replaced by TikTok and Instagram, with fellow travellers posting recommendations and suggestions instantaneously, rather than years after they returned.

"Social media was a big help in deciding where to go," says Allenden. "People posted their own Interrail routes and budgets, some had created slideshows with ideas for good places to eat and hostels to stay in." Like those on the Grand Tour, who often encountered others following the same route, Allenden and her friends quickly became part of a swathe of post-A-level adventurers, striking out for the first time.

"Grand Tour or gap year – both fulfil the same role in young people's lives," says Shona Goodall. "Once away from familial structures, you start to work out your own likes, dislikes and opinions, as well as discovering your own strengths and limitations in ways that wouldn't be possible at home. That might be how to handle not understanding the language, or working out what to do if you miss a train or flight. There's something about that first extended time away from home and parents – it's often a time in our life that we always remember."

My two-month journey across Europe has certainly stayed with me, in spite of the fact it's almost three decades ago. I remember roaring along the Amalfi coast in a police car, chasing a bus that had disappeared out of the coach park with our luggage on board while we were busy bickering about whether to have prosciutto or taleggio in our sandwich – finally catching up with it in a car park just outside

Positano. I can still hear the youth choir practising in the garden at the youth hostel they were sharing with us just outside Florence, the noise of hundreds of bikes suddenly whipping past our campsite on what turned out to be the Giro d'Italia and waking up on an overnight train from Barcelona to Granada to see the faded-gold wastes of the Almerían desert shimmering in the dawn. But what I remember most is how extraordinary it felt to be on the road, free from everything that was "normal" and "everyday", with no one to turn to, or rely on, except for ourselves.

That same desire for freedom and independence drove many of those who took a Grand Tour – and none felt it more keenly than the small number of women who set out on their own adventure, determined to escape from a society seemingly intent to treat them like children. Travel offered a unique opportunity to exercise their minds, cultivate new tastes and develop and voice their own opinions, as well as discover the delights of a freer, less judgemental society – as Lady Mary Wortley Montagu discovered on a visit to Milan in 1739.

> It is so much the established fashion for everybody to live their own way, that nothing is more ridiculous than censuring the actions of another. This would be terrible in London, where we have little other diversion ... I bless my destiny that has conducted me to a part where people are better employed than in talking of the affairs of their acquaintance.[28]

Travel writing and letters home gave women a chance to tell their own stories and share what they had learnt, often with a very different perspective from their male counterparts. While many were wives or daughters taken along by unusually broadminded fathers, there was a small band of independent – both financially and intellectually – women who were determined to escape the confines of Georgian society – which at the highest levels operated as a kind of gentlemen's club – and experience the continent for themselves.

"The number of single women in society during that time is actually quite high," says Jane Birtles, Senior Collections and House Officer for A la Ronde, an 18th-century National Trust property, set just outside Exmouth, "and those that were wealthy and confident did travel. When we look back, we often have an expectation of the past – in this case that the Grand Tour was an all-male preserve. But that's not strictly accurate."

I've come to A la Ronde to explore the history of Jane and Mary Parminter, two cousins who are thought to have taken four Grand Tours, first setting off in 1784.[29] "They were from a wealthy merchanting family," says Birtles, "both unmarried, and the family belonged to a non-conformist religion – the Moravian church – that would have allowed more freedoms than the Church of England." Their house is an extraordinary 16-sided *cottage orné*, with rooms set around an octagonal central hall, designed after they returned from Europe, and based on the octagonal basilica on San Vitale in Ravenna. It remains filled with the mementos, paintings, ornaments and decorative styles brought back from their travels; a female equivalent of Sir John Soane's house, with the same sense of passion and fascination for the continent and all it offered. In the library, I peer into the glass-fronted Cabinets of Curiosities, crammed with enamelled miniatures, chunks of quartz, Moroccan-style leather slippers and dozens of small pictures – Swiss peasants, Alpine pastures, Mount Etna spewing lava into the sky. My favourite exhibit is their original leather carrying cases, kept safely behind glass in the dimly lit hall.

"Set off from London after half five," writes Jane, in her journal, "passed thro' Greenwich, breakfasted at Dartford, very fine pleasant country; onto Rochester . . . and in a coach to Dover, very pleasant indeed the high cliffs behind the houses."[30] Sadly, only the first three weeks of Jane's journal remains, but it is known that the two women were the first to scale an Alpine peak above 3,000 metres, when they reached the summit of Mont Buet in 1786.[31] "It's tempting to think of them as eccentric, but nothing we have from that period shows they were viewed that way," says Birtles. "There were enough other women on the road that travelling without men wasn't outlandish. And they would have met up with others en route; people always carried letters of introduction, and guides would be pre-arranged to meet travellers on arrival."

Not all women were as intrepid as the Parminters; some only ventured as far as Paris, while the rare few who made the crossing over the Cenis Pass often indulged in somewhat less wholesome pastimes than Jane and Mary. Continental women were perceived to live very different, freer lives; a relaxed morality that many of those who escaped the starchy suffocation of English society took to with alacrity. Few were more notorious than Lady Elizabeth Webster, who travelled to Europe twice with her husband (whom she married at 15, when he was 38), before divorcing him in 1797.[32] Once free, she continued to travel and indulged in several affairs, once declaring, "oh, what vile animals men are, with such headstrong passions"[33] – although it seems fair to assume she was hardly a shrinking violet herself.

But while those who set out on a Grand Tour – whether men or women – might have seen it as an extraordinary adventure, there was a strong sense of disapproval from certain quarters at home. Many men were distinctly unimpressed with the idea of women packing their bags and disappearing into the dissolute world of sleazy Italian counts and Parisian aristocrats, while newspapers frequently ran opinion features about the dangers – both moral and financial – of embarking on such a trip. "The whole account of their travels is generally no more than a journal of how many bottles they've drunk and what loose *amores* they've had," sneered *Mist's Weekly Journal* – the leading Tory newspaper – in 1725,[34] as part of an article about British gentlemen out drinking in the streets of Rome until 3 a.m. Switch up the language and throw in a mention of social media, and *Mist's* lofty disapproval is interchangeable for any of the many features the *Daily Mail* runs each summer about the dissolute behaviour of Brits abroad. It seems nothing in how we holiday, even our worst behaviour, is new.

Aside from getting smashed until the early hours, there is something rather lovely about being able to trace a line from Jane and Mary Parminter to my 1990s adventure and on into Lily's 21st-century post-A-level trip. Travel has always offered an escape, a sense of genuine freedom, and although our society may be considerably less restrictive than in Georgian times, it's still no less liberating to escape the structures of home and parenting and strike out on your own for the first time. Whether it's Sir John Soane buying up ancient relics to educate his students, young noblemen pouting for their portraits in Venice or Lady Elizabeth Webster, reinventing herself as a liberated woman after years in an unhappy marriage, the Grand Tour reinforced and embedded the realisation brought about by the spa towns, that travelling somewhere different, exploring the new, could bring untold rewards, both physically and mentally.

But as the century began to draw to a close, the political landscape changed in a way that meant foreign travel was no longer the giddy pleasure it had once been. The French Revolution, which began in 1789, took Paris off the tourism map, and when the Napoleonic Wars kicked off in 1803, the door to the rest of Europe slammed closed. Twelve years later, once the conflict had ended, Grand Tours began again, although never quite to the same degree, and when the railways began to unfold, travel was revolutionised, making the whole format of the Grand Tour a thing of the past. As the new century dawned, a whole generation of young men (and a number of women) had a yen to travel but nowhere to go. The first era of the "staycation" was about to begin.

3

The Search for the Picturesque

The Wye Valley, Cumbria and the Scottish Highlands

"Scotland is the country above all others that I have seen, in which a man of imagination may carve out his own solitudes; there are so many inhabited solitudes."[1]
Dorothy Wordsworth

"There is nothing new in the world," said former US president, Harry Truman, "except the history you do not know."[2] I rather suspect his comment was made about something considerably more significant than a week of sun, sea and sand on the Spanish costas, but it's a quote that's rung true, again and again, as I've tunnelled back through the centuries to unearth how our favourite holiday traditions began. If gout-ridden gentry laid the groundwork for our current obsession with wellness holidays, and Georgian posh boys set the model for gap year hijinks, then it was the artists and writers of the Romantic era who created the idea of capturing holiday moments – gorgeous sunsets, spectacular ruins, unspoiled natural landscapes – and recreating them on paper. By the end of the 18th century, the "search for the picturesque" had almost become a competitive sport among a fortunate few, who set off on foot, horseback or in mail coaches to explore the most beautiful corners of the country.[3]

Once returned, paintings were displayed on walls, shown off at dinner parties and generally flashed about, in a battle of travel one-upmanship that wrote the 21st-century playbook for holiday snaps, postcards and ultimately Instagram itself.

In the second half of the 18th century, England was becoming a country on the move, propelled forwards by the twin forces of pre-industrialisation and new societal attitudes brought about by the Enlightenment. From the late 17th century, English thinkers, philosophers and intellectuals – along with many of their counterparts in Europe – had begun to challenge and question traditional cultural beliefs and hierarchies, including how the government was structured (hallo, wealthy, landowning elite) and the absolute power of religious institutions. A new belief in the rights of the individual and the power of reason – that humans could both understand and improve their own lives, rather than relying on divine guidance or aristocratic politicians – led to a strong focus on science and mathematical reasoning as a way of explaining the universe.[4] "Knowledge is as grateful to the understanding," said John Locke, one of the most influential Enlightenment philosophers, "as light to the eyes."[5] Put in 21st-century vernacular, *knowledge is power*. What no one anticipated was quite how much power the Enlightenment would unlock.

The era's focus on innovation and scientific thinking drove the first wave of inventions that would go on to become the foundations of the Industrial Revolution. James Watt's steam engine – able to power factories, mines and transportation – and Richard Arkwright's water frame, which, along with James Hargreaves' spinning jenny, revolutionised yarn production – were just three ground-breaking inventions that came on stream in the 1760s and 1770s.[6] Factories and mills were beginning to sprout in the North, drawing workers away from their traditional rural existences to a new way of life in fledgling towns and cities, which offered little in the way of infrastructure to support the flood of new residents.

And if the Enlightenment's ethos of individual liberties and government by consent had played a part in Britain losing its American colonies in the Revolutionary War of 1775–83, the twin prongs of industrialisation only fuelled a determination to assume power in other parts of the world. The aggressive policies of the East India Company – implemented by its own, deeply questionable private army and fuelled in no small part by forced cultivation of cash crops such as opium – saw Britain gain supremacy in India, while expanding into Asia and Africa.[7] Vast sums were channelled back into the newly emerging industries, although little – if any – consideration was given to the lives of those who toiled within them.

Many workers were forced to live in cramped and dirty new towns, while farmland was chewed up for development and waste spewed into rivers. So far, so 21st century, and the response among the leading writers, thinkers and artists of the day was not dissimilar to the disquiet felt by many today. Alongside the steady creep of urbanisation, a new appreciation of the natural world began to develop, helped along by those returning from a Grand Tour of Europe, where a new vogue for "Romanticism" – prioritising emotion and imagination over reason and scientific theory – was on the rise, as a reaction to the decades of Enlightenment thinking.

The focus on art, literature and philosophy, and the emphasis on the beauty of nature, was taken up as a rebellion by those who believed, not without reason, that Georgian Britain was becoming increasingly dominated by business and commerce in the rush to industrialise. By the late 18th century, exploring Britain's rural landscapes had begun to vie with visits to Bath and Buxton as the leisure pastime *du jour*,[8] with intrepid travellers setting out along the new turnpike roads to discover spectacular peaks, shimmering lakes and great swathes of forest that had rarely been seen by anyone besides those who lived there.

Among the early adopters of this trend was Fanny Burney, a noted novelist and diarist of the time, who set out to explore Dorset after five years at the service of the queen in the royal court.

> Hence we set out after dinner, for Lyme, and the road through which we travelled is the most beautiful to which my wandering destinies have yet sent me . . . I was fairly taken away, not only from the world, but from myself, and completely wrapped up and engrossed by the pleasures, wonders and charms of animated nature, thus seen in fair perfection.[9]

Relaxation and rejuvenation were no longer just to be found in crowded baths and ballrooms – instead, time immersed in the solitude and beauty of nature (particularly when captured on canvas and shown off to friends) became the preoccupation of the wealthy and artistic classes. This trend began decades earlier, in the small Herefordshire town of Ross-on-Wye. The Reverend John Egerton – a sociable man, with plenty of friends – could never have imagined that his habit of taking chums on a boat trip along the River Wye, through the spectacular steep-sided valley and on to the great ruined abbey at Tintern, would kickstart a whole new chapter (quite literally) in the development of the British holiday.

By 1750, so many visitors had heard of the tour and the natural wonders it offered, he commissioned a new boat specifically to offer the excursion to more people.[10] "Egerton wasn't the only one," says Ruth Waycott, Information Officer at the Wye Valley National Landscape. "The River Wye was a major highway of the day; it teemed with boats running between Hay, Hereford, Monmouth and Bristol. Local boat builders saw what Egerton was doing and recognised there was money to be made." By 1770, the trip was firmly established as a two-day journey: Wye to Monmouth on day one, Monmouth to Chepstow on day two.[11] Unwittingly, the reverend had created the first package holiday.

More than 250 years later, it's not difficult to see why this glorious stretch of border country claims to be Britain's first tourist destination. Those who visited the Wye Valley came not for medicinal benefits, or to be part of a social scene, but to explore and appreciate the destination itself: travelling, rather than holidaying; the earliest incarnation of tourism as we understand it today.

On the day I visit, the sky is duck-egg blue above the sinuous river and cloak of russet, auburn and butter-yellow woodland that covers the steep slopes on either side. It's a landscape I'm lucky to be familiar with – my sister lives in Monmouth – and I have spent years walking the footpaths that run along the lush riverbanks and sitting on the terrace at the Anchor pub, in the looming shadow of Tintern's spectacular abbey.

After a cheeky ice-cream (black cherry from the White Monk tearoom, delicious) by the river, I'm ready to tackle the 365 steps that lead up from the nearby car park at Lower Wyndcliff to the Eagle's Nest viewpoint – one of the blockbuster stops on the original Wye tour.[12] The view is extraordinary; a patchwork of fields in khaki and saffron, fringed by the wide silver ribbon of the river, ancient beech woodland rolling out to the white masts of the Severn Bridge, far off in the distance. As I lift my phone to take a picture, it strikes me I am doing exactly the same as those early visitors, trying to capture the stunning panorama, albeit on the small rectangle of my screen, rather than by hand on canvas.

It's an easy criticism that we all see things through our phones these days – too busy photographing the landscape to actually enjoy it – but the same accusation could have been levelled at those who took Egerton's tour. Most who came to the Wye would have brought bulging satchels; pens and pencils, drawing pads and sketch books, tour journals, telescope, barometer and pedometer.[13] "There would be a table in the middle of the boat so people could write or sketch as they went down river," says Waycott, "although there were plenty of stops and quite a lot of walking – up to see the view at Yat Rock, all the landscape follies and grottos at the Piercefield Estate and viewing points like the Alcove, as well as the Eagle's Nest, which boasted a double-decker viewing platform."

The most technically adept painters would also bring a "Claude Glass"[14] – the iPhone of its time. Named after the French landscape painter Claude Lorrain (no relation to Quiche), the Claude Glass was a boxed, framed mirror that reflected the landscape in miniature, blurring everything apart from the foreground and bathing it in a gentle, hazy light. More experienced artists would bring glass slides in different hues to overlay their image – very much the Instagram filters of their day. And, as with Insta, the same criticism was levelled; that those using a Claude Glass spent all their time with their backs to the view (or on their backs, having stumbled over when walking backwards to get the best possible perspective).[15]

When the artist and writer William Gilpin published his book, *Observations of the River Wye and Several Parts of South Wales* in 1782, a new tourism phenomenon was created. "If you have never navigated the Wye," he wrote, "you have seen nothing."[16] Continental travel had ground to a halt thanks to the French Revolution and those young men who had grown up fantasising about a few months of hedonistic gallivanting around Europe needed somewhere else for an adventure. A set itinerary grew up, including dining at certain inns, visiting particular viewpoints and ruins, with guides and pamphlets followed by everyone from Wordsworth and J. M. W. Turner to the author William Thackeray, who described the George Hotel in Chepstow (which still exists today) as "one of the neatest, cheerfulest, fresh-salmon-givingest inns to be found anywhere."[17]

Ironically, many who came were drawn not just by the region's natural beauty, but by its juxtaposition with the industry that grew up alongside the river. Gilpin wrote of "the great ironworks that introduce noise and hustle into these regions of tranquillity",[18] an object of fascination for those drifting by on their padded pleasure boats, with food and wine served and hauliers waiting to pull them across the shallows.

I get a chance to actually "see" an original boat when I visit Ross-on-Wye, where the innovative Museum Without Walls has QR codes dotted around the streets, creating virtual images of 18th-century life on my phone screen.

By the river, I scan the code and point my phone at the water to see a small wooden craft with a tall rectangular sail and square canopy – simple, but enough to imagine those early passengers clambering on board with easel and paints. It reminds me of the VR balloon ride I'd taken at the Buxton Crescent Experience; both examples of how technology can make history so much more engaging. I have strong memories of being catatonically bored at museums as a child; if I could have rambled round places, magicking up images and taking virtual balloon rides, it probably wouldn't have taken me until I was 40 to become an enthusiastic historian.

Predictably, it wasn't long before the popularity of the Wye created a growing curiosity about other rural areas of Britain – places that until relatively recently had been dismissed as savage and impenetrable. In 1724, Daniel Defoe had dismissed Westmorland (now part of Cumbria) as "a country eminent for being the wildest, most barren and frightening of any that I have passed over in England."[19] Sixty years later, it was on its way to becoming the second stop on the new "Picturesque Tour" that was taking shape as a replacement for the great cities of France and Italy. "Since persons of taste . . . began to make the tour of their own country and to give such pleasing accounts of the natural history," wrote Thomas West in his *Guide to the Lakes*, published in 1778, "the spirit of visiting them has diffused itself among the curious of all ranks."[20]

Cumbria's dramatic scenery – great swathes of silvery water, surrounded by glowering, auburn-hued peaks – would have been like nothing seen before for many of those who made the long journey, spurred on by either West's guidebook or Thomas Gray's *Journal of His Tour in the Lake District*, published posthumously in 1775. "Gray established a number of viewing stations that offered the best panoramas and locations for painting," says Gordon Lightburn, a Blue Badge guide based in Cumbria, whom I meet when I visit the region. "It included all the major lakes and recommended routes to get between them, with Ambleside at the centre of the southern Lakes, and Keswick to the north." Lightburn tells me that the most popular was the Claife Viewing Station on Windermere – coincidentally, almost directly opposite Storrs Hotel, where I'm based for the first night of my visit.

It's November when I stay, the lake framed by low cloud and misty drizzle that does little to mask the tranquil beauty of Windermere. On a Monday afternoon, the lake is a pale shade of platinum and creakingly silent; one stationary boat anchored a few metres offshore. Beyond, softened and blurred by the mist, the small town of Bowness-on-Windermere is just discernible. To the north, there is nothing but low hills shaded purple and khaki, watercolour woodland and a vast expanse of sky. This is how those early travellers would have seen it: utterly still, the mountains and valleys untouched save for a few, low-slung cottages and sheep in the fields. I envy them what they would have found, how overwhelming it must have felt; a time before there was any sense of just how much havoc we could wreak on somewhere so beautiful.

Dusk is falling as I stroll back to the hotel; a glow of light spooling out onto the lawn from the sitting room window where, it's alleged, William Wordsworth stood to recite his famous "daffodil" poem. No one is more synonymous with the Lakes than Wordsworth, who moved into a small cottage in the village of Grasmere with his sister, Dorothy, in 1799, calling it "the loveliest spot that man hath ever found."[21] It's still there, now part of the Wordsworth Grasmere Centre – part museum, part library, part keeper of the poet's legacy: that is, a belief in the restorative and healing power of nature, and an enduring love affair with the Lake District itself. "Come forth into the light of things," he wrote in 1798's "The Tables Turned". "Let Nature be your teacher."[22]

Dove Cottage has been preserved exactly as it was when William and Dorothy lived there, with the museum firmly focused not just on his life and work, but the landscapes that inspired them both. "We have three goals for our visitors," says Marie Batty, who joined Wordsworth Grasmere in 2016. "Slow the pace, connect with nature and have empathy with others. Seventy per cent of our work is outreach with school groups, hospice staff, refugees – we're a place where people come to share skills and experiences, but also to have a break and hopefully go away a little restored and rejuvenated. We have an immense resource – over 98 per cent of the Wordsworth collection, which is over 68,000 items. We use them to help people talk, share memories, reflect and recollect – exactly how Wordsworth would have wanted his work to be used."

As I explore the cosy, dimly lit rooms of Dove Cottage, often home to literary figures such as Samuel Taylor Coleridge as well as Dorothy and William, it's clear Wordsworth was a man ahead of his time – a 19th-century Chris Packham, albeit considerably better at turning out a sonnet. But it also strikes me, as the guide talks of his and Dorothy's life together, what an extraordinary woman she must have been; settled in this remote cottage, thinking nothing of walking to Ambleside twice daily (a ten-mile round trip) to collect the post.[23] Her *Grasmere Journals* reveal her to be as much of a naturalist and writer as her brother, with glimpses of a talent that may well have influenced William far more than she was ever (er, no surprise there) given credit for. Two years before Wordsworth's "I Wandered Lonely as a Cloud" (the poetic equivalent of "Yesterday") was written, Dorothy had been moved to write something not entirely dissimilar:

> I never saw daffodils so beautiful; they grew among mossy stones about and above them, some rested their heads upon these stones as a pillow for weariness and the rest tossed and reeled and danced and seemed as if they verily laughed with the wind that blew upon them ...[24]

The irony, of course, is that the wild beauty and solitude that drew the Wordsworths to Grasmere – and became such an integral part of their work – was already changing by the time they moved to Dove Cottage. As the cities grew, the lure of untouched and empty spaces, free of the endless clatter and rumble of construction, became more highly prized, and Wordsworth's writings only added to the region's newfound popularity. It's an accusation often levelled at travel writers – not entirely unfairly – that we discover quiet, unspoiled places, then write about them, thus ensuring they don't stay quiet and unspoiled for long; a trend magnified to an extreme with the current appetite for travel content on TikTok and Instagram. While Wordsworth wasn't actively encouraging people to visit, for many readers his words were an irresistible draw, with a steady upswing in the coaches and carriages clattering past Dove Cottage with every year that passed.

"They lived on the main road through the Lakes," says Batty, "and they would have seen all the stagecoaches going past, everyone dressed in their finery. In the early years, Dorothy and William might have heard one coach pass each day; by 1850, had they still been at Dove Cottage, they would have heard 50,000 rumble past in a year."

New ways to experience the landscapes sprung up, with "echo tourism" one of the more unusual crazes: an orchestra of brass instruments, the bassoon and clarinet installed next to a lake, spewing out deafening spurts of music to make the most of the natural echoes. The Duke of Portland took it one stage further, placing a barge with six cannons in the middle of Ullswater to create ear-splitting reverberations that boomed across the valley.[25] As more travellers arrived, the rough-and-ready inns began to polish up their acts, offering private rooms (including some that were actually clean) and meals that would have surprised the palate of many diners used to plain British dishes.

"Whitehaven was England's third largest port in the 18th century," says Gordon Lightburn. "It had links to the Americas and the Caribbean – plenty of rum and spices fell off wagons and found their way into the kitchens of inns and hotels. Cumberland sausage served with clapperbread – where the dough was slapped between hands before being placed on a hot griddle – was a classic dinner, while Rum Nicky, a shortcrust pastry filled with dates and dried fruit soaked in liquor, was a popular dessert." Such treats came at an unthinkable price; Whitehaven's "links" put it squarely at the heart of the slave trade, with much of the cargo – including rum and spices – produced by enslaved people.

As I look through the two-hundred-year-old guidebooks and pamphlets stored at the Armitt Library in Ambleside – founded by female naturalist and historian Mary Armitt in 1912 – it's clear how integral exploration and discovery are to the human condition. It's difficult to imagine how intrepid a visit to the Lakes would have been, how unfamiliar most people were with anywhere beyond the small area where they lived. For those coming from the south, with its pastoral landscapes and gently undulating hills, the scale of the mountains must have been staggering. And while it's far more familiar to us today, the region retains its pull; according to the Lake District National Park Authority, over 18 million people visited in 2022,[26] with an estimated 22 million by 2040.[27] Like Bath, over-tourism is a very real problem; even on my visit, on a damp autumn Sunday, Ambleside is packed with walkers and families, spilling out of coffee shops and striding along the pavements in cagoules and walking boots. The traffic is free-flowing, but in the summer months, the entire town – like many around Windermere – can come to a complete halt.

But while many of today's visitors come to the Lakes for the same reason as those early travellers – to walk or paint, to immerse themselves in the stunning scenery – many come simply to relax, an idea that would have been quite alien to most 18th-century visitors. The concept of "leisure travel" that had crept in on the coat-tails of the spa craze had been replaced by something more akin to a competitive sport. The "search for the picturesque" became a catchphrase in polite society, and while many travellers headed straight to the viewpoints in Thomas Gray's guidebook, those intent on bagging a rare prize went beyond the lakeshore and valleys, finding – and painting – unfamiliar mountain landscapes that could then be hung on the drawing room wall at home and boasted about over tea and warm scones.

While I can imagine the sense of awe those early visitors would have felt on encountering the craggy Cumbrian landscapes for the first time, I hadn't thought it was something I would ever *feel* in my own country. I've been lucky enough to experience that sense of wildness, of nature entirely untouched, several times in my travel writing career; the extraordinary virgin beaches of New Zealand's Coromandel Peninsula, the great sandstone mesas of Utah and Monument Valley, the brilliant, golden-hued silence in Oman's Sharqiya Sands – but I never expected to find it in my own country. But then, until last November, I had never driven along the shores of Loch Lomond and crossed the silent wastes of Rannoch Moor, to be met by Glencoe's vast, ominous mountains, glowering down over the narrow, grey ribbon of the A82. Dusk was falling as I pulled into a layby, peering through the windscreen at a landscape that felt so alien as to be almost unsettling. Outside, the air was cool and damp, the silence absolute.

Even now, months later, I remember the sense that it was like nowhere I had ever been. I had no sense of being in my own country. The mountains were forbidding, unfamiliar, none of the lush green pastures of the Alps, or the jagged outlines of the Dolomites. Down in the valley, car headlights were like fireflies in the gloom. I felt ant-like, standing beneath such great, hulking monsters cloaked in faded mauves and rust and green; nature as I had never witnessed before. Slightly spooked, I got back into the car and set off for the village of Glencoe, relieved by the first signs of human life that began to appear: the Glencoe Visitor Centre, a few houses, and then a sign to my billet for the night, Glencoe House.

Once settled in, cup of tea and a steadying chocolate digestive to hand, I reflected on the fact that Dorothy and William Wordsworth made that same journey through Glencoe over 220 years ago; a six-week, 663-mile marathon, travelling in a two-wheel, open-air cart pulled by a single horse.[28] "I cannot attempt to describe the mountains," says Dorothy, in her book *Recollections of a Tour Made in Scotland*, published in 1803. "Only that they were the grandest I had ever seen ... such forms as Milton might be supposed to have in his mind when he applied to Satan 'his stature reached the sky.'"[29] In many ways, Glencoe's mind-blowing scenery probably looked very similar two centuries ago, apart from the road; but even to attempt such a journey seems to me incredibly intrepid, verging on completely bonkers.

But the lure of the "picturesque", the search for the country's wildest, most extraordinary landscapes, drew others to follow in the Wordsworths' footsteps, and make the long journey to the Scottish mountains. Before them, the few visitors to the region had been unimpressed with what they encountered; Samuel Johnson's *Journey to the Western Isles of Scotland*, published in 1775, ended with the pithy statement that "the noblest prospect a Scotsman ever sees is the high road that leads him to England."[30] Thirty years later, when the Wordsworths made their journey, they would have enjoyed little in the way of comforts found in the Wye Valley or the Lakes; inns, such as they were, were often nothing more than a smoke-filled peasant's house with clay walls and no chimney or glass in the windows. Roads would have been little more than cattle paths and any food at all – rock-hard bread, the odd egg, a boiled sheep's head with the hair singed off – would have been a luxury.[31]

For those who were slightly less feisty, the shimmering waters of Loch Lomond and the more accessible landscapes of the Trossachs were less challenging, but still offered impressive bragging rights back home. The slow trickle of visitors – lured by the writings of Sir Walter Scott – increased considerably after King George IV sailed up the east coast of Britain in 1822, at the invitation of Scott himself.[32] The first time a monarch had visited Scotland since 1650, George dressed for the occasion in bright pink stockings and a kilt that ended six inches above his knees[33] (quite a look for a man who weighed 20 stone and was only 5 foot 2). Not to be outdone, Scott threw aside the traditional Highland costume of rough, dark green material, belted in place, and ordered vastly expensive tartan in scarlet and gold[34] – unwittingly creating a design classic that would grace shortbread tins for centuries to come.

Alongside Sir Walter Scott, one woman helped put the Highlands on the tourism map more than any other: Queen Victoria. "What began as a one-off visit in 1842," says Keren Guthrie, archivist at Blair Castle near Pitlochry, "was the start of the love affair with the Highlands that the Royal Family still has today. Queen Victoria's time in Scotland would have been the first time she ever had a holiday." Her affection for the Highlands was so strong, she and Albert returned twice more before taking a lease on Balmoral Castle in 1848; a place where, Victoria wrote, "all seemed to breathe freedom and peace and to make one forget the world and all its sad turmoils."[35] After a series of additions and enlargements to the estate, Albert bought it in 1852 and Victoria's delight in the wild tranquillity of the region – and the sense of retreat it offered – was echoed by Queen Elizabeth II, who honeymooned at Balmoral, spent every summer there, and, in July 2022, passed away at what was thought to be the favourite of all her residences.

Judging by the original letters Guthrie shows me when I visit, sent by Prince Albert to the Duke of Atholl, Queen Victoria was exhausted when they first arrived at Blair Castle, quite possibly suffering from post-natal depression and in desperate need of peace and quiet. With every whim taken care of, from meals to guided walks, Blair Castle unwittingly invented the "fly and flop", offering the royal couple a five-star, all-inclusive bolthole where they could escape the pressures of everyday life and be immersed somewhere totally different, without the pressure of gruelling spa treatments or the need to admire endless Renaissance artworks.

I'm lucky enough to visit Blair Castle on a day it's closed to the public; just Keren and I, tiptoeing up the grand staircase beneath baleful-looking stag's heads and dozens of shotguns hung in neat rows and concentric circles. I follow her along a corridor dotted with light-fittings made of antlers, past antler-shaped chairs, cabinets with more guns, more angry-looking stag's heads and, yes, another array of guns (decor by Shoot 'Em Up Interiors). Victoria's bed remains in situ, as does a huge ledger, listing everything the royal couple liked to bring on their travels, including a retinue of 100 people. Perhaps it's inevitable that the concept of travelling purely in the pursuit of leisure originated with a monarch; the only person in the country who couldn't be criticised for stepping away from their life to do ... absolutely nothing.

But while Queen Victoria might have helped invent the wilds of Scotland as a rural getaway for huntin'-shootin'-fishin' enthusiasts, it was her uncle, King George IV (formerly the legendarily hedonistic Prince Regent), more than half a century earlier, who helped kick off what would become our best-loved holiday tradition of all. While the Romantic travellers had been discovering the wild beauty of the Welsh mountains and Cumbrian lakes, another part of the British landscape had been undergoing its own revolution, slowly developing into a far more egalitarian playground than anything that had been seen before. The winning combination of health, pleasure, hedonism and leisure first invented on the elegant streets of Bath and Buxton was now being reproduced in former fishing villages up and down the coast. While the countryside was slowly unfolding, the seaside had exploded into life.

4
Beside the Seaside
Scarborough and Brighton

"The Sea washes away all the Evils of Mankind."[1]
Euripides

I have always loved the sea. It is the keeper of some of my earliest memories: a tartan rug, a striped windbreak, bright-red bucket, butter-yellow spade. I grew up with the shingle shoreline of the Sussex coast a few minutes' walk from my house; learned to swim among the tangles of seaweed and unruly waves, summer days scheduled around the rise and fall of the tide. Saturday afternoons were for long blustery walks with my sister Penny; Sunday mornings for sunlit swims before coming home to a noisy family Sunday lunch. In my teenage years, I came to love the vast skies and rippled swathe of sand that was exposed as the waters retreated; long walks beneath buffeting silver clouds that soothed whatever teenage angst I was suffering from on a particular afternoon. By the time I moved to London, the sea was knitted into my life, drawing me back regularly to swim in the summer months and sweep away the city's stresses on whip-cold winter days.

As an island people, the sea is supposedly written into all our souls. Our language is scattered with phrases that come from our seafaring heritage: "long shot" (when an inaccurate gun made an unlikely hit), "taken aback" (when a sail was unexpectedly blown flat by wind) or "in the doldrums" (a windless belt of water around the equator, where ships frequently got stuck). On the first hot days of the year, roads to the coast are jammed with cars, newspapers print the obligatory pictures of beaches crammed with visitors, and stretches of shingle and sand are patchworked with beach towels and lilos, picnics and barbecues. A day by the sea, even just an afternoon, offers a hit of that unique holiday feeling; a blast of glittering blue water, warm sun and briny, whip-clean air that sings to something in all of us.

And yet it hasn't always been this way. Three hundred years ago, in what's now known as the Age of Sail – an era of sea-based exploration, trade and warfare – the British coastline was rarely considered as anything but a gateway to a vast, underwater larder, or the jumping off point for a small number of foolhardy adventurers who disappeared off in great galleons and rarely came back. For the majority of Georgians, like generations before them, the sea was little more than a mythical concept; those who didn't live near to the coast would probably go their entire lives without glimpsing the water. For those who did, the sea was often seen as a frightening, unknown entity – quite possibly the realm of the Devil himself.[2]

Swimming as a leisure pursuit had yet to be invented; those who tried it often received quite the dressing down (Cambridge students caught swimming in the Cam were sent down after a second offence).[3] Quite why isn't really clear, although it may have been a handed-down prejudice, wrapped around stories of Playboy-style orgies associated with swimming during the hedonistic Roman era. For whatever reason, it didn't seem to occur to anyone that the sea might offer health-giving properties until the spa craze was well underway.

At the beginning of the 18th century, there was only one seaside village that could take its place alongside the spa towns – mostly because, thanks to the discovery of a chalybeate spring in 1626,[4] Scarborough was both. In 1667, a Scarborough physician, Dr Wittie, published a pamphlet, *Scarborough Spaw*, that contained a direct challenge to the likes of Bath and Buxton. "You braggard inland spaws; we have here at Scarborough such an effectual pickle for both external and internal use as none of you can boast of."[5] Wittie's words may have fallen on mostly deaf ears at the time, but 50 years later, the idea was picked up by a Buxton physician, John Floyer. "Since we live on an island and have the sea about us," he wrote, in *The History of Cold-Bathing*, published in 1702, "we cannot want an excellent Cold Bath which will preserve our Health and many Diseases."[6]

Over the coming decades, his assertion that seawater could cure everything from leprosy to deafness began to strike a chord – not just with ailment-stricken aristos, but also the physicians, medics, quacks and potion-concocters who made an extremely good living ministering to their many conditions. Most treatments centred around the belief that the deeply unpleasant business of "purging the system" was the best remedy for any number of conditions (although the cure might well have seemed more unpleasant than the original complaint). The idea was nothing new; drinking gallons of the mineral-rich waters was an integral part of the "spa cure" everywhere from Bath to Buxton. If holidays were invented as a by-product of a national obsession with health, the British seaside was born of exactly the same fixation.

Floyer's ideas began to chime with those looking to move on from spa resorts that had, unaccountably (and entirely unacceptably), been infiltrated by those ghastliest of people: the wealthy middle classes. Cities were starting to be polluted with coal smoke and human stench, streets ran with open sewers, and fresh air – particularly seaside air – began to seem increasingly attractive. But even if seawater was the new chalybeate spring, where could one go to experience it? Coastal villages were run-down, grubby and about as likely to have somewhere comfortable to stay as a doorway to the moon. Travelling was a challenge in itself, with the new turnpike roads focusing on cities and areas of industry, rather than little-trodden routes to the sea.[7] Only Scarborough – already established as a busy port – was well-connected to the growing cities of the north, although it remained out of reach to the moneyed classes clustered around London.

Even today, it feels quite a trek from my stretch of Sussex coast to Yorkshire's windswept shoreline. After several trains, refuelled by strong tea and a warm scone slathered with butter, eaten on the run between platforms at York station, I arrive into Scarborough on a glorious, blue-skied afternoon – albeit with the mercury struggling to get above zero. Growing up in the south, I'd always believed Brighton to be the first beach resort, and – with classic southern snootiness – that there was little to rival the beaches of Devon and Cornwall elsewhere in the country. Not unusually, I was wrong on both counts. When I turn the corner onto St Nicholas Close, I am genuinely stopped in my tracks by the great blue sweep of South Bay, rolling in towards the faded spa buildings that melt into the cliffs beyond.

Once I've finished gawping at the view, I check into Bike & Boot – a chic guesthouse set in the Regency terrace that sits directly across from the gargantuan facade of the town's Grand Hotel. It was designed to appeal to walkers, surfers and dog-lovers, with a mobile of Wellington boots dangling above the central table in the lobby, and a clock made of flip-flops in the cosy lounge. "We – my business partner Simon Rattigan and myself – started Bike & Boot because we thought the market needed something new," says Simon Kershaw, when I chat to him later in the sunny breakfast room. "Dog ownership shot up in the pandemic, cycling became huge, people wanted to get out into the fresh air more. We like to think we're an English ski lodge, but with facilities that are really fit for purpose: spacious bike store, somewhere to dry your wetsuit, proper dog-washing facilities."

If this all sounds a bit knit-your-own-dinner, it's anything but; my room is boutique-hotel chic, with pale grey walls, crisp white linen and pops of colour in the vintage tourism posters, cushions and rugs. As I look out towards the sea, I wonder what those early visitors would have made of the neoprene-clad surfers, sitting on their surfboards beneath the blazing January sun, waiting to catch the perfect wave. Three hundred years ago, simply getting into the water would have been a laborious process – for women, at least. "The gentlemen go a little way out to sea in boats and jump in naked directly," wrote the anonymous author of *A Journey from London to Scarborough*, published in 1734. "The ladies have the use of gowns and guides."[8]

By 1735, the town was in full swing, with money from the surrounding coal industry funnelled into new mansions, roads and infrastructure, and the flourishing smuggling trade bringing in luxury items such as silk and tea.[9] London tradesmen, cooks and upholsterers began to set up northern outposts in what had become known as the Montpellier of England, with sea-bathing an integral part of a visit, alongside a recommended intake of several gallons of seawater. Inevitably, this resulted in just about anything from a terrible thirst to violent nausea and terrifying stomach upsets. In an attempt at decorum, two "houses of convenience" were built close to the shore, with the aim of avoiding the revolting spectacle of visitors being "caught short" in public. The toilets were opened by the first governor of Scarborough, Dicky Dickinson,[10] who, it seems fair to say, was not regarded with the same degree of reverence as his opposite number in Bath. "I'll make him Sovereign of the Spaw," went a popular poem of the time, "to keep the squirting tribes in awe."[11] It's impossible to imagine the elegant visitors to Bath being described as a "squirting tribe", although doubtless chugging down vast quantities of spa waters had similarly horrible effects.

But being at the seaside released something (aside from stomach contents) in the national psyche; a shedding of British pomposity and a coarse humour that would never have been tolerated at the spa towns. Unlike spa waters, sea-bathing was open to everyone: dukes and duchesses might find themselves bathing alongside local fishermen or shopkeepers – and their wives and children, all of whose behaviour would have been a lot less refined than other gentry, and doubtless considerably more fun. Whereas the spa resorts were small, intense spaces, filled with the same faces seen at London balls and country parties, and governed by strict social rules, the seaside was a place for frivolity and fun. It strikes me, as I stroll along Scarborough's long promenade, that the sense of stepping out of one's self, the loosening of inhibitions that has always been such an integral part of the British holiday experience, may well have first taken shape in these cold waters off the North Sea coast.

As word of Scarborough's pleasures began to spread, two villages on the south coast began to see their first visitors, lured in by the promise of fresh air and health-giving seawater. The down-at-heel fishing village of Brighthelmstone in Sussex is mentioned in a letter written in 1736 by the Reverend William Clark: "We are now sunning ourselves upon the beach. My morning business is bathing in the sea and buying fish, evening is for riding out and counting the boats."[12] Nowadays we could call Clark an "early adopter", and it's fair to assume his "evening business" would *not* have included bedding down in comfortable lodgings. In the early days of the seaside, accommodation was little more than grubby rooms in a dilapidated fisherman's cottage, which usually came with a permanent fragrance of wet sardine.

Nearer to London, on the north Kent coast, the small fishing village of Margate was developing fast, helped by its proximity to the capital and the "hoys" – heavy barges – that ploughed up and down the Thames Estuary. Originally used for carrying corn and other cargo, by the middle of the 18th century, canny operators had begun to realise that good money could be made by transporting those keen to exchange the smoggy streets of the capital for some fresh sea air. The journey could be challenging – anything from nine hours to three days, depending on the weather – but the ticket price of half a crown made it an affordable getaway for London's fast-developing middle classes, along with those drawn by the new claims that seawater – and its accompanying fresh, clean air – was a universal panacea of extraordinary power.[13] "For the sake of drinking that purging draught, sea water, and bathing..." wrote *The Royal Magazine* in 1762 ". . . cripples frequently recover the use of their limbs, hysterical ladies their spirits and even the lepers are cleansed."[14]

Such claims were hard to resist, particularly at a time when there was no cure for common illnesses like consumption (tuberculosis) and no antibiotics. And once visitors arrived at the seaside, they could make use of the new, cutting-edge bathing machines; dragged across the shingle by deeply unimpressed horses, these contraptions offered both men and women the chance to "dip" without exposing themselves to the gaggles of lecherous locals gathered on the sand. As visitor numbers increased, permanent "bathing rooms" were erected. For the princely sum of half a crown, visitors could take tea or coffee and browse the London newspapers while waiting for their name to be called, before being trundled across to the water's edge, where two "dippers" awaited, thigh-deep in water, to chivvy and boss their charges into the sea.

But although Margate led the charge in sea-bathing innovation, boasted shops stocked with the best-quality lace and china and a circulating library filled with novels, to enable visitors to indulge in the fashion for reading while listening to the sea, it lacked the one thing that really mattered: the right clientele. Once Dr Richard Russell – author of the much talked about *A Dissertation on the Use of Seawater in the Diseases of the Gland*[15] – set up a clinic in Brighthelmstone (near to Hove, where he just happened to own a mineral spring), and the turnpike roads from London began to be stitched together, Margate had serious competition. The Steine Pleasure Gardens were developed from 1765, with formal promenades laid out in 1778,[16] while lodgings, assembly rooms and boutiques also began to open. Before long, a visit to the Sussex coast was increasingly discussed by those who previously would never have considered travelling to anywhere but Bath for their health-giving break.

Predictably, other seaside villages soon began to wake up to the fact that their long stretches of sand or shingle might bring in something more than the odd catch of sardines and whatever washed up from the occasional shipwreck. Unlike spa towns, which would always be limited in number due to the need for a chalybeate spring, any village with a decent beach could set itself up as a resort. The king took a liking to Weymouth (where, so legend has it, he took to the sea accompanied by a second bathing machine, filled with fiddlers playing the national anthem while he took the plunge),[17] while the Princesses Amelia and Charlotte preferred the statelier pace of Worthing.[18] But it was the visit by the Prince of Wales to Brighthelmstone – soon to become Brighton – in 1783[19] (now a sizeable town, with a population of over 4,000),[20] and its gradual development over the following years as his own personal playground, that really lit the touchpaper.

I think about this as I stroll along the Hove stretch of Brighton seafront, weaving through the plastic tables and chairs at the Lawns Café, and settle in with a cup of tea as the sun floods the vanilla-hued frontages of the elegant Regency terraces on the other side of the road. Growing up, Brighton was my playground too; a beacon of boozy evenings out that felt like the height of rebellion on the nights I escaped my staid, seaside village. Between the Prince Regent's raffish era and my teenage days of sneaking into nightclubs with a fake ID, Brighton became well-established as a place of hedonism and hangovers for everyone from weekending Victorians to 1960s mods and rockers, its health-focused origins almost entirely forgotten.

But something has changed in recent years; 350 years after Dr Wittie first extolled the virtues of seawater, there has been a massive resurgence of interest in the restorative powers of sea-swimming, spurred on by lessons learned in the pandemic and a rediscovery of how being immersed in natural surroundings can have a positive impact on mental and physical health. As I sit, muffled up in jacket, scarf and gloves, I watch a gaggle of women strip off and stride into the cold March waters, mindful of the irony that although I've spent a lifetime swimming in the sea, my unbending never-before-June rule means I'm little but a fair-weather dipper by today's standards.

"Your body adjusts quite quickly to colder temperatures if you swim regularly," says friend and Brighton resident Camille Hobby-Limon. "And the benefits are fantastic. Just being in the sea, that feeling of weightlessness... sometimes I swim, sometimes I just lie on my back like a starfish and look at the sky. The cold water's like a re-set button – I get in feeling overwhelmed, frustrated and worried – ten minutes later, everything's OK."

But if the restorative powers of the sea are unchanged, the experience would have been considerably different for 18th-century beachgoers. "We rose at six o'clock in the morn," wrote the novelist Fanny Burney, in a diary of her trip to Brighton in 1782, "and by the pale blink o' the moon we went to the seaside, where we had bespoken the bathing women to be ready for us, and into the ocean we plunged."[21] Less of a swim and more of an enforced dunking by meaty-armed assistants, an icy pre-dawn dip was just a part of the experience, with laxatives given beforehand and pints of seawater to be downed once the freezing cold immersion had been completed. Working as a "dipper" would have been a skilled job; part sergeant major, part nursemaid, with some – most notably Martha Gunn, Brighton's "Queen of the Dippers" – becoming well-known figures in their own right.

"It was a job that would have needed considerable skill," says Louise Peskett, Museum Educator at Brighton Museums. "I'm a sea swimmer, but you never really know what it's going to be like until you're in – it's uneven and deep and quite suddenly you can be in a washing machine of waves. Martha would have been able to read the wind, the clouds and the sea – and she must have had excellent people skills, because all the well-born women insisted on seeing her." For Martha, the change in the town's fortunes brought her considerable wealth and notoriety; so much so that her portrait is given pride of place in the Brighton Museum, her round scarlet-cheeked face – matching perfectly with her berry-red cloak – wearing an impatient 'Oh, come ON' expression that I suspect propelled many of her charges straight into the sea.

But the "Queen of the Dippers" wasn't the only one to benefit from Brighton's reinvention as Bath-on-Sea. The Prince Regent's regular visits, usually with an entourage of overdressed fops, lascivious earls and pimped-up playboys following in his wake, brought a tsunami of money into the town. When Boy George was in residence, the streets exploded in a whirl of pageants, balls and prize-fights, with crumbling fishermen's cottages torn down and replaced with palatial villas. The once-dilapidated roads rang to the sound of elegant carriages rattling across the cobbles, the promenade thronged with elegantly dressed women in feathers and furs, and apple-cheeked aristos galloped across the sands on gussied-up horses that spent the night in stables more lavish than many guesthouses.

The town's reputation for excess spread not just through England but across the Channel. In 1764, Gilly Williams, a renowned writer and "wit" of the time, had noted the number of French who came to sample Brighton's notorious pleasures: "extraordinary exotics . . . barbers, milliners, Barons and Counts arrive here at almost every tide."[22] Twenty-five years later, the Prince Regent would have had dozens of members of the French aristocracy to gamble and frolic with; many fleeing across the Channel disguised as sailors, desperate to escape the French Revolution, and the vicious temper of Madame la Guillotine.[23]

If pleasurable pastimes had been a side-benefit of a trip to Bath or Buxton, something to be dipped into on a Grand Tour, or occasionally experienced on a painting excursion through the Wye Valley or the Lake District, in Brighton, indulgence and excess became the whole point. The concept of "improvement" – whether physical or educational – that had been the original motivation for travelling somewhere new, became all but forgotten. "Morning rides, champagne, dissolution and nonsense," barked the *Morning Post* in 1785. "Jumble all those phrases together and you have a complete account of all that's passing at Brighthelmstone."[24] "Conspicuous leisure" was almost elevated into an art form during the Prince

Regent's era, relegating any idea of travel as "improving" to little more than a courtly joke.

Such disapproval did little to slow the town's success or stop other investors and developers from attempting to recreate its heady cocktail of indulgent pleasures and easy money at other locations around the English coastline. By the late 18th century, resorts were springing up everywhere from Blackpool and Southport to Torquay in Devon, while closer to London, Dover, Ramsgate, Folkestone and Hastings began to challenge the still busy, but much-maligned, Margate. "Should you be disposed to go to Margate by water," wrote English statesman George Saville Carey in 1799, "you must shut your eyes from seeing indecent scenes, your ears from indecent conversations and your nose from indelicate smells."[25]

While many seaside towns became known for their more relaxed social attitudes, where spacious beaches allowed all ages and classes to mingle and the tightly pulled stays of the Georgian era felt considerably looser, not all were created in Brighton's – or Margate's – image. Some were designed for those who shared the *Morning Post*'s distaste for such Bacchanalian pleasures; Bognor welcomed those looking for somewhere "respectable but unshowy" while Hastings was seen to offer a smattering of seaside pleasures without tipping over into full-on unseemliness. "Gay without profligacy," said *A Guide to all the Watering and Sea Bathing Places*, published in 1803, about Hastings, "and enjoys life, without mingling in its debaucheries."[26]

All this might sound as if everyone was hopping in carriages and cantering down to the coast for sunset cocktails and sardines on toast, but the number of those actually able to experience this new-fangled "holiday" was a tiny percentage of the overall population. Most – whether town-dwellers or farm-workers – would rarely, if ever, leave their own neighbourhoods, with about as much chance of visiting a seaside resort as joining a Grand Tour. Instead, "time off" ("holiday" in its modern usage wouldn't have even entered the vernacular) was a random combination of unofficial (but recognised) Mondays off after the monthly pay-day weekend, occasional holydays and the annual fair – often the highlight of the year. Eighteenth-century fairs often went on for several days; a whirligig of circus performers, puppet shows, exotic animals and dozens of stands selling everything from hot sausages and home-made pies to vast quantities of ale, cider and mead.[27] Seaside resorts may have arrived for the wealthy few, but it would be another half a century before the average working man might genuinely consider a trip to the seaside as a well-earned treat.

Back in Scarborough, fresh from a lemon twist ice-cream from the iconic Harbour Bar, I slip through the doors of the imposing Grand Hotel. When it originally opened in 1867, it was the largest brick building in the world;[28] an unparalleled feat of architectural design, with four towers, 12 floors, 52 chimneys and 365 rooms. It's hard, now, to imagine how glamorous it must have been; the lobby is drab and silent, save for a clutch of fruit machines, blinking and flashing beneath the wide, sweeping staircase. The bar is half-shuttered, the once-elegant lounge silent apart from the rhythmic whirr of an ancient heater, puffing dry, stale air towards the lone couple sat mutely in the vast picture window, overlooking the sea below.

On the wall by the stairs, I notice a framed reprint of a promotional poster for Dr Wittie's book, and wonder what he would have made of the town's meteoric rise and equally dramatic fall. It strikes me how integral transport is to the history of our holidays, and the extraordinary ramifications of each new development in how we move from place to place. If the new turnpike roads heralded the beginning of our love affair with the seaside and railways opened it out to a far greater cross-section of society, then it was air travel that sent the fortunes of our coastal resorts tumbling. Set against the sun-kissed shores of the Costa del Sol, and the sense of freedom and liberation at leaving rainy old Blighty behind for a week or two, Scarborough and seaside resorts like it never really stood a chance; the steep decline in visitors through the 1970s and 80s as negatively impactful as the closure of the cotton mills and factories on many northern industrial towns.

"Scarborough is unique," says Christiane, who checks me out of Bike & Boot as I prepare to head back down south. "Of course there's the beaches, but there's also great walking trails, cycling routes – there's so much right on the doorstep. The town needs investment, like all seaside resorts, but it is really loved." As I walk back to the station, I notice the number of small businesses that dot St Nicholas Street; independent coffee shops, a florist and Ginger & Gray, where I chat with the owner about how monochrome fashion is these days, and come out with a gorgeous, bottle green jumper. It reminds me of the shops that dot Brighton's bohemian North Laine area, with its vintage stores and vegan cafes, all run by people who love their town with a passion too.

Brighton may have undergone something of a reinvention in the last 20 years – unlike Scarborough, Brighton's Grand Hotel buzzes with families and couples, hen parties and wedding guests – but it suffers the same problems as its northern counterpart, although perhaps not writ so large. Homelessness, social deprivation and real poverty all co-exist alongside the bright lights and pizazz, and although there's no easy fix, I do think in some ways we are all to blame for the demise of these places that were once so cherished, so desirable. "Money has been poured into some of our seaside towns – like Margate and Blackpool," says Patricia Yates, Chief Executive of Visit Britain, "but it hasn't followed through into necessarily getting a new or different clientele. I've seen the investment, the upgrade in accommodations, but you still need to get that sense of excitement about domestic holidays, that I don't think people have."

Perhaps part of the reason there's so little excitement is because of the narrative around our seaside towns, usually dismissed as faded and tired compared to the glamorous beaches of the Mediterranean, or wherever we choose to fly to for our week by the sea. But what attracted those first visitors in the early 18th century – along with the Victorians who juddered in on their trains and our great-grandparents who settled into deckchairs to watch Punch & Judy and munch on candyfloss – still exists, and however much we might talk our seaside resorts down, these stretches of sand and shingle are the first places we want to be when the sun comes out. Look beyond the downbeat headlines and the same seaside pleasures await: warm sand between your toes, hot chips thick with salt, fresh briny air and, best of all, that great, blue swathe of nothingness. There's no better place to clear your head, raise your spirits, reflect and reconnect. Whatever else, we *are* an island people. Maybe it's time we began to value our seaside again, to celebrate our sparkling shoreline and rediscover a little of the joy these very first holiday resorts gave to so many generations before us.

5
The Wings of the Wind
Llandudno and Torquay

"I will send the locomotive as the great missionary over the world."[1]
George Stephenson

27 September, 1825. In the small town of Shildon, something is afoot. Crowds gather, journalists ready their pencils, engineers cross their fingers and the group of Quaker entrepreneurs, who have invested and believed and gambled in a ground-breaking new way of transporting their coal, cross their fingers and hope. But as George Stephenson's steam-powered Locomotion No. 1 slowly chugs its way out of the station, with 600 passengers crammed into the coal wagons,[2] whooping and waving, no one could have imagined that they were witnessing the birth of something that would change the world forever. Stephenson's creation was, said the *Durham County Advertiser*, "a stupendous work . . . a scene of gaiety and bustle was witnessed, surpassing, perhaps anything that ever occurred in that place before."[3] The locomotive was originally envisioned as nothing more than a way to move coal between the collieries and ports more quickly and easily than the existing network of canals and packhorses. The members of the public packed on board were seen as novelty-seekers, with little thought that this new-fangled contraption might be quite useful for transporting passengers as well as goods.

It's one of the great oddities of human existence that when a life-changing event happens – something that will have far-reaching consequences for decades and centuries to come – most of us are entirely unaware it has even taken place. Who knows the date at which the internet first sprang to life? When the contraceptive pill was officially granted a licence? When someone looked at their salty chips and thought, *Now, what* that *needs is a hefty slosh of vinegar*. The change wasn't immediate: Stephenson's invention, which screeched and wheezed its way across the industrialised north, had little impact at first on the wealthier classes, who continued to jaunt around the countryside in their carriages and mail coaches, while those who toiled in the mushrooming cities were probably not even aware that locomotives existed. But five years after the first passengers were carried by steam train on a public railway track, the Liverpool to Manchester line started offering regular passenger services[4] and the rail revolution really began.

"The owners of the railway were clever – they ran a very successful PR campaign," says Tom Chesshyre, travel writer and author of *Slow Trains Across Britain*. "They illuminated one of the tunnels near Liverpool, put on a band and invited the public to come and see the line before it was open. Even so, they were surprised by the passenger numbers from the start." If the public was won over, the same couldn't be said of those who owned the canals and feared – quite rightly, as it turned out – that these new, steam-belching animals would ruin the businesses they had run for decades. "Although a lot of people found it very exciting, there was quite a backlash," says Chesshyre. "Some said it was a horrible way of getting around, noisy, polluting – that your eyes would be damaged if you travelled at speed, that cows would be so upset by the cacophony of noise they'd stop producing milk."

Whatever the naysayers thought, the railway quickly became an integral part of a revolution that was as human as it was industrial – a solution to a problem that had only just begun to exist: the need for respite from modern-day life. The gradual societal changes that had begun in the 1760s – the beginnings of industrialisation, and a new, urban working class – picked up considerable pace in the first decades of the 19th century, with cotton mills, smelting factories, coal mines and ironworks swallowing up tens of thousands of workers and condemning them to long days in filthy, ear-splitting and often dangerous working conditions.

To make things worse, the new breed of employers considered "time off" an unnecessary luxury, heavily restricting the traditional freedoms to enjoy holydays or fairs that would once have been scattered through the year. A 72-hour, six-day week was the norm,[5] with just enough time on a Sunday to go to church and quaff an ale or three before the whole thing started again, with often only Christmas Day and Good Friday given as official time off.

"Whatever kind of job you do, time away from it is essential," says Mark Brocklesby, an executive coach specialising in personal resilience. "Whether just for a couple of days or several weeks, the sense of freedom it engenders is hugely important for our mental wellbeing. Holidays are ritualised for us from a young age – we mark time by them; school holidays, half-terms, Bank Holidays. The same would have been true hundreds of years ago, albeit far fewer of them – Christmas and Easter, maybe midsummer and the annual fair. For anyone who works – whether manual labourer or a CEO – time off is what we long for. Without that, life becomes pretty unbearable."

Pretty unbearable is a fairly apt description for the lives of those working in the new industrial centres, not least because the majority of employers – tough, money-hungry and entirely disinterested in their workers' wellbeing – viewed periods of forced (unpaid) unemployment – when business was slow, factories needed maintaining or mines temporarily closed – as leisure time enough. For the workers, this kind of time off usually produced the opposite of relaxation, adding to money worries and the general level of privation. Aside from the financial anxiety, there was precious little to do in the new urban centres, although some communities formed "friendly societies", while others turned to music, with cotton mill and factory brass bands slowly developing in the first half of the new century.[6] Cock-fighting and bare-knuckle boxing were still legal until the 1830s[7] – providing plenty of fodder for the ruling class, who generally believed that time away from the workplace only led to drunkenness and debauchery. More than anything, there was no possibility of the change of scene that had become so fashionable among the wealthy elite, who travelled to the spa towns and coastal resorts in their carriages, happy to pay the new turnpike road tolls for the privilege.

And then, quite suddenly, a whole new method of escape rattled and clanked its way over the horizon, slowly opening up and reshaping the British coastline into a newly egalitarian playground. Long stretches of shoreline that had been isolated and almost unreachable were suddenly connected to the world, offering those who owned the land a quick ticket to the country's newest money-making scheme: the seaside resort. "Without the railway, Llandudno might never have existed – or certainly not as it is today," says Judith Phillips, Trustee at the Llandudno Museum, when I drop in for a chat on a blustery November day. "The Mostyn family, who owned the land – and still do today – had originally thought of developing a port to link with Northern Ireland, but the anchorage wasn't deep enough. When the Chester and Holyhead Railway opened in 1848, which linked to the Liverpool–Manchester line, it offered something different: the chance to turn the land into a resort. The Mostyns looked at what was happening in towns like Brighton and Blackpool and Scarborough and decided to get in on the act."

By the time the foundations of Llandudno were being laid out, railway mania had really taken hold, fuelled by the new craze for "excursion trains" – offering the 19th-century equivalent of what we would now call the "daycation".[8] Social organisations or private companies would make agreements with the railway company to charter a train on a specific day to a specific destination, guaranteeing hundreds – sometimes thousands – of passengers at reduced prices. The Liverpool–Manchester line carried flag-waving passengers across the Sankey Viaduct – the first railway viaduct in the world, opened in 1830[9] – with interest building to such an extent that by 1840, an excursion train from Nottingham to Leicester needed four engines to pull 67 carriages, carrying nearly 3,000 passengers.[10] No matter that delays, engineering problems and frequent accidents meant there was often barely any time to actually spend in the advertised destination; it was about the journey, the experience, the sense of something new and extraordinary, of being whisked away from everyday life.

"New experiences are a key part of how our brain accrues knowledge," says chartered psychologist Audrey Tang. "The human mind is constantly on the lookout for new things that it can assess and evaluate, because it calculates everything in terms of risk. It's why we talk about fear of the unknown, and why, even though we're drawn to new adventures, we feel a need to do them as safely as possible. It's why we follow guidebooks, why package holidays are so successful. If someone else is saying it's OK, or that they'll manage the risk, we are more likely to do it."

It didn't take long for an enterprising few to realise there was good money to be made from taking the excursion train, with all its unreliable timings and crammed carriages, and offering something less chaotic and more organised. What if an excursion train was more than just a journey? What if a ticket included a meal, a musical band to welcome the train into the station and someone who would take charge of a group and ensure they reached the attraction they were travelling to see? In 1841, a certain Thomas Cook (yes, that Thomas Cook), a young wood-turner, arranged an excursion train for more than 500 members of the South Midland Temperance Association to attend a temperance demonstration in Loughborough.[11] The fare cost one shilling return, and the trip was such a success that he organised similar excursions, finally turning a profit in 1845,[12] and inadvertently inventing a role that would become an integral part of the modern holiday industry: the travel agent.

What Cook quickly recognised was that although the railways had ignited a huge public appetite to explore – even if only between different towns – there was considerable nervousness about pretty much every aspect, from booking tickets to the actual means of travel itself. Like the middlemen who organised Grand Tour itineraries a century earlier, Cook offered himself and his services as a safe pair of hands, responsible for everything from overseeing travel arrangements to ensuring a place for a restorative cup of tea and a bun after a bone-jangling train ride. For the next ten years, he ran tours around the country, before branching out across the Channel in 1855,[13] creating a business that would evolve and grow for over 150 years, before its sad demise in 2019.

Thomas Cook may be the only name that we still recognise from those fledgling days of package trips, but by the mid-1840s there were dozens of travel agents like him, as great swathes of the countryside were opened up by the unfolding rail network. "It is," said the *Manchester Guardian*, rather pompously, in 1845, "as if the wings of the wind have been given . . . to the closely confined operative, the hard-working mechanic and the counter-riveted shopkeeper. The advantages of these railway excursions are many . . . but we may notice they are greatly conducive to health."[14] It was noted, too, that days out by train were a far less raucous and more family-friendly way to spend free time than the previous favourite, horseracing, which had – until now – replaced cock-fighting as the working man's leisure pastime of choice.

A trip on an excursion train offered all manner of unfamiliar and exciting experiences – maybe a zoo, an exhibition or simply the chance to see a different town. For many of those travelling by rail for the first time, every part of it would have been mind-blowingly, unthinkably new, from the first moment the train floor began to jolt beneath their feet. Charles Dickens described the novel sensation vividly in 1848's *Dombey and Son*:

> Away with a shriek and a roar and a rattle . . . tearing on, spurring everything with its dark breath, sometimes pausing for a minute where a crowd of faces are, that in a minute more are not.[15]

But nothing could beat the lure of the seaside; a chance to visit the salty-aired, sandy-floored playground that had seemed little but a fantasy for so many years. And those who owned coastal lands, or lived in the quiet fishing villages that suddenly found themselves close to a newly opened railway station, were catapulted into the forefront of a new and hugely competitive market. The trains carried people, thousands of people, and that meant food and lodgings and donkey rides and alehouses – new jobs, new wealth and, for a part of the year at least, a whole new way of life.

"The Mostyns actually built two resorts," says Judith Phillips, as we look out over Llandudno's neat patchwork of rooftops. "Llandudno for more moneyed visitors, Rhyl for the working class. Here, they wanted to create somewhere genteel, without any of the raucousness that was developing in Blackpool. They built Mostyn Street – where the shops would have been – with wide pavements and verandas so that elegant ladies could do their shopping without getting damp if it rained. Every house on the promenade had to be the same colour." When I suggest that Llandudno is so pristine that it feels almost like a Victorian theme park, Phillips agrees. "In a way, that is what they created – Mostynworld, rather than Disneyworld. Even now, if you buy a hotel in Llandudno, you get a colour chart from Mostyn Estates. If you choose to paint the building any other colour, they'll take action."

I don't know what I had been expecting from Llandudno, but the town's pin-neat appearance is certainly a surprise to someone who's grown up near to seaside resorts that have – how can I put this? – more raffish charms. There are no fish and chip stalls on the seafront, no tacky music blaring out of amusement arcades, no blinking neon on the pier; the long, curving promenade is backed by a row of townhouses that look fresh out of the box. It's ridiculously picturesque and feels entirely wholesome, until I stroll back up the high street to be serenaded by a trio of extremely inebriated gentlemen lolling outside the Palladium pub, proof that even the redoubtable Mostyn clan has little control over the boozy pleasures of Wetherspoons.

Not all resorts were developed as carefully as Llandudno – and in some places, the demand was so extraordinary that there simply weren't enough facilities to cope. Although Blackpool wouldn't get its own train station until 1863,[16] once the line from Preston reached Fleetwood (20 miles away), thousands made their way to the coast, often arriving into towns that had a marked lack of anything in the way of attractions, including places to sleep. "The town literally swarms with human beings and every day fresh loads roll in, covered with dust and crying for beds," wrote a Bolton paper of the time.[17] Sleeping space was often in such short supply that visitors might only be allowed half the night, before being woken up and shoved out of the door to make space for another.

A lack of assembly rooms or circulating libraries – things that had been an essential part of the Georgian seaside experience – mattered little to those who had rarely been further than the end of their own street. Most came with umbrellas and a blanket – sunbathing had yet to be invented, and deckchairs wouldn't make an appearance until 1886[18] – content to stretch out on the sand and luxuriate in the new experience of not *doing* anything. For the first time, workers in the pits and the mines and the mills, for whom "time off" had been the only respite on offer from the slog of work, were able to experience a "holiday" – even if only for a day or an afternoon. Being away from the usual domestic space meant leaving behind money worries, endless chores, the monotony of the workplace and actually just *stopping*.

Not that everyone simply sat on the sand and did nothing. Some would have swum – although the fact that women managed it without drowning, clad in the long trousers and tunic that became the fashion from the 1860s onwards,[19] was quite some achievement. In more established resorts, a stroll along the pier would have been a highlight, perhaps slurping an oyster or two, or tucking into a packet of shrimps, bought from the vendors who walked the sands, long before beachfront restaurants were invented.

Those that didn't have piers and promenades soon found other, cheaper ways to keep visitors entertained, from wheelbarrow races and greasy-pole climbing competitions to treacle-dipping – where over-excitable boys got to plunge their faces into sticky syrup (with hands tied behind their backs) to find the coins dropped into the gooey depths. And all of it would have been to a soundtrack of live music, whether a brass band, a trio of fiddlers, a quartet on the bandstand or even bagpipes. Not that it pleased everyone; Charles Dickens, who, from 1837–1859, took an annual summer holiday in Broadstairs, wrote, "unless it pours of rain, I cannot write half an hour without the most excruciating organs, fiddles, bells or glee-singers."[20]

Pretty quickly, the predictable class divisions began to be apparent between resorts. Treacle-dipping, sack races and greasy poles tended to be the preserve of northern resorts like Southport, or those deliberately designed for working-class visitors. A new trend began for sibling resorts; two, set close together, each catering to a different "type". St Leonard's was created as a more refined counterpart to Hastings' saltier charms, Lytham the same for Blackpool. In 1859, the 7th Duke of Devonshire – grandson of the 5th, who had originally created the spa resort of Buxton – began to lay out plans for Eastbourne on land he had inherited in 1834.[21] A resort "built by gentlemen, for gentlemen",[22] it was a sure sign that Brighton's star was no longer in the ascendant – or had at least moved into a far less glittering galaxy.

But in spite of the photographs of packed trains and stories of towns flooded with day-trippers that filled the newspapers, the huge celebrations that took place whenever – and wherever – a new station opened, and all the new possibilities offered by rail travel, not everyone took to it so readily. In the early days, travel was, predictably, a far more comfortable experience for the wealthy, with third-class carriages barely more than cattle trucks on wheels. In 1844, a Poor Law official told the Select Committee on Railways that, "the risk and exposure of poor people in the stand-up carriages is so severe, I'd sooner pay the difference out of my own pocket."[23] When I visit the National Railway Museum in York, I can quite see his point; the gleaming, mustard-yellow first-class coach from the Liverpool–Manchester line is all soft, upholstered seating that makes the Thameslink trains I travel on seem even more spartan than they actually are (quite some achievement).

In comparison, the third-class carriages on show give an idea of exactly how the poor were treated: open-sided, with standing room only and entirely exposed to weather conditions. Accidents were common in the early days and third-class travellers would have to cling on to whatever bit of the wooden carriage frame they could reach as the train juddered its way across uneven track, often screeching to an unexpected halt. Even when the carriages had been improved, there were plenty who suspected trains were actively bad for your health, not least many members of the medical profession. In 1862, *The Lancet* published a series of articles on the effects of railway travel, citing it as a cause of everything from broken bones, cuts and bruises to memory loss, local paralysis and "slowly ensuing symptoms of intellectual derangement".[24] As someone who travels regularly on the London to Brighton line, I'm here to say that such symptoms are still very much in existence, particularly after you've been tipped off at Gatwick for the third time in a week.

Fortunately, help was at hand. *The Railway Traveller's Handy Book of Hints, Suggestions and Advice* was published in 1862, covering everything from "Preparation for the Journey", to "Letters of Advice & Supply of Etceteras" and "Treatment of Unpleasant Travelling Companions".[25] My personal favourite is the section on "Sending Females and Children Unaccompanied". "When there are ladies in the case," it says, presumably not suggesting they're actually packed as luggage, "it is absolutely necessary to allow a wider margin for the preparations for departures than is ordinarily assigned. The fairer sex *must* complete their toilet to their entire satisfaction, whatever the consequences may be."[26]

Ah, such wisdom. But as I read on, certain things dawn on me that I'd never really considered before – not least that Greenwich Mean Time wasn't established until 1884,[27] meaning that the time was different whether you set off from Liverpool or London, Bournemouth or Blackpool. Much like the 21st-century time change when flying, travellers had to note the difference between their time of arrival, London time and the length of the journey. I try to work out whether this made delays more or less likely, until I remember that I failed Maths O level three times, and go back to tips on what "etceteras" one should take – mainly cash (both notes and small change), a pocket notebook, a "card of address", note paper, envelopes, stamps, pocket pen, small inkstand – and presumably Mary Poppins' capacious carpet bag to carry it all in.

Whether or not they ever realised it, those who designed, built and operated Britain's new rail network changed the lives of millions of people – most for the better, but not all. Some places suffered simply because of geography; low-lying country along the coast was far easier for constructing railway lines, meaning that the Lake District, Highlands and Welsh mountains saw far fewer visitors than their coastal neighbours. And wealthy landowners weren't always keen to have trains screeching through their fields. "It's partly why our rail network is such a wiggly, spider's web of lines," says Tom Chesshyre. "Many of them can be traced directly back to the Victorian era, when they had to work around the country estates that wouldn't allow tracks on their land." Some seaside towns, such as Sidmouth in Devon, went into a decline after being overlooked by the railway,[28] while others took on a whole new lease of life.

"Until the railway arrived, Torquay was very much seen as a place for invalids," says local historian Kevin Dixon, when I join him for a sunny walk around the town on an unseasonably warm March morning. "Tuberculosis was very common and Torquay's mild micro-climate and reliable sunshine were seen as a natural tonic. Because of the distance from London, it had remained something of a backwater, although it was popular with poets and writers – Shelley,

Elizabeth Barrett Browning and Robert Louis Stevenson all came to the town to boost their health." Alongside health tourists, Torquay also had a number of wealthy residents, drawn to the area's beauty and relative tranquillity – surpassed only by Cornwall, which remained rather like the dark side of the moon to all but the most intrepid travellers.

Small and sedate, when the new Torre railway opened in Torquay in 1848,[29] it didn't take long for the quiet air of convalescence and moneyed sophistication to be replaced by a considerably more boisterous atmosphere. "It would have been quite a culture shock," says Dixon. "The working-class visitors that arrived – less sophisticated, with bawdy humour and a keenness for alcohol – would not have impressed those who ran the town." Within a few years of the first train pulling into Torre station, Torquay had become almost unrecognisable from the refined – if slightly diseased – resort it had once been, and the town's elders decided steps needed to be taken to realign it with Eastbourne and St Leonards, rather than Brighton or – horror of horrors – Margate.

In a move that absolutely no one called a "rebranding exercise" – but which would be viewed as exactly that today – Torquay began to market itself (perhaps not very originally) as the "Montpellier of England" and the "English Riviera"[30] – a legacy from when the town had been a stop-off point for frustrated Grand Tour-ees, whose overseas adventures had been thwarted by the Napoleonic Wars. Torre station was built with the look of a French chateau, while the hills behind the town were covered in Mediterranean-style villas and Italianate houses, clustered together in a higgledy-piggledy style, in an attempt to emulate the look of the Côte d'Azur. By 1857, the town had its own Assembly Hall and reading rooms, along with neighbourhoods named Belgravia and Pimlico, modelled on London streets in an attempt to lure more of the right kind of visitors from the capital.[31] Word of the town's rebrand even reached royal ears, and in the 1850s and 60s, the town became a favourite with European monarchs: the Russian Romanovs had their own villa built, Emperor Napoleon III came to feel the sand between his toes and Edward VII checked into the Imperial Hotel on more than one occasion.[32]

It's my first visit to Torquay, and I'm immediately struck by how similar the landscape is to both the French and Italian Rivieras. Under bright blue skies, the small, jagged hills that flank the shoreline could just as well be home to Èze or Saint-Paul-de-Vence, apart from the ugly apartment blocks, faded houses and complete lack of cicadas. Turn the other way, however, and all is Mediterranean charm: yachts bobbing in the neat marina, cafe tables set out along the promenade, a great, wide sweep of a bay, layered like a child's painting – teal sea, butter sand, low khaki hills curving in to the horizon. It's easy to see how glamorous the resort must have been in its heyday – which lasted well into the 1960s – before the steep decline began as holidaymakers began to discover the pleasures of the *actual* Mediterranean. There's clearly still wealth in the town, as evidenced by the glossy cafes and bars by the marina and the leafy neighbourhoods on the outskirts of town, with their graceful villas and spectacular views out to sea. But there's a darker side, beneath the surface; deep-rooted problems that can't be solved easily. "Are we a tourist resort, an inner city by the sea or a dormitory town?" says Dixon. "Like so many seaside towns, we need real investment, and that's in short supply."

There's an irony, somewhere, that the very beach resorts that brought about the demise of the Regency spa towns went on to suffer a similar fate. By the time Torquay and Bournemouth and Blackpool and Southport were blazing like beacons on the coast, places like Buxton, Epsom and Tunbridge Wells lay all but forgotten.[33] Bath struggled on, Buxton focused almost exclusively on spa cures, but neither could match – or compete with – the lure of the seaside and its extraordinarily restorative powers, suddenly made accessible to everyone by the new wonder of the trains.

Only, of course, it wasn't everyone. At least a tenth of those living in the crammed industrial centres would never have a day out. For most who toiled in the factories, pits and mills, the chance to explore, to get away from the harsh monotony of everyday life, might only be for one or two days a year, at least until the Factory Act of 1850, which gave half days on Saturdays to many women and younger people, prohibiting their employment from 2 p.m. onwards.[34] Many men benefited from the new law too, ushering in a new routine, whereby chores – shopping, cleaning and housework – might be done on a Saturday afternoon, leaving time on Sunday to experience a little of what the middle and upper classes had come to define as "leisure time". "The worker knows now when that which he sells is ended and when his own begins," said the Inspectors of Factories report in 1859, "and by possessing a sure foreknowledge of this, is enabled to prearrange his own minutes for his own purposes."[35] Slowly, gradually, the concept of a weekend – and all the freedoms it might offer – was beginning to take shape.

In some ways, the Factory Act marked the beginning of a new "paternalism", slowly developing among a small cross-section of more enlightened employers and politicians, born of the realisation that while an industrialised society made a small strata considerably richer, it also worsened the lives of the vast majority. By the 1870s, some clerical and shop workers could expect a week's paid holiday a year, albeit very much at the employer's discretion.[36] Although industrial workers had little hope of such a luxury, there were the beginnings of the idea that, rather than leading to drunkenness and dissolution, a little time off might actually result in a healthier workforce, as long as there were wholesome ways for said time to be spent.

In the following years, friendly societies and brass bands became more common, with football clubs beginning to appear in the 1880s. Temperance groups, often fostered by a local church, also grew steeply in number, proving that plenty of employers (and the middle class generally) still believed that giving the working man time off would only lead him directly into the welcoming arms of the nearest pub.

But for those who had money, even just a little, it was the concept of a "holiday" that was starting to crystallise; something longed for and looked forward to in exactly the way we do now. "There has been an increasing tendency of late years among all classes to find excuses for Holydays," said *The Times* in 1871. "Among those who are well-to-do, the annual trip to the seaside has become a necessity of which their fathers, or at least their grandfathers, never dreamt."[37]

Considering a holiday a "necessity" would have been laughable for many, but the coming of the trains had unleashed an innate human need for change, for different air to breathe, for a brief escape from the everyday, whether country estate or cotton mill. What no one could have foreseen was that the excursion trains and the beach resorts and the treacle-dipping and donkey rides were only the beginning; the first step on a road that would lead to holidays – and the leisure *and* pleasure they offered – becoming an integral part of life across every stratum of society. Trains had opened up more than just the country; they had opened up a world of possibility. The genie was well and truly out of the bottle.

6
A Place to Stay
Sussex, London, Gleneagles

"The great advantage of a hotel is that it is a refuge from home life."[1]
George Bernard Shaw

It seems both apt and inevitable that I sit writing these words in a hotel room. It could be anywhere, but actually it's in Alicante, en route to Benidorm (but that's for another chapter). The walls are white, the art is abstract, the TV (sadly) dominates the room. In the bathroom, there are posh smellies, a fluffy robe, a bath I won't have time to get into and a shower that will drench me in cold water while I frantically wrangle both taps, in both directions, trying to make it hot. Later, laptop closed, I'll spend a good ten minutes searching for all the light switches and when I wake up, I'll stare mournfully at the whizzy coffee machine until forced to accept that no amount of mournful staring will turn it into a kettle (nor coffee pods into teabags).

In spite of these minor annoyances, I should come clean straight away and say that I adore a good hotel. In the world of travel writing, this is sometimes frowned upon; homestays are more authentic, B&Bs more personal, villas more independent. I'd happily stay in them all, but there is just something so glamorous, so fabulously old-school, about a grand hotel, where you swish down the staircase, pay a small fortune for a ludicrously named cocktail, like a Johnny Come Lately or a Lobster Ahoy!, and sit round watching far wealthier people in posher clothes waft around unhappily, as if auditioning for the next series of the *White Lotus*.

Not that a hotel has to be grand – I'll take any of the endless iterations that have sprung up in recent decades: boutiques and minimalist boltholes, country houses and urban retreats, no-frills budget billets with pod-style rooms, opulent castles, glass spheres suspended in trees – alongside B&Bs, gastropubs and restaurants with rooms. The days when "a place to stay" meant a bed for the night and whatever the landlord's grumpy wife felt like throwing in a pot are long gone; these days, hotels have everything from Michelin-starred restaurants and world-class spas to tennis schools, private cinemas, kids' clubs and (if you're really unlucky) yoga classes at dawn.

"We're very good at hotels in this country," says Jane Knight, editor of *The Good Hotels Guide*. "I think British hotels are up there with the best in the world. If you go to America, they've got no idea – France is catching up, but they're still streets behind. Standards are so good, it's increasingly difficult to draw a line between a B&B, a pub or restaurant with rooms and a hotel. A decade ago, that was easy, but now a gastropub with rooms might have spa facilities and a B&B can have suites to match anything you'd find in a boutique hotel. Things have changed radically in the last decade or two."

Perhaps it's not surprising that we're so good at hotels in this country, when you think how long they've been part of our lives. Ever since the first human decided to break up an afternoon of rock art and woolly-mammoth wrangling with a wander off into pastures new, a place to stay has been an essential part of our innate need to travel and explore. Doubtless the Romans did a nice line in B&Bs, but for the purposes of this story, the timeline begins roughly a millennium ago, when monasteries began to open their doors to the small number of travellers and salesmen who managed to make their way across the rough-hewn bridleways and ancient Roman streets that linked the earliest settlements.[2] Hospitality was an important part of monastic life, and those who knocked on the door would have received a warm welcome from the monks in residence, delighted to have an opportunity to catch up on the salacious goings-on in the Outside World. The abbot – head of the monastery – would have been particularly pleased, as he would have been allowed to dine with the visitors, offering a night off from the usual monastic delights of porridge, vegetables and beans.[3]

By medieval times, the population was growing, and those who lived on the main routes between royal palaces and country estates began to realise good money could be made from offering shelter and food to those making the painfully slow journeys. Some of those first coaching inns are still doing business today: the Angel Inn (now the Angel and Royal) in Grantham, Lincolnshire, first opened its doors in 1203,[4] while the Old Bell at Malmesbury – built to provide accommodation for visitors to the abbey – was hot on its heels in 1220.[5] The Star at Alfriston – now one of East Sussex's plushest boltholes after a revamp by renowned hotelier Olga Polizzi – opened as a religious hostel in 1345,[6] while over in West Sussex, the Spread Eagle – a relative newcomer, dating to 1430 – remains famous for hosting Elizabeth I en route for a naughty weekend in, er, Portsmouth, with her beau of the time, Sir Francis Drake.[7]

"The London to Portsmouth road was one of the busiest during that period," says Sarah Stacey, General Manager of the Spread Eagle, when we chat beside an open fire in the inn's main bar on a chilly January night. "It takes less than two hours now, but 600 years ago it would take several days, so places for an overnight stop were essential. An inn would offer food and accommodation, but in the early days, there were very few private rooms. Everything would take place in the main hall; eating, drinking and then people would bed down for the night wherever there was space." The cramped conditions were just one reason why most guests failed to get a good night's sleep: carriages could turn up at any time of the day or night, with deafening horns announcing their arrival, horses clattering across the cobbles, doors slamming and luggage being hauled in and out of doorways.

Not that there's any sign of a similar hubbub today. When our conversation is over, I sit by the fire and let the low hum of chatter, and the dim light flickering off the low ceilings, lull me into something not far from the vicinity of a snooze. There's something hugely soothing about sitting in a lounge that has housed travellers for 600 years; its quiet sense of permanence, an oasis of centuries-old wooden beams and fireplaces big enough to seat a dinner party. Upstairs, my suite is the very one Elizabeth I slept in, complete with its own wig closet and a floor so wonky it makes me feel slightly tipsy before the evening has properly begun. The whole place feels like a great, warm hug. "It's about being looked after," says Sarah, later, when I settle back into what has swiftly become "my" chair by the fire. "Letting someone else take the reins and do your thinking for you."

Taking the reins would have been a major part of an inn's role in the early days: providing stabling for horses and space for commercial goods set them apart from the cheaper, more raucous alehouses. In the medieval era, cloth making and the wool trade were the backbone of the British economy, and there were plenty of merchants and traders looking for a place to bed down for the night and do a little business with the owner of the inn. Scarlet-liveried postboys carrying letters to and from the royal court were also frequent guests, riding at such speed (presumably fuelled by a fear of being beheaded if letters were late) that they had to give their horses a break every ten miles or so.[8] A canny innkeeper would have a number of "side hustles" on the go with many of his guests: trading cloth, importing wine, running a brewery – some even set themselves up as banks, or rented storage space. Entertainment was often thrown in: a giddy night of bear-baiting, cock-fighting or, if they were particularly strait-laced, theatre, with guests and audiences watching from the balconies that surrounded the central courtyard. In those days, innkeepers were often the wealthiest people in town.[9]

Once turnpike roads were established, the "inn business" began to boom. The rise of the spa town saw increased demand for places to break the journey en route to resorts like Bath and Buxton, while the first tendrils of industry saw growing numbers of businessmen and merchants travelling between the fledgling new towns. By the beginning of the 18th century, inns had entered a golden age, with between 6,000 and 7,000 dotted across the country.[10] It was an era that lasted for the next five decades, until a new-fangled concept from across the Channel began to take hold. *Hôtel* – like *hôpital* – was a Gallic word, taken from the Latin *hospes*, which, roughly translated, meant somewhere that had a regular number of visitors and offered food. Such a place appeared in the advertising pages of the *London Evening Post* in 1764: an invitation to stay at Madame Martin's Gentlemen's Hotel: "genteel lodgings, for one night or as long as they feel proper."[11] Guests could expect 'breakfast and dinners prepared in the neatest and cleanest manner, with the best wines of all sorts.'

This new option, a combination of the services of a (good) inn, with meals and drinks included and served to order, and the comfort of private rooms in a lodging house (which usually required an extended stay) took time to take hold. The very first Grand Hotel opened in Covent Garden in 1774, only to close again in 1780,[12] while only the wealthiest developers – such as the Duke of Devonshire, whose ground-breaking Buxton Crescent opened in 1789, housing two hotels – tried this new invention outside the capital.

By the early 19th century, the game was properly on. Mivart's, an elegant townhouse in Mayfair, welcomed its first guests in 1812,[13] with the Prince of Saxe-Coburg opening three years later.[14] In 1837, Brown's threw open its doors, run by James Brown, former valet to Lord Byron,[15] whose society connections cemented the trend for visiting noblemen, royalty and gentry to stay at one of the new breed of discreet, luxurious addresses. All three live on in 21st-century London: Mivart's became Claridge's in 1854,[16] the Prince of Saxe-Coburg was renamed the Connaught (to avoid any unwelcome German connotations) in 1917,[17] while Brown's is still, well, Brown's.

But hotels weren't going to stay small and discreet for long – and neither were they going to be restricted to London; the railways, and their whip-smart, money-hungry owners, quickly saw to that. By the mid-19th century, the sound of horses' hooves and clattering carriages had been replaced by the rhythmic chuntering and screeching whistles of the steam-belching trains that carried tens of thousands across the country each week. For coaching inns, the railway was a mixed blessing; some suddenly found themselves on deserted backroads, with carriage routes swapped for the dizzying speed (some whipped along at a white-knuckle 17 miles per hour[18]) and ease of the trains, while those close to a station often found themselves unable to cope with demand. Something new was needed; something grander, something that complemented the sense of glamour and adventure that accompanied this new, life-changing form of travel – and so, in 1839, the first station hotel, owned and built by a railway company, opened at Euston Station.[19]

Considered something of an experiment, the hotel comprised two separate units, housed in the pavilions that flanked the station. One, the Victoria, was basically a simple dormitory, with little in the way of comforts and, worst of all, no alcohol licence. The other, the Euston, was – perhaps surprisingly – let to two Europeans: an Italian called Vantini, and a Belgian, Joseph Dethier.[20] Together, they created the first hotel of its kind – smart rooms, a coffee house and restaurant – and within a year, the Euston was such a success that the Victoria was changed to run on a similar model. The Euston was the most expensive hotel ever built at the time – costing a whopping £55,000[21] – but the cost did little to deter other train companies following suit, with the Great Northern at King's Cross and the Great Western at Paddington opening within a month of each other in 1854.[22] By the time the first wing of George Gilbert Scott's Gothic Revival masterpiece, the Midland Grand (now the St Pancras Hotel), opened at St Pancras in 1873, seven years after construction began,[23] railway companies were embroiled in a competition to create the most grandiose hotels. George Hudson – chairman of the York and North Midland Railway – was determined his hometown of York wouldn't be outdone.

I get a sense of Hudson's ambition when I walk through the revolving door that leads from the chilly platform at York station into the warm, gilt-edged glamour of the Milner York, formerly the Royal Station Hotel, which opened in 1878, a year after York's new railway station became the largest in the world.[24] It's rather like slipping through a wardrobe door and discovering Narnia tucked behind the coats; the windswept train platforms and rusted ironwork of the passenger footbridge replaced by Doric columns and a great, grand lobby that could house a football pitch. "Can you imagine how it would have felt back then?" says Emmanouela Tabois-Kastouli, Hotel Manager at the Milner, when we settle in for tea on pristine velvet sofas. "For many people, it would have been the first time they ever stayed somewhere like this. The scale of the hotel, the decor, everyone dressed in their travelling finery – I'd love to have seen it."

It's pretty impressive now; Art Deco chandeliers glittering between the columns in the cavernous Garden Room, cosied up with coffee-and-cream decor, elegant, button-back sofas and velvet armchairs the colour of peppermint creams, with table lamps throwing pools of warm light across the trays of tea and cake stands. Often, these grand hotels can feel a little fusty and faded, but the Milner feels band-box fresh, humming with low-key business meetings over pots of coffee, tourists poring over their phones and couples breezing past on their way to the lifts, some with shopping bags, others with walking poles, wearing sensible windproof jackets. "I think people are still wowed by the hotel today," says Emmanouela. "It still has a real sense of occasion, of stepping away from the everyday. I think we need that – maybe now more than ever."

The Milner does still have a lovely feeling of grandeur, but the exhibition of black and white photographs in the long hallway – when 14 shillings a night (around £120 in today's money) bought a spacious bedroom and the chance to throw on a posh frock and a diamond choker and sip damn fine gin martinis in the bar[25] – does make me wistful for the languid glamour of the late 19th century. Railway travel had quickly become how the wealthy and the well-connected got about, and station hotels were designed specifically to enable moving from luxury first-class carriage to elegant foyer without having to pass more than a minute or two on the same platform as the hoi polloi, jostling to clamber into third-class carriages. In spite of the Victorians' reputation for strait-laced living, they ate up these new pavilions of pleasure with alacrity, with opulent new hotels springing up in the popular seaside resorts as well as cities. The Grand Hotel in Brighton quickly became known as the Palace by the Sea, while the Scarborough Grand (evoking memories of the stiff competition between resorts in the Regency era) was said to be the "largest and handsomest in Europe".[26]

But nowhere could out-compete London for sheer theatricality. When the Langham threw open its doors in 1865,[27] it became the city's first *grande dame*, with the Prince of Wales and the capital's young and beautiful flocking to sip champagne and marvel at what £300,000 (around £48 million)[28] could buy. The hotel boasted innovations that had never been seen before: the world's first hydraulic lifts, water closets with hot and cold running water and an early form of air conditioning. It set the standard for London hotels that reached its peak when theatrical impresario Richard D'Oyly Carte opened the Savoy in 1889,[29] a magnet for stars and celebrities, with the actress Sarah Bernhardt practically taking up residence and the opera singer Dame Nellie Melba giving her name to two original dishes: crispy Melba toast and the dessert, Peach Melba. Conspicuous leisure officially had a new address, so much so it was satirised in a 1902 novel by Arnold Bennett, *The Grand Babylon Hotel*.

> It was 7.45 on a sultry June night and dinner was about to be served at the Grand Babylon. Men . . . every one of them in faultless evening dress were dotted about the large, dim apartment. The waiters . . . moved softly across the thick Oriental rugs . . . received and executing orders with that air of profound importance of which only really first-class waiters have the secret.[30]

"Big hotels are – and should be – theatrical," says Daniel Bayrenreuther, General Manager of Gleneagles, the creation of another train company – in this case the Caledonian Railway – and described as the Eighth Wonder of the World when it opened in 1924.[31] "When you walk into a grand hotel you should have that moment of 'wow!' A sense of grandeur, of creativity – that it wasn't built by an asset manager. These great hotels were built by people who had luxury in mind; who wanted to elevate the coaching inn experience to something that really sets itself apart the moment you walk in."

I've always thought hotels have much in common with the theatre; perhaps because, as a reviewer, I'm given the unusual privilege of seeing both front and back of house. I love nothing more than being taken through one of those unnoticed doors that lead backstage, where trolleys of laundry are whisked between floors, room service orders are hastily pulled out of service lifts and staff members linger on fire escapes, having a cheeky cigarette. Hotel kitchens hum with suppliers, sous chefs bustling in and out of storerooms, pans rattling, the feverish clean-down between the end of one service and the beginning of the next. Everything is a grand illusion, that it is all done without effort, just for us, right down to the moment we close the door on a bedroom that feels new and untouched, in spite of the fact that it has hosted hundreds before us.

"The key is that guests should never be aware of what goes on behind those…unnoticed doors, as you call them," says Bayrenreuther. "At hotels, we curate a different world, one which allows you to step out of your own. Everything must seem effortless, however many numbers you are juggling. At Gleneagles, we have 1,500 staff that can cater for over 1,000 diners at lunch and dinner – the biggest five-star catering operation in the country." The numbers are staggering, but Gleneagles was built for superlatives, originally marketed as the "Riviera of the Highlands" to the wealthy young Londoners who would board the train at Euston for sporting, champagne-fuelled weekends.[32] "The dream was to fall asleep on the night train and wake up at Gleneagles," says Bayrenreuther. "It was the ultimate railway hotel."

Hotels such as Gleneagles and the Brighton and Scarborough Grands might have been a dream for London's Bright Young Things, but they were out of reach of all but the wealthiest travellers. Instead, a new breed of boarding houses and small hotels began to open up in seaside towns, catering for those who had enough money to make use of the new Bank Holidays (introduced into law in 1871 as days when banks were officially allowed to close),[33] along with an employer willing to allow them. The sense that working people might actually need a guaranteed day off here and there – a prime factor in the passing of the Factory Act – resulted in a new piece of legislation being passed, which, although not a massive game-changer in some ways, did earmark a small societal shift.

Three of the four new Bank Holidays were already in the calendar for many workers (although not legally so), but now not only were Boxing Day, Easter Monday and Whit Monday guaranteed as paid time off for all, but so was the first Monday in August.[34] Arguably, this was the first national holiday (rather than "holyday") with no religious associations, and no imperative to do anything other than to kick back and put up one's feet, opening up the concept of "leisure" to a vast section of society who'd never dreamt they might actually be *paid* while enjoying a day by the seaside or an afternoon at the fair.

As the trend for "Going-Off" clubs began to take hold in the industrialised centres – when factory and mill workers in the North saved for a week's holiday each summer – more and more accommodation was needed, reaching a peak after the Holidays with Pay Act in 1938 gave all working men and women the right to a week's paid holiday each year.[35]

By then, Billy Butlin had opened his first holiday camp,[36] youth hostels were popping up across the country and converted train carriages could be seen in farmers' fields and on riverbanks, offering cheap accommodation for poorer families. And by the time World

War II was over, a whole new concept of hospitality had evolved: the B&B, created from a need to provide somewhere to stay for the thousands of foreigners who found themselves far from home during and after the conflict. And it wasn't just the widowed or grieving landladies in Bournemouth or Blackpool who found themselves with large family homes that suddenly lay empty. World War II sealed the fate of many aristocratic families, whose way of life simply couldn't survive the social impact of two global wars. When Sharrow Bay opened in the Lake District in 1948 it created an entirely new breed of hotel:[37] a former private estate converted into a rural playground – Gleneagles with a thousand years of history – where the nouveau riche could play at being lord and lady of a lifestyle that no longer really existed.

In the first decade after the war, catering to the vast wave of newly created holidaymakers seemed like a golden ticket; a solid way to monetise everything from unserviceable train carriages to empty bedrooms or faded country piles. In the summer months, beach resorts around the country struggled to cope with the hundreds of thousands who swept in, looking for deckchairs and donkey rides and a few days to indulge in the heady pursuit of pleasure for pleasure's sake, no longer the exclusive preserve of the privileged few. No one dreamt that by the late 1950s, a new trend would drain much of the life out of Britain's booming holiday scene, that air travel would – within 20 years – be transporting those who had only just discovered the joys of Blackpool straight to the sunny shores of Benidorm. By the end of the 20th century, many British resorts – and the hotels and guesthouses that filled them – were in the doldrums, left behind, both literally and metaphorically, by the newer, sunnier resorts that all came with lashings of laid-back Mediterranean charm.

"By the 1990s, British hotels were starting to feel quite out of date," says Robin Hutson, who started the Hotel du Vin brand in 1994 and Pig Hotels in 2011. "I had been General Manager at the Chewton Glen – one of the UK's grandest country house hotels – for eight years, and to me it all felt rather over-stuffed; gold taps, marble bathrooms, lots of rules about jackets and ties and no children in the restaurant. But there had been a wave of change in society, and I didn't think hotels were keeping up; there was definitely a demand for a more relaxed style and service." Although Hutson didn't know it then, when he left to open the very first Hotel du Vin in Winchester, he was ushering in a whole new era. "I had no idea we were at the start of a revolution in hotel-keeping," he says. "But it was the beginning of 'boutique' hotels."

Ah, the boutique hotel. Never has an adjective been more overused, expanded, finessed, defined, redefined and attached to so many hotels that it's become almost meaningless. But in the early 00s, boutique hotels were the hottest trend: small, chic, informal – a microcosm of how society had evolved along with lessons brought back from Mediterranean holidays and hotels, just as the Grand Tour travellers brought back new ideas and innovations for 19th-century businessmen. Suddenly, good service meant fun without the frills; children were allowed everywhere and staff were as likely to wear jeans and a shirt as formalwear. "I worked at The Grand in Brighton 25 years ago," says Sarah from the Spread Eagle. "During the morning, we'd wear morning suits and then at 6 p.m., on the dot, we'd change into eveningwear. I can't imagine that now."

But although informality has been the defining trend for most 21st-century hotels, not all have nailed their colours to the boutique mast. Keen to see what London's most expensive hotel ever built (as of spring 2025) offers, I check into the Peninsula – the capital's first billion-dollar property, overlooking Hyde Park and the imposing Wellington Arch. Room rates start at a cool (wait for it) £1,300 a night, a signifier of its place among the diamond-encrusted clutch of ultra-luxury hotel brands catering for A-listers, oligarchs, minor royalty and any "influencers" who can blag their way through the doors. In the vast lobby, where potted palms splay tidy green leaves beneath grandiose columns, pairs of expensively dressed women with perfect manicures and Dyson-fresh blow-outs sip tea and frown disapprovingly at miniature patisserie against a soundtrack of jazz standards, floating in the artificially cooled air. Beyond it, gilt-framed doors open out into a quadrangle filled with super-cars and flanked by a row of boutiques: Dior, Chanel, Jimmy Choo. When I head to the lifts, I look up to realise I am walking beneath a long, white object suspended from the ceiling, which – naturally – turns out to be an original Concord nose cone. The lift up to the bar is designed to feel like a hot air balloon. My "room" is probably twice the size of my first London flat.

This, supposedly, is the zenith of hotel development; the last word in luxury and service, albeit designed only ever to be experienced by the super-rich. And that's where it loses me; in our imbalanced times, "Super Rich" has almost become a destination in itself: the Peninsula was in London, but I could just as well have been in Dubai or Tokyo or New York. Hotels like this are the 21st-century solution to the problem the wealthy have been grappling with for centuries: how and where to take their holidays without having to engage with those who don't own country estates or have an odd few million in the bank. Room rates that top £1,000 a night are a form of money apartheid; a guarantee of a "certain type" of guest, and quite possibly what the Duke of Devonshire was hoping to achieve when he opened the Royal Crescent Hotel in Buxton in 1789. If the Peninsula could time travel, and land in Bath in the early 19th century, just as the resort was beginning to lose its wealthiest clientele, it would probably have halted the town's decline overnight.

The following night I checked into Bike & Boot in Scarborough, where my room cost £59 and – apart from the size – offered the same things: a comfortable bed, a hot shower and a well-stocked tea tray, along with a sense of fun *and* a sense of place. It's a juxtaposition that I'm very privileged to have experienced, and it makes me think that perhaps the apotheosis of hotel development is its evolution into something that can be enjoyed by everyone, whatever budget they're on.

But hotels are not the only places to stay that have changed and evolved in the last decades. "Given the choice, I'd rather stay in a good pub with rooms than a posh hotel that costs five times the price," says Jane Knight from *The Good Hotels Guide*. "Cosy and quaint, charming bedrooms, walks from the door – and fantastic food. I feel like a 'hotel' is still considered the thing to treat yourself to, as if people haven't quite caught on to the gastropub with rooms trend yet, which is crazy." If they haven't yet, it's only a matter of time: while many of the country's pubs have shut or are struggling, there are plenty, too, who have hit on a winning combination of rustic-chic rooms and locally sourced ingredients, served up with real flair.

Hotels, gastropubs, B&Bs, guesthouses – do we have such a rich history of hospitality because we are, just possibly, good hosts? "One hundred per cent," says Mike Bevens, Group Managing Director of Sawdays and Canopy & Stars. "If you go around the country, you realise that although the accents might change, everyone wants to connect with their guests. It might not always be the slick service you get in Asia, say, but there's warmth and generosity and a real love of talking, sharing what they know about their corner of the world. I think that's created something really unique in terms of accommodation in the UK."

Jane Knight agrees. "We have a culture built around inns," she says, "and a tradition of innkeeping going back hundreds and hundreds of years. I think it's something innate in us, in a way." And there's something rather lovely, too, about the fact that many of the new breed of gastropubs with rooms are those same inns that first opened their doors hundreds of years before, reinvented for the 21st century with far fewer wig closets and much better food. It's comforting, I think, that as the world unfolds in ever more challenging and unexpected ways, something in our limbic brain is calling us back to those original places that first offered us rest and refuge, all those centuries ago.

7

The Great Outdoors

The Thames Valley and Kent

"I firmly believe that nature brings solace in all troubles."[1]
Anne Frank

It's only when I look up to meet the quizzical gaze of the pink-faced man sitting opposite me that I realise I've laughed out loud. Again. Such a sound, particularly coming from a woman sitting on her own, is not a familiar thing on a late-night Thameslink train grinding its way south from London. Normally, I'd probably be equally eyebrow-raisey, or at the very least intrigued. But on this occasion, as it's me, I shut my eyes and let myself be lulled away by the sound of Hugh Laurie's voice, narrating Jerome K. Jerome's much-loved book, *Three Men in a Boat*. Originally published in 1889, and never out of print since,[2] it is a genuinely hilarious account of three helpless chaps who decide to take a (real) week's holiday on a skiff down the Thames.

Part Jeeves and Wooster, part *Blackadder* on a boat, it's also a fantastic historical resource, giving a first-person insight into what became one of the defining trends for holidays at the end of the 19th and beginning of the 20th century – spending time in the great outdoors. While seaside holidays were now firmly established, and a handful of poets, artists and writers had begun the trend for exploring rural Britain during the early 19th century, it wasn't until a century later that the wider population began to consider the countryside as a place to step away from the pressures of everyday life, as Jerome's book shows.

> 'What we want is rest,' said Harris. 'Rest and a complete change of scene,' said George. I agreed with George and suggested that we should seek out some retired and old-world spot, far from the madding crowd and dream away a sunny week ... out of reach of the noisy world.'[3]

By the twilight days of the Victorian era, Britain was a very different place to 60 years before, when industrialisation was roaring across the landscape, railway mania was taking hold and the social structure that had held for centuries – where a small cabal of very wealthy families kept the unwashed masses in check – was undergoing serious recalibration. The young and vibrant queen of 1837 had become a dour, mute figure.[4] Britain's glittering (whatever we think of it now) Empire had suffered a series of small but nevertheless humiliating blows, with wars in the Crimea, Sudan and South Africa not adhering to the pre-agreed script of British troops arriving in foreign territories and simply absorbing them into the Empire, in a gesture of great beneficence to all concerned.[5] A new sense of anxiety had begun to creep in among the ruling classes; that the change to an industrialised society, with workers trapped indoors in factories and offices rather than undertaking good, physical outdoors work, had created a generation of soft-minded weaklings (or, as we would put it today, begun to affect both physical and mental health).

The railway era had already proved that the idea of "getting away" had great appeal to anyone who could afford a train ticket, and by the late 19th century, the positive impact of a "change of scene" was firmly embedded in the national psyche. Now, a new concept of "personal fitness" was added into the mix; a need – and desire – to exercise the body in ways the working day no longer offered. For both the wealthy and many middle-class workers in offices, shops and small businesses, exercising at home became popular.

Calisthenics – weight-bearing exercise – was the Pilates of its day, while Gustav Ernst's portable gym – mahogany boards with pulleys, weights and cords attached – was the Victorian equivalent of the 21st-century TRX.[6] But one invention, more than any other, combined the twin Victorian passions of fitness and fresh air with the newfound appetite for discovery and adventure. When the first "safety bicycles" appeared on the roads in the late 1880s,[7] replacing the completely mad-looking and ludicrously named "Ordinary" (also known as the Penny Farthing, which first appeared in 1871[8]), a new craze was born.

Cycling quickly became a way to make the most of the new weekends, with many employees now allowed to finish work at lunchtime on Saturdays. By 1895, more than 800,000 bicycles were produced in the UK,[9] while the Bicycle Touring Club – originally founded in 1878 – had more than 60,000 members, over a third of them women.[10] Every week, hundreds of cyclists poured out of the cities, with more popular routes beginning to look like Beijing before the Chinese government gave in and admitted that cars existed. The London to Portsmouth road became what we'd now call a "cycle super-highway", with the picturesque village of Ripley packed on sunny weekend afternoons with the scandalous sight of not just male but *female* cyclists gathered outside the Anchor Inn. "It is the stalking ground," wrote travel writer and author Charles Harper – a keen cyclist himself – "of self-advertising, long-distance riders, of cliquey and boisterous club men and of the immodest women who wear breeches awheel."[11]

Harper wasn't alone in his disapproval of women whizzing along the roads, particularly when daring to wear knickerbockers (eminently more sensible *and* safer) rather than long skirts. In 1899, a redoubtable female cyclist, Florence Wallace Pomeroy, Viscountess Harberton, took the Hautboy Hotel in Ockham to court, for refusing to serve her lunch due to her unseemly dress (yes, sensible and safe knickerbockers).[12] While the hotel owners may have considered her an affront to the delicate sensibilities of their other diners, the

Bicycle Touring Club – to their eternal credit – supported the case. Harberton lost, doubtless due, in no small part, to the all-male jury, but her case raised the profile of women cyclists and helped advance it as a pastime for women.[13]

If cycling was one way to satisfy the Victorian longing for holidays that offered a mix of fresh air and fitness, time on the river – particularly the Thames – was another, hugely popular choice. "1880 to 1914 was really the golden age of the Thames," says Simon Wenham, author of *Pleasure Boating on the Thames: A History of Salter Bros, 1858–Present Day*. "The railways killed much of the trade on the waterways, so a lot of boats were appropriated for leisure, heavier gigs were replaced by lighter 'skiffs' and as the population on the outskirts of London grew – particularly on the western side – so the river became a very fashionable destination." While East Enders took boats out to places like Southend and Gravesend, wealthier trippers, with more time to spare, explored the stretch from Kingston up to Oxford, gliding through peaceful waterfront villages such as Sonning and Streatley, now part of a pristine commuter belt, kept pin-neat and picturesque by the millionaires who lived in the elegant mansions that lined the riverbank.

It's not difficult to see what attracted people to lazy days messing about on the river. On a sunny Saturday morning, Goring's pretty high street looks like a pop-up from a children's storybook, as if, at any moment, Paddington might tumble out of one of the timber-framed windows. The Thames Path, which runs alongside the river for 185 miles, is wonderfully tranquil, with hardly another walker in sight – very different from the crowds that would have flocked to the riverbank during the area's heyday. "The Thames offered more than just day trips," says Wenham. "In a way, it was the birthplace of recreational camping – or certainly where it was popularised. Camping equipment at the time was super-heavy and not really portable by bike, but it could easily be transported by boat and popped up on the riverside once docked for the night." While the rich were developing their love of luxury hotel rooms, working people began to discover that it was possible to have an affordable night away somewhere lovely too, even if the standards of comfort were not quite on a par with the luxury surrounds of the Savoy or the Ritz. Camping became so popular that by the 1880s there were serious tensions with landowners, and the Thames Preservation Act was created to try and restore law and order.[14]

Sitting with a coffee on the sunlit deck at the Swan at Streatley, the other side of the river from Goring, I try to imagine the willow-strewn banks of the river dotted with tents, young men in straw boaters settled into fold-out chairs, landowners shaking their fists through the mullioned windows of the sprawling mansions behind. It's hard to imagine how extraordinary it must have been to do these things for the first time; to hop on a bike, sail down the river, sleep under canvas. Not a tradition handed down from your parents, or something people had been doing for decades, but something entirely new, slowly evolving and developing in front of your eyes. The trends we embrace as new today – glamping, say, or e-bikes – are innovative and fun, but I feel wistful for what the Edwardians had: a time when a rip-roaring adventure could be as simple as travelling a few miles from where you lived, and sailing off upriver meant venturing into worlds as unfamiliar as the Amazon itself.

And if the adventure was becoming vexed – with campers and property owners along the Thames at loggerheads – canny boat owners soon came up with a solution: producing skiffs that could be fitted with canvas covers at night to enable camping on board, as described in *Three Men in a Boat*.

> It looked so simple in the abstract. You took five iron arches, like gigantic croquet hoops, and fitted them over the boat, then stretched the canvas over them and fastened it down. It would take ten minutes, we thought. That was an underestimation. Looking back now, the wonder to me is that any of us are alive to tell the tale.[15]

Jerome and his friends' experience – wrangling the ill-fitting hoops, struggling with the canvas, bits popping out just as you fasten them – sounds remarkably similar to any time I have tried to put up anything vaguely tent-like, in spite of the fact that modern tents practically self-erect the moment you begin to unwrap the canvas. These days, tents are so lightweight that most can be packed away into a medium-sized sandwich bag, with super-clever bendy poles that only snap if you ignore the protests of your husband and insist they *will* fit into the holes if you just push a bit harder. But unless transported by boat, Victorian camping equipment was so heavy and cumbersome that the experience was restricted either to the military or to the handful of charitable camps set up by organisations such as the Boys' Brigade or enlightened employers such as Joseph Cunningham, superintendent of the Working Lads' Institute in Toxteth. Towards the end of the 19th century, Victorian paternalism had seen many "boys' clubs" begin to operate across the country, often run by genuinely philanthropic men like Cunningham (although some were simply canny employers, keen to create a more effective workforce), with the aim of giving impoverished young men a better start in life.[16] Clubs offered activities such as boxing and gymnastics, emphasising values such as a strong work ethic and self-discipline, often along with an annual camping trip away from the urban grind – quite possibly the first time many would ever have properly escaped the city. In many ways, these camps were the forerunners of the holiday camps such as Butlin's and Pontins, which became a craze of their own just a few decades later.

The real boom in camping came at the hands of one man: Thomas Hiram Holding, a tailor, who had spent much of his early life in America, where he spent five weeks camping on the wagon trail west.[17] When his family returned to the UK, he took the lessons learned amid the sprawling landscapes of Wyoming and Nebraska and began to fashion his own tents, to be taken on canoeing trips to Scotland and Ireland.[18] Holding's knowledge of fabric enabled him to use materials that were much lighter in weight – and thus far more portable – than the existing military-grade tents. In 1899, he published an account of his travels, *Cycle and Camp in Connemara*.[19] It attracted so much attention and brought him so many correspondents, keen to learn more about his new-fangled canvas designs, that in 1901 he founded the Association of Cycle Campers (ACC)[20], which became the Camping Club of Great Britain and Ireland in 1919, before eventually morphing into the Camping and Caravanning Club (C&CC), still very much a going concern today.

"A camping trip is more than just an affordable holiday option," says Andrew Robson of the C&CC. "We did a recent study with a team of academics at Liverpool John Moores and Sheffield Hallam universities, which demonstrated that campers are happier than non-campers, less stressed and more connected to nature, using their camping as a base for activities such as walking and cycling. So camping is actually good for your health." It certainly appealed to a generation of young Edwardians, with homemade tents – sewn to Holding's design and published as a "how to" guide in the ACC's members' magazine – mushrooming up in farmers' fields across the countryside. Cyclists packed them onto the back of their bikes, canoeists stored them beneath their paddles, and a whole generation discovered the joys of a few days under canvas for the first time.

According to Holding, a camping trip shouldn't have to mean compromising on daily comforts; what to take was considered as important as when and where to go, and travelling light was rarely a consideration. "Tent, poles, ground sheet, cooking apparatus," he begins, reasonably enough, when listing his essentials in *The Camper's Handbook*, published in 1908. The list then goes on: "Five little bags for tea, coffee, sugar, oatmeal and bread, marmalade or jam tin, combined knife, fork and spoon, gossamer pillow to stuff with hay, candelabra, candles, two pair flannel collars."[21] For some, a candelabra and two flannel collars were just the beginning; in 1912, *The Sphere* published an article on the luxurious camps along the River Thames that reveals glamping was invented decades before someone thought to put a duvet and a couple of throw cushions inside a tipi. "Too much has been made of the discomforts of camp life ... A piano is quite a common piece of furniture to find, gramophones are everywhere, there are comfortable beds with wire mattresses, armchairs, cushions, gate-legged tea tables and bridge tables."[22]

Camping and cycling may have been a more affordable way to holiday than staying in an inn or hotel (particularly if you left the piano at home), but many working-class families had neither the time nor money to explore either option. Instead, it was a change in the nation's drinking habits that offered many of London and Birmingham's poorest families the chance to escape to the country for several weeks each year. Ever since Flemish farmers brought hop plants across the Channel in the 15th century, the working man's pint of choice had slowly changed from malt-based ale to hop and malt-based beers, which packed a fuller flavour and had a distinctive, bitter aroma.[23] By the Victorian era, demand was so great that farmers struggled to bring in enough local help to fetch in the harvest, particularly as increasing numbers of younger people moved away from rural communities to the new urban centres.

And so, each September, an exodus took place from East End boroughs such as Hackney and poorer neighbourhoods in Birmingham and the Black Country. Families would pack up some spare clothes, a handful of cooking utensils and bits and bobs of food, and set out on open-sided trucks and specially commissioned trains for the hop fields of Kent, Herefordshire and Worcestershire. Conditions were pretty squalid in the early years – makeshift huts, floors covered with hop bines (the long stem of the plant) and usually one large iron pot and a communal frying pan, along with mattresses and blankets.[24] At its peak in the 1880s and 90s, when over 200,000 people – mostly women and children, with working husbands joining them at weekends – escaped to the countryside for a "hopper's holiday", it wasn't unusual for 70 people to sleep in one hut,[25] with six-day weeks the norm. The work may have been long and back-breaking, but for many, it was the highlight of their year. "What the banks of the Riviera are to the children of the aristocracy," wrote John Marsh in *Hops and Hopping*, published in 1892, "the banks of the Medway and the Stour are to the children of the poor."[26]

The Kentish hop fields are familiar to me to some degree, rolling out from the city of Canterbury, where I spent three gloriously irresponsible years, supposedly studying for a degree in English and American literature. A small exhibition takes me back to the vast edifice of the Gulbenkian library on campus, where black and white photographs show trains packed with families, billy-cans dangling out of windows, women with several children squeezed onto their laps, clearly as excited as if they were going to the beach for a week. Further along the corridor, there are pictures of young children picking through the hops, mothers beside them in aprons and headscarves, all gathered together around huge cooking pots. And there are extraordinary images of the "pole pullers", standing probably ten feet high on the stilts that allowed them to unhook small pieces of hop bine, caught on the highest wires. For the many families who returned each year – often for several decades – a few weeks' hop-picking, which came with negligible living costs, brought a much-needed whack of money as well as respite from the intense grind of city life.

After my visit to campus, I head to Scotney Castle, a National Trust-owned estate that is one of the few remaining hop farms in Kent. Rather than visit the house, I stroll out into the lush parkland that rolls out from the moated castle and octagonal kitchen garden, where Sussex cattle graze beneath the trees and the fields are full of neat rows of leafy green spires; the fast-growing hops already clambering up the long rows of canes. It's easy to understand why some families kept up the tradition of hop-picking holidays through three generations; the tranquil beauty of the Kent countryside must have seemed like heaven compared to the run-down streets of the East End. Later, when I read the memories of one hop-picking family on the Scotney Castle website, it seems it was exactly that. "In many ways that week was a child's paradise," says Anne, who visited a farm near Selling in Faversham. "There were no flushing toilets, showers or even wash basins. We didn't particularly notice, or care. No school, no washing for a week, and once I had picked a daily basket of hops, I was allowed to go and play with the other children."[27]

The Royal London Docks website has a section devoted to memories of hop-picking in the early-to-mid 20th century, including an oral history project that makes clear how fondly it is remembered. "Hard work but enjoyable," says Leslie Quirk, for whom it was a family tradition, started before she was born. "Something completely different from our normal lives. Fresh air and a change of scenery – spending the days chatting to friends and family on the hop bins alongside."[28] Some wives – along with the children – would go for as long as six weeks, with husbands joining at weekends (and quite often drinking most of the proceeds amassed by their nimble-fingered families). What's clear, from all the accounts I read, is that in spite of the hard work, it was regarded by most as a holiday; often the most cherished week or two of the year. "When the landlord of the Pig & Whistle called time," remembers one hop-picker in *Voices of Sussex and East Kent Hop-Pickers*, "a bath would be filled with beer and this would be placed in the middle of the road, with men dipping tin mugs in it until it was gone."[29]

By the 1920s, enjoying the benefits of time in the countryside had practically become government policy for a society ravaged by the twin legacies of World War I and the Spanish flu epidemic. It was as if, on some level, clean fresh air and healthy pursuits might go some way to expunging the horrors of the previous decade; cycling and camping associations were joined in record numbers, with the Camping Club of Great Britain & Ireland recording 4,500 members by 1929[30] and new sites opening up across the country as car ownership began to make touring camping far easier than before. New innovations increased the ease of outdoor life, from fold-up camping stoves to the zip. "It is a most ingenious device," wrote a correspondent to the club's magazine in 1923. "Imagine a row of metal paper fasteners on either side of a tent door . . . and a clip which, when pulled downwards . . . closes the opening. A fascinating and novel invention."[31]

As the decade passed, a third way of exploring – and holidaying – in the countryside became increasingly popular, stemming – ironically – from Germany. *Wandervogel* was a youth movement, a massively popular trend for yomping off into the countryside for a spot of tree-hugging, camping and yodelling as a way of rejecting the creeping industrialisation of the country.[32] Inevitably, it soon fell foul of the increasing Nazification of Germany, with weekend nature rambles replaced by enforced square-bashing at Hitler Youth meetings, but the idea still made its way across the Channel, where the idea of exploring on foot – the very simplicity of it – soon took hold. Quite quickly, those who strode out into the countryside realised they didn't want to stride back again on the same day, and a new fad for "sleeping out" – simply bedding down in a field without a tent and all the associated flummery – became such a trend, it made the papers.

"Parties bearing flea bags and blankets, provisions and on occasion even gramophones and wireless sets throng on the slopes of the Surrey Hills," reported *The Sphere* in 1931, while also estimating that around three million people would have gone trekking, either in the UK or overseas, in that year.[33] One image shows half-a-dozen young men and women wrapped in blankets and sleeping bags, one with a bottle to his lips, shoes discarded. They look like any group of teenagers on a cheeky night away and it's only after a moment that I remember how different their childhoods would have been, the losses they quite probably would have suffered, and the horrors that lay just a few years ahead. If any generation needed the restorative powers of nature, and holidays immersed in it, it was this one. As the number of young people flooding into the country continued to grow, another idea from Germany found a place in the UK. The first youth hostel opened in Llanrwst, North Wales, in 1930 (although it closed months later due to water problems)[34] – and by the end of the following year, there were 75 dotted across the country.[35]

"More and more young people were wanting to holiday in the 1920s and 30s," says Youth Hostels Association (YHA) historian Duncan Simpson. "The majority were 18–26 and unmarried – and they certainly wouldn't have been welcome as hotel guests, even if they could afford a room. The Co-operative Holiday Association and the Holiday Fellowship ran affordable holidays for workers on a low budget, but they weren't an option for anyone interested in touring around." Instead, the new youth hostels offered a low-cost place to stay, with beds costing about a shilling a night,[36] around a third of what even a room in the most basic of hotels would have cost. Newspapers were quick to pick up on the story. In May 1931, the *Daily Mirror* wrote – perhaps somewhat ambivalently – that youth hostels, "promised to cover the green places of our country with a network of clean but cheap rest houses."[37] By October, it was sounding decidedly more positive: "In these times of financial stringency, ramblers ... have discovered that a hiking tour ... is the cheapest and healthiest of holidays."[38]

Suddenly, a full-scale reclamation of the countryside was underway; in 1932, the mass trespass on Kinder Scout in the Peak District saw hundreds of walkers striding across hills and moorland as a protest against restrictions on walking across private land.[39] A handful of arrests and wall-to-wall coverage in the papers saw hiking become a national topic of discussion, along with the formation of the Ramblers – another nature-based organisation still with us today. "The mass trespass was the culmination of the frustrations of ordinary working people at not being able to access the outdoors, to be able to go up onto the Moors or into the Peak District," says Michael Duxbury of Ramble Worldwide. "It was the fighting call to get access for everyone to the outdoor environments of this country. The landowning classes were very reluctant – if not hostile – to let anyone onto the moorlands or the Dales – or anywhere people were wanting to go to fill their lungs with fresh air."

The more I learn about this period, the more it strikes me that there is a pattern in our relationship with the countryside, with the natural world; we turn to it at times of great trauma, or great change, as a way to restore some kind of balance, find some peace. I think of the pandemic, when millions of us strode out into the hills and woods, when the grass verges near the footpaths where I live were jam-packed with cars. Perhaps it's because natural landscapes are one of the most egalitarian places we can escape to: a field is a field, whether you're an earl or a pauper, there are no five-star forests, no exorbitant entrance fees to enjoy a stroll by a lake or take in a view. Of course, there are expensive hotels and country estates that cordon off their own section of the countryside for wealthy landowners and guests, but most of our landscapes are free and accessible, whatever walk of life we come from.

And, just as the Industrial Revolution drove people to explore the land to find quiet and stillness, the technological revolution we're living through is having a similar effect. "Our bookings are up across the board," says James Allen, deputy manager of Stratford-upon-Avon YHA, when I drop in for a visit. "Last year was our best year ever. Obviously, standards of accommodation are higher than they used to be, but we still keep the original ethos: the big self-catering kitchen, affordability – you can stay in a dorm for as little as £20, with private rooms from £35."

It's years – OK then, decades – since I stayed in a youth hostel and I'm struck by how appealing it is; rooms are basic, but clean and comfortable, and the Grade II listed building could easily be a country house hotel. Wooden camping pods and yurts outside are testament to how far camping has come since Holding's days, although I'm not sure he would approve of glamping. While we're looking around, a couple of families check in, parents with rucksacks, kids wide-eyed with excitement. "It's lovely with school groups," says Allen. "Often when they arrive, the teacher puts all the phones in a box and there can be some grumpiness. Next morning, they're all playing a board game or exploring the garden – phones completely forgotten."

The YHA – much like the Ramblers, the Camping and Caravanning Club and Cycling UK – may have morphed and evolved in its 95 years, but what strikes me is how closely all these organisations have kept to their original ethos, and how cyclical our holiday choices are. Growing up in the 70s and 80s, walking holidays were seen as the preserve of knit-your-own-casserole, bean-eating vegetarians, with cycling holidays not even on the radar. Now, dozens of companies offer these types of holidays in countries across the globe, tapping into our increasing need to immerse ourselves in natural landscapes as a way to switch off and go "off-grid". "The minute you lace up your shoes and step onto a walking trail, you're present in the moment," says Emma Gray, Managing Director of Inntravel, a tour operator specialising in walking holidays. "It's so grounding, it connects you back to the temporariness of our place in the landscape. Everything falls away."

At heart, what appeals to us about these 21st-century "great outdoors" holidays is no different from those racy, knickerbocker-clad women setting out on their safety bikes, Jerome K. Jerome and his friends bantering their way down the Thames, or those first campers, peering at the instructions in the CTA magazine and carefully sewing their tents by hand. However we choose to experience it, being immersed in nature has immense benefits, and exploring under our own steam – whether on foot, water or two wheels – is a very different experience to travelling around by car. A key part of a holiday – now, as then – is *difference*, and, for most of us, time spent rambling through woodland, whizzing along bridleways or sat around a campfire under the stars is about as different from our fast-paced urban lives as it's possible to get. We don't value our countryside enough, but in the years to come, I wonder if it will come to represent a new set of holiday values: sun, sea and sand replaced by space, peace and freedom – fast becoming the three things we crave most of all.

8

Wakes Weeks

Blackpool and the Lancashire Coast

"I love Blackpool. We're very similar. We both look better in the dark."[1]
Ian Holloway, Blackpool FC Manager, 2009–12

Friday night in Blackpool and, in spite of the fact it's deep into autumn and the night is damp and drizzly, the neon-flecked promenade is fizzing with life. Fairy-lit carriages, straight out of *Cinderella*, clip-clop beside the cars on the seafront; hen parties clatter along the pavement in a blaze of glittery shoes and hot pink Stetsons; groups of lads in puffa jackets tip back pints outside The Albert and The Lion pub, while families wheel prams with giddily excitable children alongside, waving glow sticks and clutching balloons. Through my car window, Blackpool Tower blazes bright blue and gold, the cabins on the sparkling Ferris wheel dangle like charms on a bracelet and even though I know I'm driving through one of the most socially deprived towns in the whole of the UK, it feels frothy and fun and wholly unexpected, as if I'd arrived at a wake and discovered a rave instead.

It's my first visit to what was once Britain's most beloved seaside town, still held in high affection by many from the Midlands northwards, but frequently dismissed by southerners as the country's tackiest resort. I should admit to being one of them; until this visit, my knowledge of Blackpool was limited to *Strictly Come Dancing* and the countless newspaper reports about the town's record levels of homelessness, drug use and social deprivation. "We are a town of extremes," says Claire Smith, owner of the rather chic Number One South Beach B&B, where I'm spending my first night in town. "We have pockets of absolute joy next to complete caverns of woe. No blending. It's either amazing, or awful."

Blackpool's story – and those of the other resorts on Lancashire's west coast – is very different from places such as Brighton and Scarborough, which exploded into life in the 18th century. The great waste of salt marsh that separated the Fylde Coast – a square-edged peninsula with Blackpool, named for the peat-coloured stream that fed directly into the sea, smack-bang in the middle – meant few people reached the town until 1840, when the train line unlocked a route into Fleetwood, seven miles north.[2] The opening of a new road from Preston to the coast in 1781 had brought a few visitors in stagecoaches from Manchester, and from Halifax a year later,[3] but even though the long stretches of sand were an ideal place for the wealthy to pursue their gender-specific favourite pastimes of gallivanting about on horseback (men) and walking slowly while gossiping about potential husbands (women), by the end of the century, the only people regularly "dipping" at Blackpool would have been hardy agricultural workers, who could walk to the beach in their clogs for a swim.[4] The town's handful of small hotels and cheap lodging houses left it way behind the nearby resort of Southport, which benefited from good transport links along the Leeds and Liverpool Canal, bringing in 20,000 visitors a year by 1820.[5]

But the key to Blackpool's success wasn't going to be the aristocracy, or the new breed of wealthy middle classes, who loved nothing more than pitching up in seaside towns and throwing money around. Instead, the resort would come to be a beacon for hundreds and thousands of workers from the cotton mills, factories and warehouses that sprang up in the new industrial cities across the north-west, most of whom had one trump card in their pocket when it came to getting time away from the manual grind of their days.

"The 'Wakes' were a tradition that went back centuries," says Richard Croisdale, when I drop into Blackburn Museum to chat with their oldest-serving volunteer. "I think they happened in other places in medieval times, but faded away. In Lancashire, they were set in stone; each summer, every village and town would have a Wakes celebration – and that meant time off from whatever work you did."

The origins of Wakes are a little misty, but the general consensus is they originated in the medieval period, growing up around the annual tradition of "rushbearing", when the old rushes – long skeins of plant, woven together and used as flooring in churches – were ripped up and replaced by fresh.[6] Once the work was done, the rest of the day would be taken as a holiday, often a pretty raucous one, with plenty of ale taken, songs sung, and thanks given to whichever saint the church was dedicated to. In a spectacularly fortuitous bit of planning, most Lancastrian Wakes days took place in the summer, and in the early days of the mills, employers might find an unexpectedly quiet factory when a Wakes celebration was taking place. While there's no *actual* proof that the first members of staff to "pull a sickie" were a group of Bolton cotton workers, many employees risked a dressing-down, or worse, for failing to show up to work during the annual Wakes festivities.

Inevitably, the canniest of the new employers began to see how the Wakes tradition might actually work in their favour. No mill or factory could operate 365 days a year; machines needed an annual clean and tune-up, often taking several days to a week. Tying the two together seemed an obvious answer, not least as the Wakes Weeks were staggered, with each town holding its festivities on a different date, saving the seaside resorts from becoming overwhelmed with too many visitors at the same time. But while this was a handy solution for the mill-owners, it wasn't quite the same boon for workers, most of whom were forced to take their Wakes Week holiday as unpaid leave. As Charles Booth noted in *Life and Labour of the People in London*: "Enforced idleness is a poor substitute for a holiday."[7]

Enforced *unpaid* idleness was even worse, but as it became clear some workers were going to be subjected to a summer holiday whether they liked it or not, a new trend for "Going-Off" or "Wakes Savers" clubs began to take hold, with a small amount contributed by each man on a weekly basis, to be drawn on – and gleefully spent – during the Wakes Week break. In Oldham, Werneth Spindle Works was the first to run a Going-Off club, with workers contributing sixpence a week, for a £1.25 payout (around £125 in today's money), while workers in Burnley, Bolton, Preston and other nearby urban centres paid into similar schemes.[8] The rapidly unfolding train network finally gave workers the chance to spend a day or two somewhere away from their own town, and nothing appealed more than the bright lights and bustle of Blackpool, which, by the end of the 19th century, was finally coming of age.

Innovation was key to Blackpool's success, beginning with the Illuminations, first experimented with in 1879, as a way to lure in visitors during the darker, autumn months. Eight lamps, positioned on 60-foot poles, were dotted along the seafront, creating what came to be known as "artificial sunshine", drawing crowds in their thousands.[9] When Blackpool Tower opened in 1894 – then the tallest building anywhere in the British Empire[10] – it capped several decades of development, with three piers – one for open-air dancing (hallo, Brighton, are you listening?) – pleasure gardens, swimming baths and one of the country's first all-electric theatres alongside the Illuminations themselves.

It was Scarborough on steroids, a Brighton for the North – slightly brasher, unashamedly dedicated to pleasure and firmly targeted at those who toiled in the nearby cities, while those who employed them, or white-collar workers who felt themselves to be above such plebeian frivolity, immersed themselves in the altogether more refined resorts of Southport and Lytham. In summer, the promenade thronged with workers who had put in double shifts or longer hours in the preceding weeks, while the early Wakes Week-ers gleefully spent the proceeds of their Going-Off fund on donkey rides or a cheeky bag of cockles, sharp with vinegar and pepper, eaten while strolling on the prom. Most, however, still came just for an afternoon, jolting in and out of the town on trains that would have felt like moving sardine cans.

By the beginning of the 20th century the "holiday" had become a concept known to everyone, through the countless newspaper photographs and stories of packed beaches and crammed trains, the postcards sent by friends and neighbours and the creeping realisation – by more enlightened members of the ruling class, at least – that time off might be a right for all, rather than just those with a little money in the bank. Some shop workers and clerical employees were beginning to enjoy a week's paid holiday, while in 1906, an agreement was reached in Lancashire which standardised the closure of the factories and mills, each on a set week between June and October.[11] But for many, the annual holiday was simply a day out to Rhyl or Blackpool, while others might afford a night or two at a lodging house in Llandudno or Morecambe. "We all lived in terraced houses, amid the muck from the great mills, factories and pits," writes Pat Mancini, arguably Blackpool's most famous landlady, in her autobiography, *Queen of Blackpool*.[12] "Manchester in those days was just often covered in a sort of industrial fog, and we had smog masks during the winter, but when you came up to Blackpool, the air was clear and fresh, and somehow the sun always seemed to be shining."

The concept of paid holiday for every worker, regardless of position, was still a long way off, in spite of the Trades Union Congress passing a resolution in its favour in 1911. The same resolution was passed for several years afterwards, and yet it never became a priority – mostly because the majority of employers saw paid holiday as a stealth pay increase.[13] Many argued that the wage increases already negotiated for their workers were intended to cover luxuries such as holidays and they had no intention of bumping up their wage bill twice. The economic depression of the late 1920s made the idea seem more outlandish than ever, and it wasn't until the late 1930s that it finally gained some traction.

One of the main drivers was the "Seaside Campaign", waged by female members of the Labour Party, who handed out over a million leaflets, and convened 150 meetings at 40 seaside resorts, calling for paid holiday for the working man.[14] That same year, 1938, the Departmental Committee on Holidays with Pay pronounced: "It cannot be, in our view, denied that an annual holiday contributes in considerable measure to work people's happiness, health and efficiency ... and the taking of consecutive days of holiday annually would be of benefit to the community."[15] Their recommendation was unanimous. Of the 18.5 million people earning less than £250 a year (around £26,000 today) in Britain, only 7.5 million had some form of paid holiday.[16] It was time to level the playing field: a minimum of one week for all (two, for full-time domestic servants), ideally taken in the summer months. In the face of such definitive findings, Neville Chamberlain's government had little choice but to act. Finally, in 1938, the Holidays with Pay Act was passed.[17]

"The irony is," says clinical psychologist Shona Goodall, "that time away from work actually makes people far more productive. There's been some Danish research that shows just one day of holiday increases performance by 8 per cent. The NHS knows from their sickness rates that people who don't take enough leave will be less well." I suspect the cotton mill workers in Burnley and Blackpool didn't need a study by the Danish Happiness Research Institute to tell them they'd feel better for time away from the clattering and banging of machinery, but the lesson was starting to be learned – holidays brought workers back refreshed and invigorated, rather than bitter and resentful at having to return.

For some, the Holidays with Pay Act was an opportunity to be taken as quickly as possible. "We have had a good holiday," wrote an anonymous factory worker from Coventry, in an August 1938 issue of the *Midland Daily Telegraph*, "... feeling for the first time we could

Gossip and gout; queuing to drink the water in Regency Bath

Wealth in search of health, the New Baths at Buxton Crescent, 1854

Rome, as discovered by the very first Grand Tourers, 1745–1794

The rural pleasures of the River Wye, 1700s

Packed carriages for a day trip to the sea, Llandudno, 1905

Blackpool brings in the crowds, 1920

Festival vibes on Box Hill at the height of the camping craze, 1930

Sunny days under canvas at Walton-on-Thames, Surrey, 1938

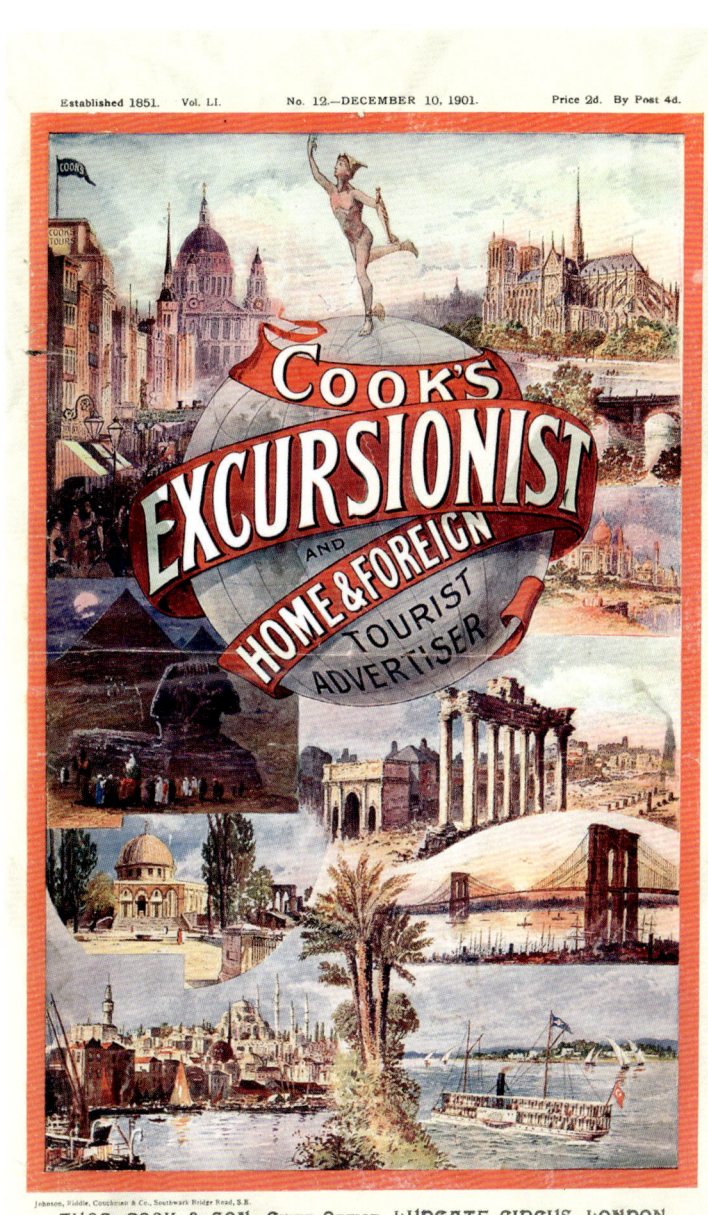

Thomas Cook blazes a trail for foreign travel, early 1900s

Fun and games at Butlin's, August 1939

The holiday camp phenomenon begins in earnest, 1945

Dancing on deck; the glamour of cruising, P&O

The British love affair with Benidorm begins, April 1966

The world – and Blackpool – shuts down, Autumn 2020

Residents of Barcelona make their feelings clear, Spain, April 2024

afford to pay for it without having to apologise to the butcher and the baker for being unable to meet his bills the week after. I am justified in saying 'thank you' to whoever did the trick."[18] But the mass exodus expected in the summer of 1938 failed to materialise, with many opting to holiday at home and bank the extra cash, while some workers lost the subsidised visits that had been their annual treat.[19] The number of seaside visits actually dropped; a stroke of luck for the unprepared resorts, who simply wouldn't have had the infrastructure to cope with such a sudden swell in numbers.

It took five years and a world war to really let the stopper out of the bottle. In the summer of 1946, wages were high, there were jobs for everyone and 11 million workers were entitled to paid leave.[20] Blackpool's Golden Era began, with ten million visitors flocking to see the Illuminations or twirl across the floor in the ornate ballroom – many of them friends, neighbours or fellow workers, arriving on packed trains and buses that couldn't squeeze in another body, leaving behind a ghost town, as the streets of Burnley or Oldham, Blackburn or Bolton fell silent for the Wakes. Rooms left empty by sons and husbands who never returned from the war were opened up to visitors, with women who had never dreamt of being anything but wives and mothers suddenly catapulted into whole new careers as landladies.

On the morning after my spangly drive along the prom, I walk through the streets to find Blackpool's imposing baroque library and begin to wonder if all the Friday night frivolity was just a figment of my imagination. In the bright light of day, the town's dilapidation is clear: closed-down shops, litter-strewn alleyways, the imposing frontage of the Winter Gardens looming up like a ghost from the past. In the library, I flick through countless images of the resort in its heyday – smiling women with crimped hair, wearing simple floral dresses and splashing in the shallows – and read about when the Wakes Week was the highlight of a year, with every part of it – from spending a little of the holiday club payout on a new dress and lipstick to scrambling to find space on a crowded train – recounted with warm, wistful nostalgia. "Our holidays were more special than almost anything we can imagine today," writes John Hudson, in *Wakes Weeks: Memories of Mill Town Holidays*. "On a day apparently written in tablets of stone, the entire town took to the coast: Blackpool was Oldham on Sea, Morecambe became Bradford-super-Mare."[21]

For those workers, the down-at-heel streets around the library were a fantasy world they could step into, filled with music and dancing, fairground rides and candyfloss, with deckchairs to snooze in, regardless of whether skies were blue or stony grey. I get the same sense of a disappeared world when I drive inland to visit Blackburn museum, through long rows of small, cramped houses originally built for mill workers and factory machinists, just some of the tens of thousands of jobs that no longer exist. It's sobering, to see such an entirely different world from the one I've been reading about; when I park the car, the town's main square feels eerily quiet and slightly dystopian. The brightly lit windows of Marks & Spencer shine out in the gloom, a beacon of 21st-century life among the faded facades of the imposing Victorian buildings, monuments to a time when the city blazed with wealth and industry.

"In our part of Blackburn, there were a lot of mills, and we all looked forward to our Wakes Week," says Richard Croisdale, slight, white-haired, effortlessly dapper in a neat waistcoat and watch chain. "The mills would close down on the Friday night – as you walked home, there'd be a deafening roar as they released the steam from all the boilers before powering down. You'd hear one, then another – in the end, it was so loud you couldn't hold a conversation." In spite of just having passed his ninetieth birthday, Croisdale's memories of his holidays to Blackpool are still pin-sharp; joining five-deep queues at 3 a.m., alongside those waiting to catch the train to Fleetwood, or the ferry to the Isle of Man. "The first time I went it was during the war, so it was full of airmen and they'd painted the bottom of street lamps and telegraph poles with white rings so you didn't walk into them. But we always had a good time. You'd walk on the prom and always see people you knew; there were penny slots, amusement arcades, deckchairs to hire for a few pence. And the boarding house ladies were smashing." He twinkles at me. "Some were very strict though. You had to be in by a certain time, or the door was locked."

What strikes me, the more I read and learn about Wakes Weeks, is how much has changed in what we expect from a holiday. These days, no respectable B&B is complete without homemade cake on arrival, en suite bathrooms with heated towel rails and power showers and welcoming hosts happy to chat through everything from local restaurant recommendations to the best walking routes nearby. Seventy years ago, the cake might be homemade, but there the similarities ended; rooms were basic, bathrooms were shared and the welcome from the flinty eyed landlady would often land somewhere between Nurse Ratchet and Professor McGonagall (without the hat). "They had to be tough," says Jilly Martin, whose grandmother ran a six-room B&B in Southport in the 1950s. "Nana used to say that the war left so many of her generation with big, empty houses – Victorian family homes where sons and husbands never came back. Those women had to find an income – I don't think they started out tough, but most of them had to become that way to survive."

In the early post-war years, just managing to keep a business going would have been an achievement in itself. Most lodging houses expected guests to provide their own food – particularly until post-war rationing began to be phased out, with separate pigeonholes in the kitchen for each family's provisions. Business-savvy grocery shop owners, who might have one branch in, say, Preston and one in Blackpool, quickly saw the potential for an Ocado-esque delivery system, with orders placed in the city-based shop phoned through to the seaside branch, and delivered to the relevant lodging house in Blackpool, Fleetwood or Rhyl.

Any idea that a holiday might offer the chance of a break from your annoying neighbour, or a few days free of bickering colleagues, simply didn't exist. Trains would be packed with families who lived cheek-by-jowl all year, only to find themselves in rooms along the same corridor when they went on holiday. "I remember families from Burnley coming to stay at my grandparents' B&B," says Mark Smith, who runs Number One South Beach alongside Claire. "Whole streets would come together. Number 1 Hill Street would have room 1, number 3 Hill Street would have room 2, number 5, room 3 – and so it went on." A third-generation hotelier, Smith's memories of working with tourists reach back to long before he was of officially employable age. "When I was a boy, my brother and I would take an old pram base down to the station and wait for the train to come in – then we'd offer to take people's luggage to where they were staying. It was quite a walk from the station to the lodging houses, and it was an easy way to earn a bob or two."

On arrival, guests would be informed of a daily schedule so regimented it wouldn't have been out of place in Beau Nash's Bath. Breakfast was at 9 a.m. – not at ten to, or quarter past, with guests expected to sit on their beds and wait until the bell, or gong, was rung. Everyone had to be out by 10 a.m., and they weren't allowed back in until 11.45, when lunch would have been a sandwich, piece of cake and cup of tea. The doors closed again at 1 p.m., before reopening at 5 p.m. "And it had to be five," says Smith. "The working men's clubs opened at 6 p.m., and if you weren't in the queue, you wouldn't get a seat. It didn't matter there were dozens of them, they were all packed." The sheer number of guests that poured into Blackpool in its heyday meant that *everywhere* was packed, with no bed – and no flat space – left unused if it could be pressed into service. "We'd go out to the pub on a Friday night," says Claire, "and come back to find Mark's mum had let his bedroom – and theirs too. She'd say *No, no – don't go in!* We'd all sleep in the lounge, like sardines, then get up and start work. All the B&Bs did it. And if there wasn't a bed available for the coach driver, we'd just put a board across the bath and he'd sleep on that."

So many of the things we prize so highly in holidays these days – privacy, space, peace, comfort – simply weren't part of a Wakes Weeks jaunt. Many B&Bs and lodging houses might sleep 30 people with just two toilets and one shower. "I remember people queueing on the landing in their dressing gowns," says Claire. "They'd all be clutching their toothbrushes and towels, chatting away quite happily. People didn't expect much, but they were happier then, I think. More grateful." And no one went looking for peace and quiet; there were theatres and concerts, funfairs, gaming machines, fortune-tellers and photographers – entertainment was even made out of guessing people's weight, with jokey recriminations for those considered too fat or too thin. Blackpool and other seaside resorts would compete to pull in the biggest names, from George Formby and Gracie Fields in the 1930s to Ken Dodd and Morecambe and Wise in the 1950s and 60s.

Not everyone took the trains and coaches to the resorts on the Fylde coast. Liverpool workers could take the paddle steamer to Llandudno in North Wales, or across to the port of Douglas on the Isle of Man, which became big business in the 1950s.[22] By 1955, nine passenger ships sailed from Fleetwood and Heysham to Douglas, as well as from Belfast, Dublin and Ardrossan.[23] Many Scottish mills and factories operated on a similar system of summer shutdowns, with plenty of romances between Scousers and Scots. Some who made the crossing to Douglas on the Isle of Man found themselves in such rough seas, they wished their holiday over before it had begun. In *Wakes Weeks*, Michael Johns remembers "some evil trips ... times when I would have gladly swapped a swift and painless death for what I was going through."[24]

But however people travelled, and wherever they arrived – from Llandudno to Lytham, Blackpool to Rhyl – nothing else in the year topped the Wakes Weeks holiday. Years turned, summers came and the towns fell quiet like dominoes, with workers surging back after a week of silence, clutching miniature Blackpool Towers to put on their dressing tables, postcards to tape to workplace lockers and memories of flirtations and those few short days of freedom saved up to be pored over in the dark winter months. "The more rigid and structured your working life, the greater the benefit of a holiday," says Executive Coach Mark Brocklesby. "There are so many pressures – to be on time, to be reliable, dependable, to achieve targets, and all of it occupies our minds. On holiday, there's none of that. Suddenly, we have time to daydream. People underestimate how good that is for our brains – like taking them out for a long walk, before cooping them up again."

For a time, it seemed as if the resorts on the north-west coast were destined to be holiday hotspots for generations to come. No one could have foreseen how quickly it would all end. While London swung its way through the 60s, the North began to falter, with factories and mills unable to compete with the cheap, imported textiles flooding the British market, made with technology they didn't have, and labour costs far below what was acceptable (thankfully) in the UK. By the late 1960s, mills and factories were closing at the rate of one a week,[25] and the easy comfort of Wakes Weeks holidays began to fracture, as streets where neighbours had worked and holidayed together became an uncomfortable mix of those still lucky enough to be employed and those doomed to an interminable search for an ever-diminishing number of jobs. Blackpool held out for a while, but the days of shared bathrooms and dinners of gammon and pineapple and Peach Melba were slipping fast from its grasp.

And yet, somehow, the town endures. More than Morecambe, which feels drab and dejected when I pop in, although there are ambitious plans for a new Eden Project (set to open in 2027 ... or possibly 2028) and to restore the Winter Gardens, which won a £2.74 million grant from the Department for Culture, Media and Sport in 2023.[26] It's worth a visit just to understand the sheer scale of the beach – the largest swathe of intertidal sand flats in the UK, with a shoreline stretching for five miles – and to imagine those first Victorian visitors galloping around on their horses and swishing across the sands in full-length frocks and bonnets, and the trainloads and charabancs of working men and women who followed, many of them seeing the sea for the first time.

I buy some chips and stroll along the promenade, trying to picture it in summer, when I'm sure the beach is packed, but even the statue of my all-time comedy hero, Eric Morecambe, striking his best "Bring Me Sunshine" pose feels a little forlorn. I'm not sure there's anywhere more haunted by its ghosts than a forgotten seaside town on a damp Saturday morning, although, as with so many of the resorts I visit, there's clearly real passion and enthusiasm for restoring the town's fortunes. For so many of us, these places are the repository of cherished memories; if not ours, then our parents' or grandparents', captured in faded photographs and crumpled postcards, passed down from one generation to the next.

Fortunately for Blackpool, enough of its original attractions remain to still draw in a loyal crowd of day-trippers, even on a damp, chilly November Sunday. Before I leave, I set out for a walk along the prom, heading towards the gates of the Pleasure Beach, where great metallic tentacles weave and twist up towards the sky. The park has just opened when I arrive, and the crowds are streaming in: groups of teenagers, frazzled-looking dads with over-excited kids, the air fracturing as the first lines of carriages hurtle across the rollercoaster lines suspended above the walkways. "We don't profess to be the cultural capital of the North," Claire had said to me, as I checked out of Number One South Beach. "We just say . . . come and have fun."

And that, it strikes me, as I watch a pair of giggling teenagers clamber into a carriage on the Revolution coaster, is what lay at the heart of a Wakes Weeks holiday. Instead of self-improvement or practising painting or focusing on health, they were about a lightening of the spirit, a chance to be silly, giddy, to really laugh – to have fingers sticky with candyfloss, flirt a little, forget the harsh realities of everyday life. Until I came to Lancashire, I'd never really understood the seismic, devastating change the region went through in the 1960s and 70s; the extraordinarily difficult legacy it has been left with, after decades of under-investment and the failure of any government to properly tackle the problems of the region's post-industrial landscape. And so I'd never been able to understand what Blackpool means – then and now. Deprived it may be, down-at-heel definitely, and yet on a damp Friday night in the depths of autumn, it still blazes like a beacon; ready and waiting for girls – and boys – who just want to have fun.

9

Good Morning Campers!

Bognor and the New Forest

"Our true intent is for all your delight."[1]
Billy Butlin via William Shakespeare

"Bong! Bong, bong! Good morning, campers!"

It's hard to make a glockenspiel come off the page, but anyone who remembers the 1980s will probably also remember Gladys Pugh's daily morning announcement, as Chief Yellowcoat at the fictional holiday camp of Maplins. *Hi-de-Hi!* was a hit show on the BBC from 1980–88, lampooning everything Butlin's had once been famous for, from knobbly-knees competitions to Glamorous Grannies and brylcreamed sunbathers by the pool. Holiday camps might have been ripe for affectionate mockery by then, but in the first half of the 20th century they had been an integral part of our developing love affair with holidays, as essential to our story as Beau Nash and Blackpool Tower.

Ninety years after Billy Butlin opened his first camp in Skegness, holiday parks – as they now tend to be known – remain a hugely popular choice for an active, affordable break. Companies including Parkdean, Away Resorts, Haven, Center Parcs and Butlin's generated £12.2 billion in 2024,[2] according to the UK Camping & Caravanning Alliance, and even those of us who have never been near a holiday park will have an image in our minds, whether from *Hi-de-Hi!*, or the classic black and white photographs of Butlin's that have come to symbolise holidays in the 1950s. They look charmingly quaint now – neat wooden chalets and crowded poolsides – but back in the 1930s, Butlin's, Warner's and Pontins became a success story almost overnight,[3] appealing to families looking for an affordable way to experience the newly accessible concept of a "holiday" that was fast becoming a national preoccupation, thanks to the 1938 Holidays with Pay Act.[4]

"When Butlin's started, it was aspirational," says CEO Jon Hendry Pickup, when we chat via Zoom. "In those days, most people aspired to what the landed class did – and the idea of 'taking a holiday' had always really been seen as the preserve of the rich. Butlin created something that people could actually afford: a week's holiday for a week's wages. It was a social gathering space – full of fun and activities – that people wanted to be part of."

The canny Billy Butlin – known as the man who brought dodgem cars to Britain (and made a fortune with his travelling fairs) – was also tapping into the trend for active, outdoorsy holidays, partly created by the new pastimes of hiking, cycling and camping, and building on a tradition of communal camping holidays that had begun almost 30 years before. Perhaps surprisingly, the very first holiday camp was at Howstrake on the Isle of Man, set up in 1894 by Joseph Cunningham – previously Superintendent of the Working Lads Club in Toxteth. He and his wife, Elizabeth, who lived in the North End of Liverpool, an area of docks with perilously low standard of living, created Cunningham's Young Men's Holiday Camp, with the aim of offering a week away to inner-city workers who would otherwise never get a break. The first site could sleep up to 600, in neat rows of white, circular tents (albeit with strict temperance rules to quash half the fun); in 1905, another five acres of land were added, along with 1,500 tents and a dining pavilion, offering such joys as kippers with jam and fruit and vegetables grown in the camp's own garden.[5] Others quickly followed: the Socialist Holiday Camp in the Norfolk village of Caister-on-Sea opened in 1906[6] – notable for being advertised as an "ideal holiday resort for Suffragettes" in *Votes for Women* magazine[7] – with several others springing up along the coast during the pre-war years. In 1920, having stayed at Caister before the war, Herbert Potter took the £500 he had won in a newspaper competition and invested it in creating a camp of his own, building a clutch of timber huts in Hopton-on-Sea.[8]

As the new decade dawned, others were following Potter's idea, replacing tented camps with makeshift huts and cabins that offered slightly more protection against the unpredictable British weather. But it was a retired military captain, Harry Warner – rather than Billy Butlin – who first took the basic, charity-based holiday camp idea and super-charged it into an early form of all-inclusive resort, albeit with a marked lack of swim-up bars, teppanyaki restaurants and kids' clubs designed with the sole purpose of ensuring wealthy parents don't actually have to spend any time with their offspring. The first Warner Holiday Camp opened in 1932, offering four-course meals, a bar and entertainment, and Captain Harry quickly appointed Butlin, a friend and fellow holiday camp evangelist, to the board. For a few years, they were the Lennon and McCartney of the holiday camp world, until Butlin opened his own camp in Skegness, in 1936.

Two years later, in a spectacularly fortuitous confluence of events, the Holidays with Pay Act came into force. Butlin himself couldn't have planned it better; suddenly, there was a vast new market for his innovative camps, which brought together all the new experiences Britain had to offer. Cheap public transport meant people had begun to travel easily beyond their own town or village, and the dizzying magic of the radio opened up new aspects of the world to those who had barely strayed beyond their front parlour. Dance halls, cinemas, swimming lidos and racing circuits were just some of the ways people now had to spend this curious new concept of "leisure time" – and Butlin, more than anyone else, understood that combining all these things with somewhere comfortable (rather than basic) to stay, would have mass appeal to the millions able to take a *real* holiday for the first time.

"The most modern camp in the world," ran a Butlin's advertisement at the time. "Free golf, tennis, bathing, bowls, dancing and concert parties. FOUR good meals a day, cosy Elizabethan chalets and first-class sanitary arrangements – ALL FOR 45 shillings PER WEEK."[9] And to ensure guests engaged with everything Butlin's had to offer, an army of Redcoats – young men and women – were on hand to make sure days went with a swing, overseeing everything from poolside games to ensuring every guest had a dance partner in the evening (whether they wanted one or not).

Success was instant, and almost overwhelming; one advertisement in the *Daily Express* newspaper generated 10,000 queries and the resort was instantly booked out for the whole of the summer. Butlin seized the opportunity, opening Clacton in 1938 and starting construction on Filey in 1939,[10] before Hitler appeared over the horizon, sending holidays to the very bottom of the country's collective to-do list. Within months, Warner and Butlin found their camps requisitioned as army bases and training camps, while the Dovercourt Camp was used to house German refugee children who had arrived in England as part of the Kindertransport programme. "The camp leaders are very keen, full of human kindness," reported a visitor from the Women's Voluntary Services in 1939, ". . . and great efforts are made to stress the future hopes of the children and help them to forget the past."[11]

Once the war was over, the boom really began. Something about the carefully curated holiday camp spirit tapped into the brisk, best-foot-forwards, all-in-it-together mentality that – according to the government at least – characterised a population determined to move on from five years of hideous conflict. Returning soldiers would have felt particularly comfortable with the structured days of activities, classes and entertainments – not least because, at some camps, the wartime station commanders remained in charge. London newspaper *The Sphere* quoted the Filey camp controller in November 1946: "It's exactly the same as when I was commanding here during the war," said Group Captain Borthick-Clarke. "If a group of youths ... start making a noise after 1 a.m.... I inform them that if they do not guarantee to behave themselves, they will be compelled to leave. They always behave after that."[12]

If ex-army group captains weren't enough to keep the racier elements from sullying the good Butlin's name, the Archbishop of York was appointed as the honorary "Ecclesiastical Advisor to Butlin's Holiday Camps".[13] Butlin was clear-eyed about the kind of guests he wanted: not the factory and mill workers who were flocking to Blackpool, but middle-income families who were looking for something a little more glamorous than a repurposed train cabin or an unfriendly lodging house. Chalets were the boutique apartments of their day, with electric lights, carpeted floors, running water and baths – the height of luxury for many guests who would still have had outdoor toilets and bare floorboards. Days were packed with sports and dancing, funfair rides and competitions – but the long-held belief that holidays should also offer some form of worthwhile improvement was cleaved to by Butlin, who also ran a programme of debates and high-end entertainment, including concerts by the San Carlo Opera Company in the summer of 1946;[14] a kind of continuation of Victorian paternalism, albeit with Glamorous Granny competitions alongside more cerebral pastimes.

"My holidays are no more like barracks than the *Queen Elizabeth* is like a tramp steamer," Butlin wrote in an open letter, published in the *Paddington Mercury* in 1951, as a response to a letter from two ex-soldiers, wanting a good holiday that didn't involve "roughing it". "You can go to a luxury hotel if you like, but you will not stay in more delightful surroundings, sleep in more comfortable beds or eat better food."[15]

Quite whether the wealthier classes – who were very happy to settle back into their cruise ship cabins, Thomas Cook tours across Egypt and villas in the south of France – would have agreed with Butlin is up for debate. Certainly, no duke or earl would have been seen dead by a Butlin's pool; instead, the camps were just the newest manifestation of the trend towards ghettoisation between British holidaymakers, first seen in the 19th century, with the wealthy sequestered in Eastbourne and Llandudno and the great unwashed carousing in Margate and Rhyl. The irony, perhaps, is that Butlin's belief in "improving" activities for his guests was exactly the same belief that knitted Thomas Cook's "educational" tours together.

For the next two decades, Butlin's dominated the holiday camp market; by 1966, there were nine resorts around the UK, welcoming a million holidaymakers each summer.[16] Others tried to emulate the success. Fred Pontin opened his first resort in 1946 – a smaller-scale, lower-key take on the Butlin's formula – and quickly expanded, with 30 Bluecoat-filled Pontins dotted across Britain by the 1970s,[17] while Haven opened its first caravan park in 1964.[18] Ladbrokes took over some of the Warner camps and some enterprising farmers opened simpler holiday parks, but nowhere could match the original. For many visitors, the parks held a kind of otherworldly feel, from the billowing flags that welcomed guests into the resort, to the sky-blue and primrose-yellow decor that illuminated everything from the chalets to the dining rooms, dance halls and entertainment venues. Every corner of the park seethed with life; unpaid barrow boys racing between car park and chalet in hopes of a tip, fairground rides whirling, the air thick with whoops and screams from passengers on the Wild Mouse rollercoaster, deliberately designed with wheels at the very back of the car, to give the impression it was about to go over the edge every time it took a corner.[19]

"Butlin's has never been about coming away for a quiet, peaceful time," says Jeremy Pardey, Strategy Director at Butlin's, when I drop into Bognor for a visit. "We're about high-energy fun for the whole family, and great value for money. Our history and traditions are important, but we've worked to become more contemporary – to not just keep up with what's on offer on the High Street, but match it, surpass it." I don't mention that I know Bognor Butlin's of old, that I grew up on the south coast a few miles' drive away, and that it had always been somewhere seen as a bit of a joke, a bit faded and tragic. (Apart from when we were allowed a day trip and it suddenly became quite exciting and considerably more fun than double maths – at least until I almost threw up on the waltzer.)

I'm surprised, then, by what I find on a wet February Friday. It's the beginning of half-term and kids are scrambling out of cars in the car park, while early arrivals are whizzing down the flumes in the scrupulously clean Splash Waterpark. There are only three Butlin's left now – Minehead, Bognor and the very first in Skegness – but clearly there's been a major reinvention, with Adult Weekenders offering 80s and 90s themed music festivals, while on-site attractions include a VR gaming suite that looks like something out of the latest Netflix sci-fi drama. Jeremy leads me into the Lasertag suite, where a gaggle of kids stream past, a troupe of middle-aged dads behind them, all looking equally excited. While I'm not invited to view the more old-fashioned chalets, the bedrooms in the upscale Wave Hotel are slick and modern, with fun neon touches and contemporary design – rather like a Premier Inn room, all dressed up for date night.

It's all a far cry from the days of competitions to see how many things you could get in a matchbox, or games like Find the Pirate, where a Redcoat dressed as Captain Kidd had to be found somewhere in the resort, before being marched to the swimming pool to walk the plank. Girls competed for the much-coveted title of Holiday Princess while boys watched wrestling bouts between the same pot-bellied, pantomime fighters who threw each other around on Saturday afternoons on ITV, before heading to the discotheque – little more than two flashing lights in an unlit room, with fluorescent paintings on the wall and a Redcoat hovering uncertainly behind a couple of record decks. But some aspects remain the same: at night, the resort still lights up with neon illuminations and familiar faces from Saturday night TV ramp up the entertainment – Stephen Mulhern instead of Des O'Connor or Bob Monkhouse, with concerts by everyone from Jason Donovan to Fatboy Slim.

"We're the home of entertainment now," says Jon Hendry Pickup. "It is a reinvention and it needed to happen. The 80s and 90s were particularly hard for us – package holidays to Europe were more and more accessible and so much cheaper, and people suddenly had so many other options. The problem with being an iconic brand is that you have an image everyone knows in a particular way. We did a lot of work at understanding what people want from their holidays; for our market, at least, it's not about boutique accommodation and fine dining – our guests want to be entertained, have fun things to do and most importantly have value for money."

After my visit, I take a deep dive into the world of online Butlin's nostalgia, both on the company's own website, but also on some of the forums dedicated to sharing memories about the holidays taken everywhere from Ayr in Scotland to Minehead in Devon. What comes across in so many of them – much like the Wakes Weeks reminiscences – is the absolute sense of wonder, of stepping into a world where everything was new and exciting, from ice-cream floats for tea and chow mein in the on-site Chinese restaurant, to the first time on a rollercoaster or first dip in the sea. But many of the posts come with a coda, a sad acknowledgement that by the 1970s, many of the resorts had become faded and shabby, unable to match the guaranteed sunshine and sense of adventure that Mediterranean travel offered. In 1972, Butlin's son, Bobby, sold the company to the Rank Organisation for £43 million, and the downhill slide picked up speed.[20]

But not all sites fell out of favour so fast. "I became a Bluecoat at Pontins Brean Sands in 1997," says Paul O'Brien, who donned the coat for three seasons and worked in holiday parks until 2005. "I was lucky to catch the tail end of the glory days. There were 15 of us Bluecoats to 3,000 guests and we worked a six-day week, often 15-hour days, for £1.63 an hour. It was exhausting, having to keep your energy levels up – sometimes you'd be greeting people for breakfast, doing activities through the day and then DJing till 3 a.m. But 99 per cent of the time it was absolutely brilliant. The camaraderie, the people you met, the relationships you had (some of which you probably shouldn't have) – there was nothing like it."

O'Brien believes that holiday parks fell foul not just of the new vogue for foreign travel, but also through failing to keep up with changes in society. "Even in the late 90s, for most people, entertainment just meant TV – so they were happy to come away, switch off their brains and be entertained by us. We'd do *Blankety Blank* or *The Generation Game* – our Entertainments Manager was this fabulous drag queen, which was really rare back then. By the mid-00s, the internet meant people had far wider entertainment choices, just at the click of a mouse. Ten average singers and dancers up on stage just wasn't going to cut it." By 1999, there were just three Butlin's resorts left and Pontins was down to eight. Diehard fans continued to visit but, according to O'Brien, it became a steady slide downwards. "By the end of my time, budgets were being slashed and parks sold off. There was no investment – they just went for the real budget end of the market."

If Butlin's and Pontins weren't moving with the times, a new type of holiday park was proving that there was still huge demand for activity-based family breaks, albeit with a distinctly different ethos. The first Center Parcs opened in the UK in 1987 in Nottinghamshire's Sherwood Forest, followed by Elveden Forest in Suffolk in 1989 and Longleat in 1994.[21] Owned by Dutch entrepreneur Piet Derksen, who opened his first camping site in Europe in 1968,[22] Center Parcs swapped Butlin's garish colours and whizz-bang pace for a calmer, more stripped-back feel. Slick woodland lodges with dishwashers and en suite bedrooms were dotted through the trees, with bicycles for exploring and a signature vast dome, housing the 'Subtropical Swimming Paradise' with lazy rivers and towering flumes. "The wild water rapids swirl past glistening rocky banks and the lush foliage of palms and banana trees," said the *Daily Express* in 1987. "The 450-acre development at Sherwood Forest, costing £34 million . . . is as far from the old concept of *Hi-de-Hi!* as it is possible to imagine."[23]

Suddenly, a family break to a holiday park was not just acceptable, but positively aspirational for many of those who had long been sniffy about the dubious delights of Butlin's. Center Parcs was a perfectly judged mash-up of nature retreat and indulgent getaway, with guaranteed Caribbean temperatures in the Subtropical Dome, an on-site spa for weary parents and upscale dining if rattling pots and pans in the woodland lodges' well-equipped kitchens all felt a bit too much. Inevitably, such grandeur was reflected in the cost: £400 for a week in August in 1987 (around £1,137 today), with no meals included;[24] price once again ensuring that different "classes" of holidaymaker stayed in their lanes. An all-inclusive week in Butlin's at the same time would have cost a quarter of the price, firmly establishing Center Parcs as the Waitrose of the holiday market, clearly targeted at the "Volvo and Claret set", as the *Express* tagged the red-trouser wearing dads and Laura Ashley-clad mums who swung into the car parks in their 4x4s every weekend.[25]

Regardless of the price tag, this new version of family camping – surrounded by nature, with a focus on outdoorsy activities, but without the need for leaky tents and inflatable beds that always, *always* deflated at 4 a.m. – quickly became the latest holiday trend. In spite of a lack of either a Volvo or Claret (or, thankfully, trousers of any hue besides denim or light beige), we have had several extended family weeks at Center Parcs, where we spent so long in the lazy-river rapids that by the end we looked like a gaggle of prunes, wobbling back to our lodge on bicycles, my youngest niece shrieking with delight at the squirrels, as she trundled along in the toddler carriage attached to the back of my brother-in-law's bike. It was the right holiday recipe at the right moment for millions of families; a glamorous way to go back to basics (kind of), before portmanteau words became a national epidemic and "glamping" became An Actual Thing.

"We've been on around 15 Center Parcs holidays," says Justine Campbell, a mother of three, who often holidays with her sister's family. "It's the best option we've ever found. The safety of the village is a massive advantage if you've got small children, as no cars are allowed after drop-off has finished. The pool complex is included in the price, and we used this every day, sometimes all day." Campbell believes Center Parcs' success is that it offers as much to weary parents as over-excited children. "Now our kids are adults, they still want to go – as do us fifty-somethings. It's just a lovely place to spend some quality time with your loved ones."

It's more than a decade since I stayed at a Center Parcs, and in the intervening time, the world of holiday parks has changed again, with the tough economy transforming it into a sector that's booming once more. Pontins may be on its last legs, but Butlin's successful reinvention sits alongside Parkdean, Haven and Away Resorts, all offering an updated take on the classic holiday park experience, boasting everything from static vans and camping pitches to eco-pods, glamping and luxury lodges with private decks and hot tubs. And some of the original businesses still survive; four generations and 105 years after Herbert Potter opened his camp on the Norfolk coast, Potters Resorts recently came top in an independent *Which?* survey of the best holiday parks in the UK. "The sector is absolutely brilliant right now," says Carl Castledine, MD of Away Resorts, which now has 22 parks around the country. "There aren't many countries where there's such choice for working-class families to go and have a lovely holiday on the beach in such a cost-effective way."

Castledine, whose grandfather ran the Caister holiday park in the 1970s, started the business in 2008, buying Whitecliff Park on the Isle of Wight, and redesigning it for the needs of 21st-century families. Seventeen years later, there are 27 Away Resorts around the country. "In a way, it was the glamping trend that kickstarted my thinking," he says. "I couldn't get my head round why families wanted to stay in a tent with no heating or bathroom, when they could be staying in a warm, comfortable van. But then I realised – no one wants to go into the office on a Monday morning and say they'd spent their weekend in a static caravan. The holiday park concept needed a revamp – but I was sure there was still a market there."

Castledine's vision is Butlin's, reinvented for our times; Holi-esque colour festivals rather than beauty contests, mass custard pie fights and family Pride events rather than knobbly-knees competitions. When I check into the Heartwood Lodge at Sandy Balls in the New Forest, it's clear he also has Center Parcs in his sights. I'm genuinely blown away by what's basically a good-sized holiday cottage, with a huge widescreen smart TV in the lounge-diner, an en suite master-bedroom with a free-standing, in-room bath, a well-equipped kitchen and a small private terrace that I shiver on in the early morning light, listening to woodpeckers tapping against the tree trunks that wrap around the van. There are simpler options on the site – from basic camping pitches, through to wooden lodges and classic static vans – as well as the kitschily pink Esme Lodge, with neon lighting, liquorice-stripe wallpaper and plush velvet furniture.

It's quiet when I stay, out of the main holiday season, but when I stroll up to the shop to buy coffee and a croissant, it brings back memories of caravanning holidays, that lovely moment of opening the door and stepping onto grass thick with dew, the silence broken by the occasional sound of awnings being unzipped and the quiet rattle of kettles being set on gas stoves. I pass by an elderly couple, sitting in fleeces and scarves, sipping coffee on their deck, and a family peering at the details of the day's activity programme on the signboard in the village square. "Every year we host thousands and thousands of families," Castledine tells me, when we chat over Zoom. "They've all got their individual needs and wants – whether it's being part of lobbing 6,000 cans of shaving foam around or watching an NT live broadcast of *La Bohème*. Whatever they want, we aim to provide it. Life is so overwhelming now, there's such tyranny of choice, that we want to make it as easy as possible; that feeling that once you've made the booking, we've got you."

As I wait for the barista to make my coffee, I think about how Castledine's words chime with what I've heard from so many people in the industry. The internet has given us infinite holiday choices, on everything from destinations to accommodation, experiences and flights, with endless booking sites – Expedia, booking.com, Airbnb – all insisting they offer the best experience and can do us the best deal. It can be daunting, even overwhelming, and so it's unsurprising that holidays which offer everything sewn up in a neat and tidy package – from all-inclusives to cruise ships and holiday parks – are doing so well. The sense that everything is taken care of – that you can arrive and just dive into an array of entertainments and experiences that even the most *ennuied* teenager will love – is what many of us want when planning our precious time away.

"You can't have a one-size-fits-all holiday," says clinical psychologist Shona Goodall, "because everyone finds relaxation and rejuvenation in different things. Some people might go on a yoga retreat and come back totally rested, while their partner might find it the dullest thing in the world. Someone else might come back from holiday saying 'I feel so rested' when they've spent the entire week white-water rafting. Holidays that include a big choice of activities – along with the chance to do nothing – can help counter the problems this can cause. Everyone can have exactly the type of holiday that suits them, that they find relaxing."

Of course, holiday parks aren't for everyone and some remain faded, justifying their dilapidated state by offering rock-bottom prices.[26] But at a time when the need for affordable family breaks has never been greater, it's good to see that, instead of the slide to the bottom that took place in the 80s and 90s, this new generation of parks is competing to outdo each other. Whether bringing in the biggest names from Saturday-night TV, creating events that have real appeal for 21st-century families, or putting together affordable, adult-friendly weekends that offer a chance to step away from all the everyday worries and responsibilities, it does feel as if the choice of affordable breaks has never been greater.

Castledine and Hendry Pickup are both evangelists for their holiday parks, the latest in a long line of those determined to ensure a holiday is a universal pleasure, accessible to everyone. You can trace this line back through Warner and Butlin, the determined group of Labour women in the 1930s, pushing for the Holidays with Pay Act, and those before them, who set up Going-Off clubs and Wakes saving schemes to ensure workers could have at least a few days' holiday. "There's still snobbery out there," says Jon Hendry Pickup, "but Butlin's is a 90-year-old brand. It's up to us to change the narrative and be clear on who and what we are. We're not about status. We're not about peaceful beach holidays. We're about families coming together, having fun and not worrying about the cost to their pocket."

Carl Castledine agrees: "There are still barriers to break down. I feel like it's part of my job to let 66 million people know there are really cool places on their doorstep, where they can have a holiday that will give them real time together. Every family has its stories – they're so important to who we are – but I think that gets forgotten, there's just never enough time. A good holiday should give you that chance – to tell the old stories, and create new ones." I'm sure Billy Butlin would agree.

10
The Rush to the Med
Benidorm and Menorca

*"Oh! This year I'm off to sunny Spain, Y Viva España.
 I'm taking the Costa Brava plane, Y Viva España!"*[1]
"Y Viva España", Leo Roozenstraten & Leo Caerts

The human memory is such a curious thing. In some ways, our brains are like giant filing cabinets, tucking away moments and places, sunsets and suppers, until they are suddenly evoked by revisiting a specific place or reminiscing with old friends. Now that I am older, nowhere evokes memories for me like the sunny shores of the Mediterranean. I can't sit on a beach without drifting back to the holidays of my twenties; whizzing around Corfu on a moped with my girlfriends from uni, dancing with my sister until the early hours in Bar & Bar in Kalkan, late night skinny dips and breakfasts at lunchtime, all kitted out in sparkly flip-flops and sarongs from Accessorize, bought on an over-excited shopping trip a couple of weeks before. My summer as a holiday rep is indelibly printed on my mind too; airport runs and welcome meetings, customers complaining about overly loud chickens and too much sun; file after file of pin-sharp, nostalgia-filled memories that flood back with that first sip of ice-cold Efes beer.

I think my wistfulness stems not just from a sense of lost youth, but also for a time when everything – and everywhere – was new: picturesque old towns with tangles of alleyways, shaded by terracotta-walled houses that leaned towards each other like gossiping neighbours, great sprays of cerise bougainvillea cascading over whitewashed cottages, beachfront tavernas with rickety wooden tables and blue wooden chairs. For me, it's always been the eastern Med – Greece and Turkey – and even now, there's nothing I love more than a lunch of cold rosé and a plate of crispy calamari, eaten while the sea clatters gently over pebbles, or oozes into the sand just a few feet from my table. I've been lucky enough to travel the world for my job, but if I could only have one week's holiday a year it would be somewhere in Turkey, probably in mid-September, when the sun has just started to dip a little in the sky, and the light is golden and languid and inexpressibly beautiful.

Of course, there's nothing unique about my love affair with the Med. Nowhere calls to us quite like its sparkling shoreline, stretching from the southernmost tip of Andalucía to the sun-drenched coast of Turkey, over 2,000 miles away. More than 75 years after the first charter flight took off from Gatwick, our infatuation shows no sign of slowing down. According to the national tourist boards, 18.4 million of us landed in Spain in 2024,[2] with France welcoming 12.7 million holidaymakers[3] and Turkey playing host to around 4.5 million Brits.[4] "It's close, it's different, but culturally we understand each other," says Noel Josephides, who began Sunvil Holidays in 1970, and remains chairman of the Sunvil Holiday Group today. "The UK has always played, worked and fought in the Mediterranean and we go back many generations."

Even so, the numbers are pretty staggering – particularly for an industry that only really began in earnest with the first charter flights from the UK to Europe, a few years after the end of World War II. But the vogue for Mediterranean holidays began at least a century earlier, most notably in 1838, when a British aristocrat, Lord Brougham, found himself stranded in Cannes on the way to Genoa.[5] With time to kill, he toured the area, pronounced himself in love with the "delightful climate of Provence, its clear skies and refreshing breezes" and promptly splashed out on a swathe of land where a palatial holiday villa could be constructed.

Friends who visited were quick to follow suit, with the hills around Cannes and Nice soon echoing to the sound of grumbling Gallic construction workers building ever-more palatial villas for Brougham's aristocratic chums, many of whom may have passed through France on a Grand Tour, but never made it as far as the sun-drenched south. By the late 19th century, when the British coast was seething with visitors, the Prince Regent was gallivanting around Brighton and Lake District residents were already complaining about overtourism, artists such as Vincent Van Gogh and Paul Cézanne were rhapsodising about the beauty of the Provençal light and landscapes, paving the way for Picasso, Matisse and Gauguin in the following decades. Even royalty got in on the act, most notably the Russian Romanovs, who regularly pitched up in Nice for vodka-fuelled weekenders,[6] and Queen Victoria, who travelled down by train in a carriage of blue-padded silk, refusing to eat any filthy French muck and indulging instead in days-old Irish stew, brought in leather saddlebags from Windsor.[7]

By the early 1920s, the Côte d'Azur was the desirable holiday spot for the well-to-do; British holidaymakers could take the Golden Arrow Train to Dover, and then the Flèche d'Or from Calais to Paris. From there, the overnight Train Bleu – famous for its elegant restaurant and chic Art Deco wagons – chuntered its way down to the sun-drenched south.[8] The glamorous hotels brought together British aristocracy and wealthy Americans, who sailed across the Atlantic on the new breed of ocean liners, bringing a new obsession with the "body beautiful" to European shores. Days were spent playing polo or tennis, swimming or sailing, with the idea of lightly tanned skin taking hold as the fashionable look. By night, the starriest celebrities of the day could be spotted on the Croisette in Cannes; Rudolf Valentino and Charlie Chaplin propping up the bar at the Hôtel Martinez, with Ernest Hemingway and F. Scott Fitzgerald quite possibly under it. Zelda Fitzgerald described the appeal in her novel, *Save Me the Waltz*.

The riviera is a seductive place. The blare of the beaten blue and those white palaces shimmering under the heat accentuates things ... a small horde of people wasted their time being happy.[9]

"Travel has been made so easy and expeditious," said *The Sphere*, in 1931, "that even a holidaymaker with only two weeks at his disposal can reach any corner of Europe that attracts his fancy."[10] While this made it sound like half the country was high-tailing it across the Channel, in reality, foreign travel remained the preserve of those whose great-grandfathers would have set off on the Grand Tour, alongside *nouveau riche* industrialists. And the ease and expeditiousness didn't last long; by the late 1930s, even those who could stump up for a suite at the Negresco, Nice's most opulent hotel, began to find their travels curtailed by the gathering storm over Germany. Hotels were requisitioned by the armed forces and the Train Bleu was left to gather dust in a railway siding, until it was smartened up and relaunched in 1946.

But although the war put a brake on travel to the continent, it also left a legacy that helped open up the delights of a Mediterranean holiday to a far greater number of people. Five years of war in the air meant Europe was scattered with airfields, while huge numbers of experienced pilots were available to fly the countless aeroplanes no longer needed for dropping bombs on terrified cities. Hundreds of thousands of men had spent years hunkered down in the French countryside, or fighting their way across Sicily, through Naples and Rome, while millions at home had seen countless images and hours of newsreel sent back from the European front. By the time VE Day was celebrated, most British people knew a great deal more about the geography, landscapes and culture of our continental neighbours than they'd ever done before.

Five years later, just as the new decade turned, the very first mass-market package holiday was about to launch. In May 1950, Horizon Holidays, set up by Russian émigré Vladimir Raitz, took its first group of holidaymakers on a DC3 Dakota – a repurposed war plane – from Gatwick to the Campo Franco-Britannique on Corsica.¹¹ The business had almost failed to get started at all, thanks to the monopoly held by British European Airways (BEA) as the exclusive carrier of holiday flights to Europe. After six months of waiting for a licence (and in spite of the fact BEA didn't even fly to Corsica), Raitz was told he could only take students or teachers. "I chose three publications," he writes, in *Flight to the Sun: The Story of the Holiday Revolution*. "*Teacher's World*, the *Nursing Mirror* and the *New Statesman*, explicitly inviting their teacher and student readers to have a marvellous holiday in the sun."¹²

Raitz was one of the first to take advantage of the fact that thousands of ex-military aircraft were now surplus to requirements and needed to be put to use. Commercial passenger flights had already been in service for over 30 years, albeit (sound familiar?) for the privileged few. In 1919, Aircraft Travel and Tourism Ltd (a forerunner of British Airways) launched the world's first daily scheduled service between London and Paris.¹³ In 1927, Thomas Cook ran its first package – from New York to Chicago for a boxing match – and by the late 1930s, it was offering flights on various routes from London to Europe.¹⁴ Flying was not for the faint-hearted, or anyone but the wealthy, but all that began to change in the years after World War II.

Those who took up Raitz's offer paid £32 each (around £1,400 today), for six-hour return flights with a refuelling stop in Lyon, and two weeks' accommodation under canvas with meals in the open-air dining room and "as much local wine as they could put away" before a spin on the campsite's dancefloor. Horizon had just 180 clients that summer, but slowly word began to spread; by 1952, Mallorca was added as a destination, with Alghero in Sardinia coming on stream in 1954.¹⁵ Raitz wasn't the first to package up flights and accommodation. Alongside Thomas Cook, several other companies, most notably Cox & Kings and the Polytechnic Touring Association, offered similar tours, but they tended to have a more highbrow focus – cultural visits, academic lectures – rather than the newer holiday pleasures of breakfast at lunchtime, an afternoon of intense snoozing and a shimmy on the dancefloor before bed. But Raitz was the first to make a package holiday accessible to working people.

It's hard to imagine now, when most of Europe is so familiar to us and the Spanish costas have long been dismissed as Anglicised and overdeveloped, what it must have been like to step onto a plane for the first time and arrive somewhere so entirely different. Everything – from the sunlight and the warmth, to the cypress trees and rhythmic click of the cicadas – would have been overwhelmingly, extraordinarily new; those first overseas holidaymakers experiencing the same sense of stepping into the unknown as early Victorian railway travellers, crammed into third-class carriages, jolting out of their towns and villages for the very first time.

In those early days, infrastructure barely existed – travellers arriving at smaller airports might be met by little more than a dusty airstrip, with a horse and cart waiting to move the luggage.

"We each had to be weighed, as well as our bags," remembers Anne Jones, a particularly well-travelled aunt of one of my friends. "People took all sorts of things with them – tinned food, cereals, cleaning products. There was a sense of not knowing what you were going to find. And the beach was packed with vendors, selling castanets and sombreros. I remember one had a baby chimp you could have your picture taken with."

Where Raitz led, others quickly followed. Holidays to Italy began with flights to Basel from Manston Airport in Kent, before travelling over the Alps by coach. "A trip to the continent in the mid-50s would have been quite the adventure," says Dave Richardson, author of *Let's Go: A History of Package Holidays and Escorted Tours*. "It was seen as pretty intrepid – often with good reason. Planes were small and very uncomfortable, and when you arrived, the hotel might only be half-built."

On YouTube, I find British Pathé archive film of those early Mediterranean holidays; sweeping sandy bays edged with just a handful of low-rise buildings, men with slicked-back hair and skimpy shorts running dinghies into the sea, women in stiffly boned swimsuits watching local fishermen haul their boats onto the shore. It looks both incredibly different and remarkably similar: the same thatched umbrellas dotted across the sand, inert bodies snoozing poolside, but just so much *less*; less of everything – people, cars, jet skis, Coca-Cola signs, flip-flop stands, ice-cream fridges – everything that crowds and clutters those same resorts now. As I watch, I think how little anyone knew, back then: that hundreds of thousands of lives would change, these quaint fishing villages reborn as city-sized resorts, the original tangle of streets now the "old town", filled with souvenir shops and bars.

There were those, however, who did have an idea what the future might hold – and nowhere more so than Spain. "It was a match made in heaven," says Dave Richardson. "The legacy of the Civil War and 15 years of Franco's regime had left Spain pretty much poverty-stricken by the mid-1950s, just as resorts on the Mediterranean were starting to develop." The problem for any Spanish town that might fancy itself as a rival to Cannes or Nice was the strict social restrictions imposed by Franco's regime; beaches had to be segregated, with separate sections for men and women, foreign women could be (and were) arrested for wearing revealing clothes, while just the idea of a bikini was enough to have respectable Catholic women swooning in the streets.

"Spain was a very backwards country in those days," says Leila Bilbao, Director at Visit Benidorm, when I visit on a sunny February weekend. "But Benidorm was different. From its earliest times, our men were sea captains and tuna fishermen – they travelled the world, saw different places, and brought their knowledge back with them. It made Benidorm different, more open-minded, and Pedro Zaragoza was a product of that."

Zaragoza, the town's young mayor, was determined to revive the town after the closure of its last tuna canning factory in 1953, by monetising its two long stretches of sandy beach – both south-facing, unlike most on the Costa Brava. Legend has it that he drove on his moped from Benidorm to Madrid for a meeting with General Franco, where he suggested that letting foreign women prance about in bikinis, and opening up the sea to the racy idea of mixed bathing, might help top up Spain's groaningly empty coffers. "Did he really go all that way on a moped?" asks Leila, arching an eyebrow. "We know he left Benidorm on his scooter, and that he arrived in Madrid on one. But in between, who knows? But why spoil a great story?"

However Zaragoza reached Madrid, once there he gained an audience with Franco and – quite possibly to his own surprise as much as anyone else's – achieved the unthinkable. Franco granted Benidorm the social freedoms it needed and the mayor returned (possibly by moped, possibly not) a hero, at least to those who could see beyond the scandal of scantily clad women to the pile of pesetas waiting beyond. He immediately began to draw up a General Urban Development Plan: to build upwards, rather than horizontally, to ensure the largest possible number of visitors and still retain plenty of green space. In 1956, the plan was launched, with 61 per cent of the Benidorm area to be kept undeveloped; a ratio that still holds today.[16]

Not that it seems that way, looking out of my taxi window as we speed along the coastal road towards the town from Alicante. "We call it the Spanish Miami," says the driver, Pedro. I don't say that Benidorm gets called much less flattering things in the UK; that in the last 30 years the town has become a byword for the very worst kind of tourist development, and the worst kind of British behaviour abroad. Admittedly, many who judge it so harshly will never have actually been or – even more unfairly – base their opinions on the TV series *Benidorm*. I watch an episode before I visit. It does nothing to raise my expectations.

"We know there's a lot of snobbery about our town," says Sergio Frau, who also works for the tourist board, as we stroll towards a bike-hire shop from where, apparently, I'm going to e-bike along the prom and up into the Serra Gelada National Park. "But there are many Benidorms. If you want to drink and party, there is Levante.

But Poniente beach is much quieter. There is the National Park, the mountains, 85 miles of bike lanes. You have to understand – tourism is all we do. It's the one industry we have. So everything is here.'

As we set off along the palm-lined promenade, flanked with cafes and restaurants already doing swift business at 11 a.m., I'm reminded of my Friday night in Blackpool. There's the same sense of giddy release, of being somewhere designed for the express purpose of kicking back and having fun. Sergio was bang on about the snobbery; I don't know quite what I'd expected, but it certainly wasn't the pristine beach that I cycle past, the wildness of the Serra Gelada National Park, which literally overlooks the town, or the vibrant *pintxo* bars that I visit later in the evening. Levante might be studded with Great British Boozers and Coronation Street Cocktail Bars, but Poniente – where beachfront apartments go for a cool €2 million[17] and we tuck into great platefuls of seafood-rich paella (always at lunch, never at dinner) – oozes authentic Spanish charm.

Not that there was any snobbery about Benidorm 50 years ago – or the resorts that came after; Tossa de Mar, Sitges and Lloret de Mar. Torremolinos – now a byword for cheap tourism – was the most glamorous of them all, opening Spain's first five-star hotel in 1959 and playing host to everyone from Pablo Picasso and John Lennon to Brigitte Bardot and Frank Sinatra.[18] It became Spain's most broad-minded resort, welcoming gay and queer travellers at a time when everywhere else would have shunned them – a laudable and brave openness that, predictably, ended up costing the town dearly. In 1971, a huge police raid saw over a hundred people arrested and several bars closed[19], sending the resort into a downward spiral from which it's never really recovered.

But by then, there were plenty of other resorts to choose from, as canny businessmen began to realise there was excellent money to be made by following Thomas Cook's original package holiday model. Some worked together with Spanish developers, part-funding hotel projects which they guaranteed would be filled with British visitors, while travel agents brought allocations of rooms, negotiated seat prices with the airlines and wrapped them all up in an easy, one-price package that usually included the services of a British overseas rep, on hand at all times to provide a reassuring bridge between uncertain travellers and Johnny Foreigner. Many travel agents offered two weeks in the sun for around £30 per person (around £500 per person in today's money), and British holidaymakers, lured in by the promise of the same pleasures as a seaside break in the UK, only without the need for a windbreak, half-a-dozen sweaters and a stack of wet-weather board games, couldn't snap up the packages fast enough. Rumours of unheard-of luxuries such as en suite bathrooms – removing the dubious holiday ritual of polite conversation with complete strangers in skimpy dressing gowns on draughty guesthouse corridors – only made the lure of an overseas holiday even more irresistible.

Although the cost would have been prohibitive for many working people, for some, the chance for an adventure was too good to miss, even if it meant spending savings or scrimping on other things. "We went to Lloret de Mar in 1966 – or possibly 67," says Chris Bulpitt, a close friend's mum. "I was a nurse and the cost – about £20 for flights and accommodation – was pretty much a month's salary, but it still seemed cheap for a holiday abroad." Bulpitt remembers a fried breakfast on board, grappling with unfamiliar calamari and plenty of (cheap) champagne. "We had our meals in the hotel, where there was a disco and a swimming pool – we spent very little when we were there, not least because there were currency restrictions at the time, and we couldn't take much out of the country."

"People began to realise that once they'd got to these unknown foreign climes, it was often cheaper than at home," says Sean Tipton, spokesman for ABTA (the Association of British Travel Agents). "Package operators offered menus 'tailored to English tastes' and made sure hotel staff spoke English. Even if they didn't, there was always a British rep on hand to help navigate the situation." The only bum note was Harold Wilson's policy, implemented in 1966 (and not repealed until 1979), restricting the amount each person could spend on a holiday to £50 (around £700 today).[20] The cost of the package was deducted, and whatever sum was left could be taken in traveller's cheques; an attempt, in part, to slow the exodus that was threatening the livelihoods of those trying to make a living in beach resorts at home.

It didn't work. "Whatever history may decide on the first ten years of the second half of the twentieth century," said an editorial in *Travel Trade Gazette* in early 1960, "it must surely be marked as the decade when mankind really got on the move."[21] By 1967, the total number of Brits going abroad had reached around five million, with the new breed of jet aircraft able to carry 130 people at a time, rather than 30 or 40.[22] "That was the real gamechanger," says Dave Richardson. "Flights were quicker, more reliable – and the economies of scale meant prices came down."

As a new decade dawned, other countries began to follow Spain's lead in raking in the tourist dollar (or pound). In what was then Yugoslavia, communist leader Josip Tito decided what was good for Franco was good for him, with Soviet-style hotel blocks cropping up in Opatija and around Dubrovnik, and companies such as Yugotours offering package holidays to British visitors. Bulgaria also tucked away its communist principles in the back of the wardrobe and began to develop Sunny Beach as a resort. While the number of those who chose Bulgaria was relatively small, Yugoslavia became a huge success story, with Yugotours sending over around 500,000 British visitors on holiday in its 1980s heyday.[23] Greece joined in, with Corfu leading the island pack and Crete not far behind – although it offered something different, a quieter, simpler type of holiday.

"When we started Simply Crete in 1978, villa holidays didn't exist in the way they do now," says Graham Simpson. "My wife is Greek, and the previous summer, my brother-in-law had asked if we might be able to help rent out a couple of houses he'd built in the summer months. I put an ad in *The Times* and we were inundated." The following year, Simpson launched Simply Crete, targeting a very different clientele from those flocking to the Spanish costas. "Crete was very simple then, very authentic. In our first brochure, we said our holidays would 'appeal to the person who doesn't just want to go on a package tour'. We had 80 clients that year. Twenty-one years later, when I sold Simply Travel, we had 40,000."

For many, it was a simple choice: Spain meant "holiday", Greece meant "travel": the unspoiled islands, and network of ferries that ran between them, creating a new breed of independent traveller – younger, less wealthy, with rucksacks strapped to their backs rather than carrying embossed suitcases. "I always remember my first trip to Greece, bumming around the Cyclades and the Peloponnese," says Dave Richardson. "The whole essence was simplicity; simple tavernas, simple accommodation. It makes me a bit sad now to see the big resorts and all-inclusives. If there was a destination where mingling with local people was key, it was Greece, not Spain."

Inevitably, the idyll couldn't last. While Greece might not have followed the build-em-high, pile-em-in model to quite the same extent as Spain, many islands underwent massive changes in the 1970s and 80s, as large-scale developments took the place of the elegant Xenia hotels that the government had previously funded and promoted. Islands such as Corfu, Rhodes and Crete lost long stretches of their coastline to sprawling apartment blocks and hotels with hundreds of rooms, along with the rustic charm that had lured the first holidaymakers, looking for something different to Spain's built-up costas.

But not everywhere in Spain fell prey to the worst excesses of development. From Benidorm, I fly on to Menorca; the smallest of the "big three" Balearics, behind Mallorca and Ibiza. It's my first visit to an island often dismissed as quiet and family-focused – even slightly dull – and certainly in the shadow of its two glitzier neighbours. "And that's fine by us," says Alvin, my guide, as we stroll along the boardwalk onto the silent, pristine beach at Es Grau. "People think Menorca was slow to develop compared to Mallorca, but the truth is, islanders didn't want tourism on that scale. The island already had two successful industries, shoe-making and agriculture, and the idea was to develop more slowly, to keep a balance between welcoming tourists and not destroying what makes the island special."

It's a policy that's worked to some degree; Menorca welcomes 1.5 million visitors each year, as opposed to the 13 million that flooded into Mallorca in 2024,[24] and as a first-time visitor, I'm amazed by the lush, unspoiled interior and quiet coves. The island's status as a UNESCO Biosphere Reserve has helped considerably, along with the policy of keeping the bigger, mass-market resorts contained on certain small stretches of coast. I'm aware though that visiting in February, when the whole place is practically mothballed, doesn't give an accurate picture of what it will be like in summer. "It's not as bad as Mallorca, but high season can bring problems," says Alvin. "Roads get jammed, you can't get anywhere – it's not fun for anyone."

While Menorca may have fared better than some places, by the end of the 20th century, tourism to the Med had become a juggernaut that swept aside everything in its wake. Holidays became increasingly hedonistic: Club Med became a byword for booze-fuelled weeks, where inhibitions were left in the suitcase (if they'd been packed at all), nude sunbathing was acceptable and rooms were more like cell-blocks than sea-view suites. Club 18-30, originally begun in 1970 to appeal to younger travellers, became famous for the havoc its bar crawls and all-night parties wreaked on places like Magaluf in Mallorca and Kavos in Corfu. Ibiza, once Mallorca's sleepier sister, became the epicentre of Europe's club scene, with a whole subculture built up around the White Isle and the DJs who flocked to play at clubs like Pacha and Space.

Small, specialist tour operators were gobbled up by huge international companies like TUI, the new budget airlines massively increased not just capacity but also the frequency of the holidays we took, and the internet basically lit a torch under the traditional model of travel agents and packages, ushering in a free-for-all era that has just grown more and more out of control. "There's hardly any small, independent companies left like us now," says Noel Josephides of Sunvil Holidays. "We take full responsibility for what we do and look after our destinations. We pioneered many places: the Alentejo in Portugal; we were the first to fly to Skiathos, Lemnos, Chania and Kalamata. Unfortunately, we were watched by the giants, who then pile on capacity, sell cheaply and change the very nature of the destinations themselves."

In recent years, it's become clear that – in some areas at least – our love of the Mediterranean is becoming an extremely mixed blessing, and one not always appreciated by those trying to live in the countries we visit. Protests across Spain – in the Canaries, Balearics and Barcelona in particular – as well as some Greek islands, have grown increasingly heated, with a strong resentment at the impact tourism is having on lives and livelihoods. "I can't imagine ever being able to afford to buy a place with my girlfriend," Pedro, my taxi driver in Benidorm, told me sadly. "At least, nowhere we'd want to live." In January 2024, the Spanish government talked of imposing a 100 per cent tax on homes bought by non-EU residents, although at the time of writing, no law had been passed.[25]

Elsewhere, governments are starting to take first, tentative steps to try and control the number of visitors flooding in each summer. Venice has imposed a daily tourist tax for both day-trippers and overnight stays; Dubrovnik has limited cruise ships to two a day and Barcelona is aiming to phase out all short-term rental properties (around 10,000) by the end of 2028.[26] "One of the biggest problems is Airbnb," says Sean Tipton of ABTA. "When hotels and villas were the only options for tourist accommodation, that kept visitor numbers to a manageable level. When a town was full, it was full. Now every house can become a place to stay – and that means an infinite number of beds."

The problem for governments is that tourism is a money-spinning behemoth of an industry; in 2023, it accounted for 12.3 per cent of Spain's GDP.[27] Imposing restrictions or levying taxes can bring problems of their own. "It is vexed, but I think there's a real risk to the industry, unless the problems of overtourism are talked about openly and addressed," says Mike Bevens of Sawday's. "There are no national policies yet, but unless it's dealt with carefully, there will be a major impact – what Venice is doing will become a lot more common. The industry has gorged on communities with little consideration for the social implications of huge numbers of tourists at concentrated periods of time."

As I write this, news websites are full of new anti-tourism protests in Mallorca, with water-guns fired and slogans chanted. It might be difficult to admit that our much-loved holidays are beginning to have a detrimental impact on some of the places we visit, but there's a need to recognise the fact that how, where and when we take our breaks does affect local communities. I look at my nephews, nieces and godchildren setting off on trips to the Med and I want them to have the same extraordinary experiences I did; that joyous sense of newness, of discovery, of a different adventure every day. "We all have a role to play," says Noel Josephides. "Many of those in Mediterranean resorts and businesses feel exploited – but companies like Jet2, easyJet and TUI are never going to worry about overtourism. In many ways, it's up to the destination, but there are things we can do as visitors – don't stay in all-inclusives. Eat out at local restaurants. Explore."

Amen to that.

11
Cruise Control

Bergen

"The sea, once it casts its spell, holds one in its net of wonder forever."[1]
Jacques Cousteau

It's a sunny September afternoon in Bergen – one of Europe's rainiest cities, with an average of 235 wet days a year[2] – and the sun is cracking the flags. Sitting outside, on deck nine of the *Viking Saturn* cruise ship, the city is laid out before us like a Legoland village: scarlet and blue tugs chugging through the water, fishing boats clanking masts on the quayside, onion-domed churches and clean, white office blocks dwarfed by the bottle-green mountains rising behind. We're halfway down ice-cold beers; behind us, a group of Americans are noisily playing outdoor checkers, apart from one who has broken away to shout loudly into her phone, presumably on Skype, about the poor amount of effort her sister is putting into maintaining her plants. Suddenly, one of them lets out a whoop and I realise we are moving. No fanfare, no brouhaha, just a slow, silent glide into the infinite blue.

The *Saturn*'s silence (apart from the Americans) is extraordinary, given its size: a 48,000-tonne, 745-foot behemoth, carrying 930 passengers and 470 crew,[3] drifting out of Bergen like a paddleboard. The ship seems huge to me, but it's relatively compact and bijou compared to the monsters operated by lines such as Royal Caribbean. Their Oasis-class ships move around the oceans like floating cities;

the largest, the *Icon of the Seas*, can carry up to 7,600 passengers and 2,350 crew,[4] with everything from an ice-skating rink to a glass-domed entertainment venue and more than 40 places to eat. It's the perfect metaphor for the cruise industry itself: a vast, multi-billion-dollar global phenomenon that's growing faster than any other tourism sector, with a jaw-dropping 34.6 million passengers in 2024,[5] according to Cruise Lines International Association (CLIA). With over 310 CLIA-registered ships visiting 1,200 ports around the world,[6] it's the rush to the Med gone global, a packaged-up, all-in, admin-free holiday that, for many, is the perfect antidote to the overwhelming nature of modern life.

"It's not difficult to see why cruising has become so successful," says clinical psychologist Dr Shona Goodall, who specialises in emotional health and wellbeing. "Everything comes with such a huge amount of choice these days, and holidays are no exception. Do you go for a lazy week on the beach, or a city break? And if so, which city? Hotel or Airbnb – again, which one? There's a serious amount of overwhelm involved in booking a holiday, and it's easy to feel swamped." Cruise holidays offer the luxury of choosing a destination – and maybe an excursion or two – with everything else left in the hands of Viking, Royal Caribbean or one of the other 78 ocean and river cruise lines that send their ships around the world.[7] "It also gives a new perspective on destinations – even if they're very familiar," says Wendy Akin-Smith, MD of Viking UK. "Sailing out of Paris on the Seine from a sprawling urban city into beautiful countryside, or into Hong Kong harbour at dawn before docking next to the Star Ferry with the iconic skyline in full view. In Basel, lots of local residents commute to work by swimming or rowing with their clothes in a waterproof pack, so it's fun to watch – all unique experiences you wouldn't get any other way."

Like so many of our 21st-century holiday trends, cruising has its roots in an industry that had nothing to do with leisure. It was originally a cheeky side hustle by the whip-smart owners of the Peninsula Steam Navigation Company (later to become P&O), Captain Richard Bourne, Brodie McGhie Wilcox and Arthur Anderson.[8] Originally created in 1822 as a trading steamship line between London and the Iberian Peninsula (Spain and Portugal), the company was such a success that in 1837, the government gave them the contract to deliver mail to Gibraltar and Spain. Three years later, a new contract was awarded for Alexandria in Egypt, with the company re-named the Peninsula *and Oriental* Steam Navigation Company.[9] The service began in 1840, the same year Canadian businessman Samuel Cunard signed an agreement with the British Admiralty for a transatlantic mail service, sending the wooden paddle steamer *Britannia* across the rolling waters of the Atlantic, taking around 13 days to reach the Eastern Seaboard of the USA.[10]

It didn't take long for the owners of both companies to realise that taking passengers on board was a way to increase revenue and fill empty cabins. Charging passengers wasn't a new idea – merchant ships, making their way across ocean trade routes, had been taking intrepid travellers for decades, albeit those who could stomach both the basic conditions and the length of time it would take to get anywhere, if the wind wasn't in the right direction. But steamers and packet ships would inevitably take quicker, direct routes. "In those early days, it was just about transporting passengers from point A to point B," says Gary Buchanan, a cruise journalist for over 30 years. "That's where the word 'liner' comes from – the ships simply ploughed a line back and forth between ports." Cunard's passengers – including Charles Dickens, who travelled from Liverpool to Boston in the 1840s[11] – set sail purely with the aim of reaching the other side of the Atlantic. Crossings could be tempestuous, but, as Dickens described in *American Notes*, passengers were kept well fed and oiled (at least those who could stomach it):

At one, a bell rings, and the stewardess comes down with a steaming dish of baked potatoes, and another of roasted apples; and a plate of pig's face, cold ham, salt beef; or perhaps a smoking mass of rare collops. We fell upon these dainties; eat as much as we can (we have great appetites now) ... if the fire will burn (it will sometimes) we are pretty cheerful.[12]

It was P&O who offered the first ever leisure cruise, unwittingly birthing a gazillion-dollar industry with one small advertisement in *The Times* in March 1843. Beneath the heading "An Interesting and Classic Excursion", the itinerary offered an impressive amount of stops, calling at Constantinople (now Istanbul), Gibraltar, Malta, Athens, Smyrna (now İzmir), Mytilene and the Dardanelles.[13]

Enough readers got in touch for P&O to plan a late summer cruise, and on 15 August, the paddle steamer *Tagus* – at 182 feet, slightly longer than two tennis courts, and 26 feet wide – juddered its way out of Southampton, to begin its 22-day itinerary.[14] Take-up was small – according to the *Illustrated London News* there were just 12 passengers on a ship that could take up to 65[15] – made up, predictably, of wealthy aristocrats with perhaps an artist and one of the new breed of wealthy interloper, spending a little of the fat profits made in the factories and cotton mills of the smoggy north-west.

Comfort, luxury, indulgence: these are not words that would have described the *Tagus*. Staterooms – originally used by hard-living sailors for little more than sleeping off copious amounts of rum – were more like dark, dingy cupboards, with spectacularly uncomfortable bunkbeds and portholes usually slathered with so much grime it was impossible to see out. Taking the air on deck might involve an encounter with a bemused chicken or pig, desperately trying to escape from a holding pen that was just a temporary stop en route to the dining table, where meals would have been taken communally, rather than served by white-gloved waiters. One thing the *Tagus*, and those that followed, did have in common with their 21st-century counterparts was a copious amount of booze, fortunately included in the price of a ticket.[16] Sloshing back the wine and getting stuck into whisky were the two best ways to blur just about everything, from the endless din and constant rat companions to the pungent whiff – part creosote and tar, part bilge water, part human unmentionableness – that thickened the air below deck.

Uncomfortable or not, it soon became clear there was an appetite for sea-going trips that offered more than just moving from A to B; a water-based version of the Grand Tour, particularly for aspirational industrialists who hadn't caught on to the fact that the vogue for continental travel had begun to wane among old money. In quite possibly the first example of influencer marketing, P&O sent famous writer William Makepeace Thackeray on a Mediterranean cruise in 1844, and he turned the experience into a book, *Notes of a Journey from Cornhill to Cairo*, published in 1846. "Lisbon, we owned, was a failure. Athens a dead failure. Malta very well, but not worth the trouble and sea sickness."[17] While it might not have been quite the glowing review P&O had hoped for, Thackeray brightens up when the ship reaches Smyrna. "Some men may read this who are in want of a sensation. Let them book themselves on board one of the P&O vessels and try one dip into Constantinople or Smyrna. Walk into the bazaar and the East is unveiled to you . . ."[18] The sighs of relief from the 19th-century marketing department are almost audible, even now.

Thackeray's book makes fascinating reading, not least for the ending, which perfectly encapsulates what 21st-century psychologists like to call "Fading Effect Bias", where the mind cleverly keeps hold of all the happier holiday moments (snoozing, cocktails, sunsets) and conveniently forgets the rest (sunburn, arguments about whether a third glass of rosé at lunch is too many, rain). "I forget what seasickness is now . . ." writes Thackeray, safely back in Blighty, ". . . when the bitter ale was decidedly muddy, the cook deserting at Constantinople. The sorrows have passed away with the soothing influence of time; the pleasures of the voyage remain."[19] Frankly, if Fading Effect Bias didn't exist, the travel industry would have found some way to invent it.

In spite of Thackeray's (mostly) glowing write-up and P&O's continuing small-scale Mediterranean voyages, most 19th-century passengers used steamships simply as liners, until P&O launched their next innovation in 1881. The *Ceylon* was a small former liner converted into a more comfortable cruising yacht than the *Tagus*, with a capacity for 40 passengers, which left Southampton on 29 October 1881 for a round-the-world cruise, calling at India, China and the US before finally returning to Hampshire in August 1882.[20] In Germany, the shipping magnate Albert Ballinn was doing a similar thing with Hamburg America liners, although it was increasingly clear the ships were far from ideal for leisure purposes, with great hulking bits of machinery obscuring views and causing, to put it in 21st-century parlance, considerable health and safety issues. Ships were often too big to dock in the smaller ports convenient for tourist sites, necessitating much inelegant scrambling up and down rope ladders into smaller boats, which frequently ended up with both sailors and passengers tipping into the sea. Instead, Ballinn decided to create the first ever purpose-built cruise ship, and in 1900, the *Prinzessin Victoria Luise* launched from Hamburg: a 407 foot, 4,419-tonne vessel that would hurtle around Europe at a white-knuckle 16 knots (19 miles) an hour.[21]

"It was the first time the ship was the point of the holiday, rather than the means of reaching your destination," says Gary Buchanan. "There was a library and smoking room, a ballroom for dancing and a palatial art gallery surrounding the dining room. The 120 staterooms were luxurious to a degree never seen before on a cruise ship." Not everyone was impressed. Legend has it that when Wilhelm II, King of Prussia and Germany's last emperor, visited the ship, he was distinctly underwhelmed to find it slightly longer than his own yacht, the *Hollenzollern* – a frankly unpatriotic show of shipbuilding oneupmanship.[22] But for wealthy (just not quite *that* wealthy)

American and European travellers who dreamt of having their own yacht but who couldn't quite afford the upkeep and maintenance, the *Victoria Luise* – and those that followed – offered the chance to experience life at sea in giddy style.

If the cruise market is competitive now (bigger pools! Higher climbing walls! More restaurants! Make the sea bluer!), it was no less so 120 years ago, albeit with considerably fewer ships. The launch of the *Victoria Luise*, and Germany's increasing domination of the transatlantic route, ruffled Samuel Cunard's gilded feathers to such an extent that when he revealed the *Mauretania* in 1907, it was the largest moving structure ever built, with a capacity of 2,300 passengers.[23] He was determined that his transatlantic liners would offer the same luxury and glamour as Ballin's touring ships, while offering the chance to travel between New York and London faster than ever before. Two years later, the ship set a new record for a transatlantic crossing of just four-and-a-half days, which it held for the next 20 years.[24] Size-wise, it was briefly beaten by White Star Line's *Titanic*, until it set sail on its maiden voyage on 10 April 1912 and was promptly sunk by an iceberg five days later.

When I re-watch James Cameron's seven-hour long (at least) *Titanic*, what comes across – apart from how bad the CGI is by today's standards – is the extraordinary glamour, the vast amounts of money that would have been spent on the grand staircase, gilded Parisian cafe and lavish staterooms, rather than on unnecessary fripperies such as lifeboats, a couple of pairs of binoculars and rivets that didn't snap like twigs. *Titanic* is no one's idea of a documentary, but it does give an idea of the scale and ambition of the world's greatest unsinkable ship, and the horror that ensued (and I don't mean 40 minutes of Kate Winslet rushing around watery corridors in an increasingly damp frock).

"Cruising is evolving faster than any other form of travel," says Gary Buchanan. "But it is moving further and further from what it used to be. *Icon of the Seas* has seven different neighbourhoods – you could quite happily spend your holiday just in one, without needing to visit the other six. When cruising first took hold, the ships were like elegant, floating hotels, often with just one restaurant. The irony is that cruise companies have managed to persuade travellers the larger the ship, the better the cruise, but in my opinion, that's definitely not true."

It certainly wasn't true for the *Titanic*, whose sinking was the beginning of an incredibly challenging era for the nascent cruise industry. Two world wars saw many ships lost to bombing raids, with others pressed into war service – some openly, some not. In World War I, the Germans issued a specific threat that any transatlantic cruise liner suspected of carrying arms or supplies to the UK would be bombed. In 1915, the *Lusitania* sailed from New York – carrying 42,000 cases of rifle ammunition and 100 cases of empty shrapnel on board, alongside 1,200 passengers and 700 crew. It never arrived in Liverpool; torpedoed and sunk off the coast of Ireland, with 1,201 passengers and crew declared dead.[25] Other lines were converted into hospitals or troop carriers, with many ships performing a similar service in World War II. Some were repainted with what became known as "dazzle paint" – black-and-white stripes that made them look like gargantuan zebras, galloping through the water, thought to make it difficult for distant enemy ships to calculate their size and heading.

All of which meant it took several years after the war for most liners to be re-adapted for leisure passengers, and it was the 1950s that marked cruising's most glamorous era. Ships became their own social world; sunbathing and shuffleboard by day, the evenings a chandelier-decked, cocktail-fuelled whirl of black-tie dinners and ballroom dancing, the newest movies on show and a midnight buffet to power partygoers on through to the small hours. Cunard ran an all-American star cruise, with Frank Sinatra, Elizabeth Taylor and Walt Disney on board, with Noel Coward – possibly the least all-American person on the planet – booked to keep the guests diverted with witty repartee and arch songs at the piano.[26] Through the 60s, the cruise liners dominated what would come to be known as "long-haul" travel, where the journey – salt-tinged, diamante-flecked and giddily indulgent – meant that, in many cases, it really was better to travel than arrive.

Few foresaw how short the era would be, but within a few years of the first jet aircraft zooming across the sky – cutting journey times from days to mere hours – cruise liners had had their day. Getting from A to B by sea was no longer the choice of anyone who wanted to get somewhere in a hurry; many trans-ocean liners were refitted as holiday cruise ships, and re-settled in Miami, for tours around the Caribbean or between the historic ports dotted around the Mediterranean. New companies began to spring up – Princess, Royal Caribbean, MSC and Carnival – with a more informal ethos that did away with the traditional three-tier class system, dating back to the days of the *Titanic*, and added new on-board entertainments from casino nights and live concerts to late-night limbo dancing, creating the brand new concept of a "holiday resort at sea".

Keen to get an idea of how cruising looked half a century ago, I dip into YouTube, which proves to be a treasure trove of vintage clips from the era. None is more entertaining than a 1970s American advertisement for the "Fun Ship *Carnevale*", with shirtless, moustachioed chaps rolling balloons up and down their wives (hopefully) in on-deck competitions, elderly grannies pulling slot machine handles with ferocious intent and female diners showing their appreciation of the on-board cuisine by inappropriately kissing nervous-looking waiters.[27] The British equivalent for the P&O ship *Oriana* is hilariously stiff in comparison – neat bow ties, thrill-a-minute bingo games and the giddy heights of a calypso band by the pool – while also being spectacularly lascivious: "Lunch in your bikini, madam? Oh, yes!"[26]

But it wasn't just the Americans and the British who were starting to see the potential in this new, mass-market form of cruising. Germany, France and Greece were quickly developing their own brands, and by the mid-1970s, even the Russians were in on the act. "It was a company called CTC Lines," says Steve Gatenby, a lifetime cruise fan, with around 70 sea-going trips under his belt. "They were Russian-owned, with maybe five or six ships dotted around the Med, and their trips were sold through British travel agents." In 1977, Gatenby took a two-week cruise with CTC, paying £190 – considerably less than a P&O or Cunard cruise – which covered all meals (including caviar) and as many shots of vodka as you could drink. "The rumour at the time was that the ships were deliberately put into service to spy," says Gatenby. "There was lots of talk about plain-clothes passengers, who clearly weren't there on holiday. But it was probably more likely they were there to keep an eye on the crew and stop any of them trying to defect."

In the same year Gatenby took to the seas courtesy of the KGB (possibly), cruising sailed into a far wider section of the public consciousness, thanks to an American TV series, *The Love Boat*, which pepped up the interminable Sunday afternoons that characterised 1970s weekends, before shops were allowed to open and "doing nothing" had become an aspirational pastime. Each episode focused on the captain and crew of the MS *Pacific Princess* and the romantic entanglements of their passengers. Light-hearted and comedic, it helped reinforce the message cruise operators were keen to put across – that it was no longer just for toffs in tuxedos and their jewel-encrusted wives.

"Cruising was still a lot more formal back then," says Sue Bryant, Cruise Editor for *The Times*, who has covered the industry for 25 years. "But companies began to understand that if you wanted to have wider appeal, it needed to become more relaxed, less stuffy. Slowly, over the next ten years or so, things began to change; black tie dinners started to be just one or two evenings, rather than the norm. Now, a lot of ships don't even have that; instead they're gala or 'dress up' nights. After all, who wants to wear a tuxedo in the Caribbean?" Some, though, still retain a hint of the old glamour; Cunard still sails with "gentlemen hosts" on board, whose sole job is to be a genial dance partner for any single women travellers (or those with unenthusiastic husbands) – which makes me long to book a Cunard cruise immediately, just to hear some of their stories.

Along with easing up on the formality, cruise companies began to realise that if they filled the ship with different activities and a better standard of entertainment, it could become a destination in its own right. "Twenty years ago, a climbing wall was considered the height of innovation," says Sue Bryant. "Now big ships have go-kart tracks and skydiving simulators, bespoke treatment programmes in state-of-the-art spas and celebrity chef restaurants – essentially they're floating resorts." There are certainly plenty of passengers on *Viking Saturn* who seem to view the ship – with its sizeable pool, well-stocked library, late-night cocktail bar and particularly fine chocolate cookies available at seemingly every corner – as the destination in itself, in spite of the myriad excursions that leave port each day. But the company's ethos is far closer to Thomas Cook's Victorian-era tours, or a *cicerone*-accompanied Grand Tour (or even, dare I say it, Billy Butlin's foray into opera): the idea of travel as educative, even transformative, rather than simply being about leisure.

"We have a team of experts on board every sailing, providing lectures on everything from geology and oceanography on an expedition ship, to art, music and geopolitics on ocean itineraries," says Wendy Akin-Smith. "Many of our guests want to travel as a way to learn and to connect with different peoples and cultures." While Viking's smaller ships don't have the same impact as the giant cruise lines (which can disgorge over 5,000 passengers at one time),[28] it's still a model of holidaying I struggle to understand; an immersion, really, in cruise-ship life, rather than a particular destination – one that, for me at least, simply doesn't allow enough time to truly get under the skin of any of the places visited.

But if cruising doesn't sing to me personally, there are millions – 2.4 million Brits in 2024,[29] to be exact – for whom it is the perfect holiday. I suspect a large part of the attraction is the same reassurance that Thomas Cook offered those who took his trips in the 19th century; the chance to visit far-flung (or close to home) destinations that would feel a bit daunting to explore independently. Whether Madagascar or Mallorca, cruising offers a few short hours on land before returning to the familiar cocoon of the ship. It both sings to our inner explorer and soothes our sense of anxiety about travelling to lands unknown, just as those first holidays to Spain – with waiters trained in English, and hotel kitchens serving up familiar dishes – strove to overcome the nervousness that often goes hand-in-hand with the excitement of being somewhere new.

"On a practical level, it's just so easy," says Glynis Gatenby, who has joined her husband Steve on almost 50 cruises. "You just unpack once and then you miraculously turn up in all these different, really amazing places. And it's always such an adventure, on every trip something happens you don't expect. On one trip it was so rough, I ended up sliding from one end of the bed to the other at such speed that my satin pyjamas actually sparked into flame from all the static. But – even on the choppiest of cruises – it's still such a safe, secure way to see the world."

It's an irony, I think, that as cruise ships increasingly become floating playgrounds, packed with every activity, food and 1970s disco hit imaginable, it's actually the ease of cruising, the very simplicity of it, that has such mass appeal. "These days, health is the new wealth," says Shona Goodall. "We are coming to understand the importance of rest – not just sleep, but resting our minds and bodies, which has a hugely positive impact on our physiology. Travelling and holidaying are two different things; one is about actively broadening your mind, the other about soothing it. I suspect cruising has become so popular because it offers the chance to do both in one easy package."

There's certainly something blissfully relaxing about drifting across the ocean with nothing to do but stare out at the vast horizon – although I'm not sure how tranquil it would be surrounded by 5,000 other people, all trying to do the same thing. Sue Bryant believes value for money is also a major factor. "It's great if you're on a budget," she says (and who isn't, these days?). "On many ships, all your transport, food and entertainment is included – and standards are really high now, with concerts and theatrical events on a par with the West End." But the drive for good-value pricing sometimes masks hidden costs. "It's called 'nickel and diming,'" says Gary Buchanan. "Where cruise companies add more and more activities and extras that have to be paid for on board. The ideal for the grey suits in the Miami head offices would be for passengers to never actually get off, but stay on board paying for everything from zipwire rides to spa treatments."

Ironically, it's not just the suits and bean-counters that wish cruise passengers never got off – because when they *do*, the numbers can create serious problems with overcrowding, particularly in the Mediterranean and the Caribbean. Nassau in the Bahamas can take seven ships at one time,[30] leaving streets gridlocked and locals unable to simply go out and do their shopping. In the Mediterranean, towns like Dubrovnik and Oia in Santorini are swamped when cruise ships dock; friends who holidayed in Croatia in the last couple of summers have talked about needing to be in and out of Dubrovnik before 10 a.m., to have any chance of walking the historic walls and exploring the city in any kind of quiet. Some destinations have started to take action; at the time of writing, Venice, Palma and Barcelona, among other ports, have imposed restrictions on the number and size of ships that can dock at one time,[31] but even so, the numbers remain overwhelming.

"I don't believe cruise lines are entirely to blame for overtourism," says Sue Bryant. "They are just more visible. Places like Barcelona and Amsterdam have more issues with Airbnb than with cruise ships. I don't particularly like seeing giant cruise ships towering over small Caribbean islands, but they do contribute to the economy." But do they, really? Often, it seems, the cruise industry's answers to the problems it causes are rarely of benefit to the local communities they visit. In an attempt to remedy the problem of overcrowding at Caribbean ports, some of the biggest cruise lines are increasingly buying land and private islands to build their own "beach resorts", spending $1.5 billion since 2019, according to Bloomberg analysis released in May 2024,[32] with increasing environmental implications. While the cruise lines insist many of the new projects are locally owned and offer hundreds of new jobs, it also means every dollar spent goes straight back into the cruise company's giant pockets, rather than small local businesses. "I think it's an awful trend," says Steve Gatenby. "Cruise companies pay a massive premium to rent or buy land or islands outright, local people aren't allowed access, and there are often wire fences to stop them coming in. We went to an island off the coast of Haiti, and it was so sanitised and Westernised, no Haitian character, other than a few tacky souvenirs. A lot of long-time cruisers like us think the whole idea is hugely detrimental, but Americans seem to love it."

Few other forms of holiday divide people as much as cruising, from those – like me – who question the environmental impact and the increasing tendency for the big cruise companies to wreak havoc on some of our most beautiful destinations – to committed cruisephiles who would never think of taking their holiday any other way. But as the environmental impact of our holiday choices becomes ever more apparent, these divisions are becoming more polarised; just as "travellers" look down on "tourists", so anti-cruisers can be pretty damning about those who choose to take their holiday at sea.

The situation is vexed. There's no question that large cruise ships have a detrimental effect on many destinations around the world, but sitting in judgement on how other people choose to spend their precious free time is hardly an answer either. Because just as all cruise companies aren't the same, so every cruise passenger is different, from those – like the Gatenbys – who explore independently wherever they can, and only sail on small ships, to those who book their cabin on a 5,000-berth ship and rarely leave the bar.

While I'll never be a cruiser, there is something extraordinary about actually *being* at sea; a glimpse of how it might have felt to explore, to be Dickens, bouncing across the Atlantic, or Thackeray gliding into port at Istanbul. My foray into cruise ship travel opened up a whole new world going about its business: oil platforms and vast cargo ships, sailing yachts and ferries, sea lanes bustling like a watery network of motorways and B-roads. On sea days, we stared out at infinite, royal-blue skies, at night we came back to our cabin to sit on the balcony, while midnight-green waves rolled out into the vast, empty darkness beyond.

"When someone says, where's your happy place? I always say the balcony of a cruise ship," says Glynis Gatenby. "The sound of the ocean, the rhythm of the movement – it's the perfect feeling for me." That, at least, is a sentiment I can share; my favourite memory of our cruise was sailing out of Bergen on that blissfully sunny Sunday afternoon. We sat up on deck for more than two hours, watching the rugged coastline drift by – clapperboard houses tucked into quiet inlets, motorboats moored up outside – all the more beautiful when the shouty Americans went inside for dinner, and the vast Scandinavian seaway belonged to no one but us.

12
Holidays on Screen
A Variety of Sofas

"What, may I ask, did you expect to see out of a Torquay hotel window? Sydney Opera House, perhaps? The Hanging Gardens of Babylon? Herds of wildebeest, sweeping majestically across the plains?"[1]
Basil Fawlty, Fawlty Towers

Cruising, camping, kicking back on the Costa Brava – by the second half of the 20th century, holidays were knitted into the fabric of almost everyone's lives, whether Blackpool, Benidorm or, for the privileged few, Barbados. In summer, newspapers were full of stories about the number of Brits in Spain,[2] the new boom in caravanning[3] or the *Wacky Races* driving style of coach operators offering bargain-basement trips across the Channel. As the world began to open up, holiday stories were swapped in the pub, at the office and on the bus, with travel no longer just for the wealthy. And in film studios and TV companies, programme makers, directors and producers began to realise that few things sat bums on seats more quickly than a glamorous location, ideally with an uplifting, transformational storyline woven around it.

From its earliest days, cinema tapped into audiences' fascination with exotic and different locations. In 1921, surrounded by a sea of slapstick comedies starring the likes of Charlie Chaplin and Buster Keaton, *The Sheik*, set mostly in the Algerian desert, broke all box-office records, showing in 250 movie theatres across America.[4] A classic boy-meets-girl love story with an exotic twist (Arabian sheik meets feisty upper-class English woman, carts her off into the desert and keeps her prisoner, where – naturally – she falls in love with him and they live happily ever after), it kickstarted Rudolf Valentino's brief but stratospherically successful career, and pulled in over $1 million at the box office.[5] It also started an "Orientalist" craze, which – in spite of how problematic we might find it now – fuelled everything from fashions to furniture, books and music infused with Arabian style, fuelled further by two sequels.[6]

But it was in the 1950s and 60s, as holidays – however simple – were becoming a reality for a bigger percentage of cinemagoers, that movies began to reflect the new fashion for travel, and the power of a holiday to effect real change in our lives. In 1953, the world swooned as Audrey Hepburn's frustrated royal, Princess Ann, escaped into anonymity on the back of Gregory Peck's Vespa for an unforgettable *Roman Holiday*, while Katharine Hepburn flew the flag for frustrated singletons everywhere, when she took a solo holiday to Venice in *Summertime* (1955), only to embark on a sizzling affair with an Italian married man.

"Holidays are a chance to shed our existing persona and slip into someone slightly different, even if only for a few days," says psychologist Audrey Tang. "Being in a different environment allows us to shake off who we traditionally are – whether that's a mum or a princess, an unhappy singleton or a frustrated wife. We get the chance to rediscover who we were, or explore who we might like to be, without all the expectations that we constantly carry."

Summertime's underlying theme – the transformative power of time away (obviously involving a man, because how could a woman possibly transform without one?) – is a storyline that worked just as well 30 years later in 1989's *Shirley Valentine*. Jettisoning a life that had become so wearisome she ends up having conversations with her kitchen wall, Shirley takes a two-week holiday to Greece, where she also embarks on an affair, this time with Tom Conti's Greek lothario, Costas, and his spectacular Greek moustache. Her decision to stay on Mykonos and become the woman she once might have been (or, as the *Guardian* put it recently, "undergo a mid-life, feminist makeover"[7]) gave a name to the tens of thousands of women who embarked on a holiday romance and never returned home. In the 1980s and 90s, newspapers regularly ran features on women who threw off their British lives to "do a Shirley Valentine" somewhere in the sun.

Reader, I was one of them. While I can't entirely lay my decision to spend a summer living in Turkey with a boat captain called Mustapha entirely at Shirley's door, she definitely had a hand in it somewhere. But in my teens I ate up everything that showed me different parts of the world and what they might unlock; re-watching Meryl Streep as Karen Blixen in *Out of Africa* so many times I could recite it, cheering on Shirley as she told her lugubrious husband she was going to Greece without him, transfixed by the idea of zipping around Rome on a moped, particularly when attached to Gregory Peck. By the time Frances Mayes' book[8] on the transformative power of buying a villa in Italy was made into *Under the Tuscan Sun* (2003), it felt almost hackneyed – at least until Elizabeth Gilbert's *Eat, Pray, Love*[9] came along, which tackled the theme of the life-changing potential of travel with all the subtlety of a frying pan-wielding carthorse.

Alongside the empowerment of women, plenty of movies threw in glamorous locations simply to offer viewers the pleasure of armchair travel. The James Bond films became almost as famous for their globe-trotting backdrops as Sean Connery's smooth style. The first, *Dr. No* (1962), introduced cinemagoers to the palm trees and sandy shores of Ian Fleming's beloved Jamaica, while *From Russia with Love* (1963) took viewers on a whirlwind tour of Istanbul, Venice and, er, Scotland. But even with glorious locations and a bevy of Bond girls, Connery's second outing only just managed to hold on to first place at the box office, with a movie about a very different kind of holiday coming in a very close second.[10]

Summer Holiday – a 1963 musical fronted by Cliff Richard – is proof yet again that there is no such thing as a new travel trend. Much as the Romantic era's Claude Glass was the forerunner of

Instagram, so Cliff was a "van lifer" (the trend of converting old commercial vans into holiday campers) 50 years before the first penniless surfer had looked at a battered old Caddy and thought, *Hmm, I could do something with that*. The story of four young bus mechanics who convert a bright-red London double-decker into a mobile home for a driving holiday across Europe was a smash hit; a kind of souped-up (or possibly just soupy) *Roman Holiday*, where Cliff saves the bus stowaway, Barbara, who inevitably falls in love with him, from her stultifying life with an overbearing mother.

While Cliff was warbling his way around Europe, Sean was cutting a swathe around the Caribbean and women were having all manner of life-changing holiday romances, TV execs were realising there were other, small-screen ways to make the most of the public's new appetite for travel. In 1959, a new type of programme launched on the BBC: a weekly travelogue, with reports from locations around the globe. Originally a segment on the *Tonight* programme, *Whicker's World* was fronted by Alan Whicker; the living embodiment of the slightly stiff, "tally-ho chaps!" kind of Brit, with a neatly trimmed moustache, endless collection of spotless safari jackets and a delivery that had more than a hint of Austin Powers. "I always pack books, bug-repellent and a blazer," he said, in an interview with *Wanderlust* magazine in 2004. "It's a useful piece of kit you can wear either at the beach or at the governor's reception."[11]

I find his swansong programme, *Journey of a Lifetime*, on YouTube, in which he reflects on that first series: leaving London in July 1958 and not returning until the end of October, having covered 30,000 miles and filed 50 reports from six different countries.[12] As a travel writer, it sounds the absolute dream assignment, particularly at a time when so many destinations were still untouched by mainstream tourism. But Whicker's programmes went far beyond the beaches and the souks: a former war reporter, he met everyone from Martin Luther King and Muhammad Ali (in his Cassius Clay days) to Papa Doc, the much-feared Haitian ruler.[13] Although most of his travels would have been to places most viewers would never visit, his travelogues created a new genre of programmes that would be handed on to Michael Palin, Clive James and today's Simon Reeve.

But if *Whicker's World* – and those that came after – was about broadening the minds of its viewers through travel to exotic destinations, by the end of the 1960s it was clear there was an appetite for another type of show, focusing on far more familiar destinations. When the BBC launched *Holiday* in 1969, it was ground-breaking;[14] a sunlit mix of location reports and advice for viewers on how to actually get away themselves. The programme was presented by the earnestly bespectacled Cliff Michelmore, already known as the man who had presented the BBC's coverage of the moon landings, sitting behind a desk in a cream-walled studio, designed to be a neutral counterpart to the glamorous locations for which he provided the links.

"When *Holiday* started, it firmly targeted the Beeb's more affluent viewers," says Peter Hughes, editor of *Wish You Were Here...?*, which launched on ITV in 1974. "Alongside beach holidays, they made expensive-looking films about long-haul trips to the Caribbean and Florida, and more adventurous type holidays – safaris, walking tours. A lot of people watched it as armchair travel, although every segment ended with a price and company to book with."

I manage to find the first ever episode of *Holiday* on YouTube, where the credit sequence mostly involves cut-up strips of newsprint placed at racy angles, interspersed with classic holiday ingredients of the time: water-skiing in tiny pants, sun-cream smeared into slightly sweaty skin and a bikini-clad body (head out of shot) sashaying past a pool. The first report was from Torremolinos, where interviews with guests at the Hotel Azor reveal not much has changed in 60 years: complaints about the unclean beach and particularly the food at dinner, although as Michelmore notes, somewhat condescendingly, it would have been the first time many holidaymakers encountered foreign dishes such as pasta and paella. Other reports focus on the parade of skimpily clad "beauties" competing for the title of Miss Pontinental at the Pontintental Holiday camp, and a distinctly lecherous commentary over the footage of Club Med Tuscany. It's tempting to re-watch the entire programme with a couple of Gen Z-ers, just to see them burst into flames.

"Once mass travel began to make a foreign holiday a reality, it was viewed with as much trepidation as expectation," says Hughes. "Many viewers would have been contemplating getting on a plane and going abroad for the very first time. One of the strongest planks of *Wish You Were Here* . . . ? was that we removed the suspicion of going abroad, without extracting the perception of glamour." In spite of its eventual 20-year run, for a time it looked as if *WYWH* would never make it past the first series. "At first, we were denied a second series," recalls Hughes. "The prime minister, Edward Heath, had imposed the three-day working week and holidays were considered too frivolous a thing to be making programmes about when the country was in crisis."

Heath's government may have considered them frivolous, but Thames Television's then Director of Programmes, Jeremy Isaacs, was wise enough to realise that holidays were fast becoming a non-negotiable, whether a week in a metallic miniskirt in Mallorca or a rainy few days at Skegness Butlin's. The hiatus was short-lived; in 1976, *WYWH* was back in a primetime slot, regularly pulling in between 13–18 million viewers for the next two decades. Targeting a more mass-market audience than the BBC's *Holiday*, half the location reports were UK-based, giving British hotels and destinations a much-needed boost. "Sometimes it could be a mixed blessing," says Hughes. "Hotels would get in touch to say they'd had phones ringing off the hook. Once we covered a canal boat holiday, and the chap whose company it was got in touch to say the phone had started ringing before the programme was even over. People watching had scribbled down the number on the side of the boat and started calling." Mediterranean holidays made up the majority of the other segments, with the unholy triumvirate of Judith Chalmers, Anneka Rice and Anthea Turner unleashing a teeth-gnashingly annoying brand of bubbly blonde brightness onto an unsuspecting public.

But while *WYWH* – and *Holiday*, at times – continued to champion UK-based trips, others saw the country's old-fashioned hotels and holiday camps as ripe for comedy. In 1975, a new sitcom aired that lampooned the traditional British seaside hotel, with ex-Monty Python John Cleese storming onto TV screens as the manic Basil Fawlty, proprietor – alongside his long-suffering wife Sybil, played by Prunella Scales – of the aptly named *Fawlty Towers*. Cleese based the character on a Torquay hotelier he had met while staying in the town with the Python team, once calling him "the most wonderfully rude man I ever met".[15] The series poked fun at everything from the British class system (and corresponding xenophobia) to terrible food, questionable hygiene standards and the overwhelming sense that having to actually deal with hotel guests was the thing Fawlty liked least of all.

The second series of *Fawlty Towers* aired in 1979, and just one year later, another holiday-based sitcom landed, this time sending up the traditional pleasures of the classic British holiday camp. *Hi-de-Hi!*, with a real Warner's holiday camp doubling for the fictional Maplins,[16] regularly pulled in 20 million viewers between 1980–88,[16] mining the knobbly knee and buns for tea ethos for every laugh it could get. Even though we'd never been to a holiday camp, it was appointment-to-view TV in our house: Ted, the sleazy Head of Entertainment, and Spike, his wide-eyed protégé, Yvonne and Barry, the purse-lipped dance pros, Peggy the ditzy chalet-maid and Gladys Pugh, chief Yellowcoat and head of glockenspiel-led announcements, which always began with "Hi-de-Hi campers!"

Other sitcoms took the long-favoured route of finding much to laugh about in the strange ways of Johnny Foreigner. *Duty Free* (1984–86), set in Marbella, charted the exploits of two couples on holiday in Spain, and the secret affair between two of them. *French Fields* (1989–91) followed a middle-aged couple navigating their way through the, er, hilarious eccentricities of Gallic behaviour after relocating to Calais. Watching a little of both proves that although – hopefully – our attitudes to other cultures and countries have changed considerably, our attitude to travel itself remains remarkably similar. The first episode of *Duty Free* begins with one character wishing he had more travel stickers on his suitcase. "Dubrovnik or Nairobi," he says, wistfully. "Maybe Sri Lanka." "But you haven't been to any of those places," says his wife, witheringly. Whatever else changes, one-upmanship seems destined to always be a part of how we travel and the stories we tell.

While neither series achieved the cult status of *Fawlty Towers*, they received considerably more positive reviews than the next big comedy series set in a holiday destination. *Benidorm*, which ran from 2007 to 2018, with guest stars including everyone from Joan Collins to James Corden, was as loathed by the critics as it was loved by viewers. In 2016, the *Guardian* summed it up in a spectacularly, well, *Guardian*-esque review: "drinking, misunderstandings, farts, blow jobs, big bellies, belly flops, boobs, innuendo, pork balls, a little light racism . . ."[17] None of which put seven million people off watching it every week.[18]

But TV reviewers weren't the only ones who didn't appreciate *Benidorm*'s depiction of Spain's original holiday resort. "I watched an episode," says Sergio Frau, of the Benidorm tourist board. "And I didn't like what it showed. It really didn't help with what we're trying to do here, and it definitely didn't show the Benidorm I know." It's a sentiment echoed by Jon Hendry Pickup, CEO of Butlin's. "When millions of people watch something, it has a very real, long-lasting effect. Most of our guests under 40 won't have even heard of *Hi-de-Hi!*, but it still gets mentioned all the time in relation to Butlin's, and journalists still ask about Glamorous Granny and knobbly-knee competitions. That's so not what we are now, but it can be very hard to shake the association."

Not all destinations and businesses saw a downside from exposure in TV or film; the *Fawlty Towers* effect still sees visitors coming to Torquay to find the original hotel, in spite of the fact exterior shots were actually filmed in Buckinghamshire. The Gleneagles is now a retirement home, albeit one called Sachs Lodge in memory of

Andrew Sachs, who played Manuel the waiter, with a commemorative blue plaque on the wall. "*Fawlty Towers* has been very good to us," says local guide Kevin Dixon, when he drives me around the town. "And it's not just English visitors – people come from all over the world to see the home of Basil Fawlty." Other locations saw a boost in tourism numbers after featuring in series that had nothing to do with holidays; Jersey basked in the *Bergerac* effect for a decade from 1981 to 1991[19], while Oxford saw its tourism revenue increase by millions during the *Inspector Morse* years.[20] But a picturesque backdrop was no guarantee of success: the Spanish costas saw little benefit from the car-crash that was *Eldorado*. Launched with great fanfare in 1992, the BBC's flagship new sun-soaked soap opera about expats living in Spain was so spectacularly awful it never got past the first series.[21]

Far more successful – almost unexpectedly so – was a series about another former member of Monty Python gently and politely making his way around the world in the footsteps of Jules Verne's fictional character, Phileas Fogg. *Around the World in 80 Days* aired in 1989, with Michael Palin proving to be everyone's favourite Englishman abroad, apart from the extraordinary stiffs at the Reform Club, who refused to let him enter, 79 days and seven hours after he'd set off from their front door, because they had a function on.[22] "I almost decided to go round the world again," he said, in a recent interview,[23] and in a way he did, with ten further travel series over the next 25 years, taking him everywhere from the Sahara to North Korea.

Palin's programmes may have been popular, but as the 1990s swung in, TV execs realised they needed to find a programme to cater to the new breed of holidaymaker: young backpackers and budget travellers, for whom Jill Dando's *Holiday* reports, Judith Chalmers' perma-tan and even the languid charms of Michael Palin were the very antithesis of cool. Spotting a gap in the market, BBC2 had launched *Rough Guides to the World* in 1988, presented by the uber-hip, sunglasses-addict Magenta Devine who, along with co-presenter Sankha Guha, took very different kinds of trips to the packages offered by their BBC1 and ITV equivalents. *Rough Guides* aimed to really get under the skin of a destination: going to football matches with locals, knocking back cocktails in dimly lit bars and talking to anyone who would stop in the street – a kind of *Whicker's World* for the Hacienda generation. It ran on BBC2 until 1999, by which time the internet was beginning to make such seismic changes to how we travelled that programme makers were forced to realise traditional holiday programmes – whichever type of traveller they targeted – were fast becoming redundant. "The internet was the death of *Wish You Were Here . . . ?*," says Peter Hughes. "People could find all the information we were giving them online, along with a huge range of other choices. We couldn't compete."

WYWH was cancelled in 2003; *Holiday*'s final series began in 2006. For a while, programme commissioners tried various other travel show ideas, from *Holiday Showdown*, where two families with contrasting holiday preferences spent a week experiencing each other's choice, to *Perfect Holiday* – a frankly bizarre mash-up of *Through the Keyhole* and *Ground Force*, where one viewer nominated a worthy chum for the holiday of a lifetime, and a group of "experts" sneaked into their house to have a nose around and decide what kind of holiday would suit them. As with *How to Holiday* – where two presenters visited the same location, one on a budget and one on a luxury ticket – it was thankfully short-lived.

If TV was struggling with how to package up the recalibrated holiday industry, films were also grappling with a switch in viewers' habits, from armchair to *actual* travel. *The Beach* (2000) – a hugely successful adaptation of Alex Garland's bestselling novel about a backpacking trip to Thailand that goes horribly wrong[24] – was arguably the first that had a serious impact on a holiday destination. Shot on the little-known Thai island of Ko Phi Phi Le, the film sent tens of thousands of backpackers on the trail to Maya Bay, adding to the damage allegedly done at the time of filming. Over the following years, 90 per cent of the natural coral was destroyed by up to 200 boats each day, bringing thousands of people to the beach.[25] In 2018, the Thai government closed the area to tourists in the hope of some environmental regeneration; it reopened in 2022, with visitor numbers heavily capped, periodic two-month closure periods and a new jetty to avoid boats coming into the bay.[26] During the four-year closure, 30,000 pieces of coral were replanted, with blacktip sharks, clownfish and lobsters returning to the waters – although a full recovery is still some way in the future.

Other destinations were quicker to embrace and manage increased tourist numbers, following the model of Salzburg, with its numerous *Sound of Music* tours and experiences. New Zealand saw visitor numbers rise by 40 per cent between 2000 and 2006,[27] mainly down to the grandiose *Lord of the Rings* epics, while Dubrovnik's reinvention as the capital of Westeros in *Game of Thrones* birthed countless King's Landing-themed boat trips and walking tours.[28] And it wasn't just films that could put a new tourist destination squarely on the map; Michael Palin's travelogues proved so popular that they became known for creating the "Palin effect", with cities, towns and resorts seeing a notable upswing in visitors once they had been featured in his shows.[29]

But the Palin effect was about more than where people chose to take their holidays – it also opened the floodgates for literally dozens of travelogue TV programmes, fronted by everyone from Joanna Lumley to Joe Lycett. In a 2024 interview with the *Radio Times*, Palin admitted that he "didn't know" how to approach *Around the World in 80 Days*. "In the end," he says, "I realised the best thing was to be myself. And a new kind of travel programme came out of that, something less formal. Alan Whicker would never have been seen in the shower or eating camel, but people want something more personal now, to feel as if they've been taken on a journey."[30]

Certainly, contemporary travel programming is as much about the presenter as the destination itself. In the space of one afternoon, I go crane-spotting in Hokkaido with Joanna Lumley, soak in a Hungarian sauna with Richard Ayoade, whizz through the Canadian countryside in a black cab with Stephen Fry and shiver with Billy Connolly on the Northwest Passage, while passing up the chance to go on a road trip with Gordon (Ramsay), Gino (di Campo) and Fred (not sure who) – a televisual equivalent of Dante's fifth circle of hell. *Race Across the World* is also as much about the people who don the backpacks as the destinations they rush through, and has become so popular that it has inevitably spawned a celebrity version.

"Travel programmes have changed radically in recent years," says Carmen Roberts, who has been a presenter on BBC World's *The Travel Show* for over two decades. "People know how to travel, they don't need to be told that. So it has to have an edge, an angle, whether that's celebrity-based or some kind of reality TV format." Roberts believes that thanks to Instagram, TikTok and YouTube, we are in a new era of how holidays are featured on screen, with destinations very much playing second fiddle to the presenter. "Everything is about the individual now – even on news-based travel shows, you're no longer just a reporter or a mouthpiece. You need to be personally involved, on your own 'journey'. Everyone wants to know your story – if there's some hardship or tragedy in it, the better it will sell."

With the exception of the excellent Simon Reeve – whose thoughtful travelogues and quietly reflective narratives continue the Palin-esque style of presenting – holidays and travel on the small screen are increasingly a backdrop for celebrity presenters, with foreign locations used in dramas that are more likely to make you *not* want to visit, rather than get straight onto Expedia. Last year's execrable *Crossfire* played into our increasing anxieties about travel, with Keeley Hawes' Mediterranean family holiday derailed by a terrorist gun attack that, naturally, only she could thwart. And holiday tropes are now so well established they can be used for social satire, most notably in *The White Lotus*, where a group of utterly ghastly, super-rich holidaymakers gather in an uber-luxurious tropical resort until one of them dies in suspicious circumstances; Agatha Christie with a hefty dose of cocaine and incest thrown in.

Fortunately, Hollywood shows no sign of switching up its reliance on the transformative power of holidays to create its favourite type of feelgood film. *The Holiday* (2006) might just be the ultimate example, with Cameron Diaz swapping her LA mansion for Kate Winslet's English country cottage, giving both the chance to embark on new chapters of their lives (albeit with Jude Law and Jack Black). Others are more subtle; *The Way* (2010) is a quietly charming study of a buttoned-up father, played by Martin Sheen, dealing with grief for his son while walking the Camino de Santiago in Spain, while *Ticket to Paradise* (2022) sees bickering divorcees George Clooney and Julia Roberts travelling to Bali to try to stop their daughter from marrying a seaweed fisherman and, spoiler alert, rediscovering their true feelings for each other in the process. And of course, the phenomenon that is *Mamma Mia!* is built on the premise that free spirit Donna's (Meryl Streep/Lily James) post-university, liaison-filled trip to Greece changed her life forever.

Mamma Mia! may have been made over a century after *The Sheik*, but the central theme remains the same: however much the way we holiday has evolved, however much the internet has demystified the world, holidays still have the same, almost alchemical, power to change our lives. And although the consensus seems to be that there's no longer a place on TV for a traditional "holiday" programme, I'm not sure that's true. Holidays are more precious, more necessary, than ever in these overwhelming times, and as a travel writer, I'm endlessly asked for tips and recommendations, reliable companies, nice hotels. There's such a tyranny of choice that perhaps a programme which curates the very best options, that cuts through all the noise, would actually be a very timely thing. If anyone asks, I'm available.

13

The New Wave

Everything Everywhere All at Once

"I think the potential of what the internet is going to do to society ... is unimaginable. We're on the cusp of something exhilarating and terrifying."[1]
David Bowie

It was sometime in late autumn 1999 that I got a phone call that would change my life. After a couple of summers in Turkey, I was living in London, combining working as a secretarial temp with trying to write a novel *and* break into travel journalism. I had no idea, really, what the travel desks were looking for, and no contacts in the industry, but I figured if I just kept sending ideas in – usually by fax (remember that?) – and pestered enough editors enough times, sooner or later one of them would give me a break, if only to shut me up. It took months, but it worked; Cathy Wood, then travel editor at the *Daily Mail,* gave me my first assignment, and after two pieces in the *Mail*'s travel section, I wangled my first feature in *The Times.* The call came not long afterwards: "Why don't you come in for a trial shift?" I had no idea that marked the beginning of an extraordinary quarter of a century working as a travel writer, at a time when travel – already a national obsession – was just about to go stratospheric.

Until the late 90s, holidays had continued – for most – much as in the previous decade; an annual treat, perhaps a fortnight soaking up the sun in Spain or Portugal, a week in a French gîte or a few days in a caravan or holiday park at the mercy of the British weather gods.

Every high street had at least one travel agent, windows papered with last-minute deals to Tenerife and Mallorca, shelves stacked with blue-skied brochures from dozens of different companies – Thomson, First Choice, Yugotours, Instasun – with Thomas Cook still right at the forefront, 150 years on. Once the holiday was booked, guidebooks were bought, a handful of foreign phrases committed to memory (usually involving the words "beer" and "please"), Alka Seltzer and Imodium chucked in with factor 8 sun lotion. Stores like Snappy Snaps and companies such as Truprint did a roaring trade in photo processing, with paper envelopes bearing 12, 24 or – if you were really pushing the boat out – 36 photos excitedly opened in the hope of finding at least a handful of pictures without camera shake or a thumbprint hovering in the corner.

The internet – still very much in its infancy by the mid-90s – seemed of little relevance to the holiday industry at first, save for buying some cheap holiday reading on Amazon, which launched as a cut-price bookseller in 1995,[2] or bidding for second-hand suitcases on eBay, which appeared in 1997.[3] Most people looking for a holiday deal used Teletext and Ceefax; a kind of Fred-Flintstone-does-the-internet information service, accessed through the TV, where you scanned pages of eye-searing, analogue graphics to find the deal you wanted, only to phone up and be kept holding for at least half an hour to find the holiday had already been sold. A few early adopters took advantage of a new site called Expedia (1996),[4] which offered the chance to book flights, hotels and car hire directly, without going through a travel agent, but few – if any – realised it marked the beginning of another seismic change in how we took our holidays.

At first, many people were understandably nervous about this new-fangled way of booking a holiday. In those early years, the internet was a wild west, with none of the security measures and password protections we take for granted now. Dipping into *The Times Holiday Handbook*, first published in 2006, the chapter "Growth of the DIY Traveller" makes clear the anxieties many people felt. "The internet has freed us up to become our own travel agents from the comfort of our homes," writes Cath Urquhart. "In this chapter, I explain how to book flights and hotels in safety ... and explain how to make the most of the online revolution that has brought us lower fares and greater choice."[5]

Over the next 37 pages, Urquhart tackles everything from budget flights to hotel cancellations, which sites to trust and what protections to look for. While the book was perhaps aimed at more mature holidaymakers, younger travellers had already grown used to this new way of planning trips, with sites like lastminute.com, which launched in 1998,[6] bringing a whole new spontaneity to booking holidays, offering low-priced deals that almost became a competitive sport. "I remember when you used to ring round different hotels to see what the prices were," says Patricia Yates, Chief Executive of Visit Britain. "When the internet came along, suddenly you could just see what everything cost. Booking became so much easier and made smaller, independent businesses so much easier to find."

And it wasn't just hotels. The internet, with its virtual high street of infinite shop windows, meant that anyone with a tourism business – from a five-star hotel to a rural B&B – could suddenly have global reach. Holiday cottages and overseas villas – once advertised in the back pages of *The Times*, or through small specialist companies that few people knew about – were suddenly discoverable at just the click of a mouse, while long-haul travel became a far more realistic possibility. Being able to *see* destinations and hotels online encouraged more travellers to venture further, opening up more far-flung countries to a wider cross-section of holidaymakers, and expanding the market with places such as the Maldives and Mexico beginning to appear on tour operator websites.

For some, the lure of the Mediterranean had given way to more exotic, long-haul destinations as far back as the late 1980s, with Richard Branson's Virgin Holidays leading the charge to the USA and islands in the Caribbean. Competition for the routes became so intense that in 1993, British Airways was found guilty of a 'dirty tricks' campaign against Virgin in an attempt to put them out of business, including tampering with confidential company files, poaching employees and undermining Branson's reputation in the City – a strategy which cost them £3 million in legal fees and a £500,000 payout to Branson.[7] In 1994, the ABTA Travel Industry Report showed the US was the third most-visited country from the UK, after Spain and Greece, with Mexico, Jamaica and Barbados also making it into the top 15.[8] Countries like Thailand and Malaysia were encouraging more intrepid tourists to dip their toes into South-East Asian waters, while Jordan and Syria were picking up a small number of visitors who had done Egypt, and wanted to explore more of the region's extraordinary historic sites.

"Working for a tour operator in the 1990s was like being a modern-day explorer," says Sue Biggs, Managing Director of Kuoni from 2001 to 2007, the first tour operator to launch online booking, in 1999. "Until then, long-haul was mostly the Caribbean or Kenyan safaris, places that had been under British control during the colonial era and still had a lot of visitors from the UK, with friends and family links. I remember a discussion about the Maldives in the late 1980s – people were saying 'you can't take people there, there's no infrastructure, nothing there'. Those first years, it was very rough and ready, there was no fresh water, a lot of imported food – I remember eating a lot of tinned pineapple. And we had to arrange our own charter flight, because no scheduled airline would take the risk."

And if package operators were branching out into more distant lands, independent travellers were doing the same. Suddenly, "gap year" travel was a huge thing, as the children of those whose parents had Interrailed around Europe, backpacked around Greece or followed the "hippy trail" across Asia, came of age. As the internet made every aspect of travelling abroad – from finding hostels to booking bungee jumps – easier, so a new Grand Tour began to take shape: to Australia, India, South America or Asia, as immortalised in *The Beach*, Alex Garland's *Heart of Darkness* for the backpacker generation.

"Maybe it's because I was so young, and really not that worldly, but my memories of Australia are still *so* vivid, even though it was over 30 years ago," says Katie Nesling, who travelled around Australia for several months in the early 90s. "It taught me budgeting, self-sufficiency and legendary skills with a self-service buffet. My dad put me on a plane at Heathrow and I only had one phone call home the entire time. I was super nervous, but a friend who had already been reassured me I would meet other travellers along the way and have a great time (he was right). Backpacking in Australia was definitely a well-worn path in those days."

In Thailand, Bangkok's Khao San Road, a former rice market, became the first stop for a generation of teenagers and twentysomethings; an Asian equivalent of Rome's Piazza di Spagna, 250 years earlier. A low-rise, ramshackle neighbourhood, it welcomed backpackers from every corner of Europe, America and Australasia, who slept (sometimes), ate, drank, dodged tuk-tuks and bartered for harem pants and tie-dyed T-shirts, all beneath a mind-boggling patchwork of multi-coloured signs for hostel rooms, massage parlours, restaurants, money exchanges and stalls selling bowls of *tom yum* soup. For many, it was a gateway to a year of exploration, not yet encumbered by the pressure to post every breakfast and bungee jump on Instagram and TikTok, with the occasional postcard sent home rather than a daily download onto email.

By the early 00s, the internet had really found its feet, and innovations in holidaymaking were coming so thick and fast it was almost impossible to keep up. "When I joined *The Times* as travel editor in 1997, we had four or five pages at the back of the review section," says Cath Urquhart, who held the role until 2007. "By the turn of the century, we had a standalone, 60-page section. I remember we did a front cover with 'www' in the headline – everything was new and things were changing constantly."

Barely a week passed without a new, travel-focused internet start-up opening for business – booking engines, budget airlines, couch-surfing and home-swapping – with websites offering everything from price comparisons to personal reviews of everything from hotels to hire cars. Booking a holiday began to feel a little like ordering a hot drink in the new-fangled Starbucks coffee shops that had first appeared in London in 1998: "Just a black coffee, thanks," had been replaced by a low-fat, double-strength, extra hot macchiato and a week's holiday was now a mid-haul, all-inclusive, twin-centre getaway for two, with car hire on the side and quite possibly sprinkles on top. The internet put a rocket underneath the familiar holiday routine that had now existed for more than half a century, exploding it into hundreds of different choices. A whole phalanx of new phrases came into common usage: long haul, short haul, weekend break or gap year, staycation, daycation, road trip or river cruise; all comparable and bookable all in one place.

And nothing was more integral to those changes than a radical upheaval in the airline industry. In 1984, three businessmen based in Ireland decided it was time to challenge the duopoly held by Aer Lingus and BA on the routes between Ireland and the UK.[9] When Ryanair took to the skies in 1985, with just 15 passengers on board,[10] it was the first salvo in an airline revolution that really took hold after the EU approved a new "Open Skies" policy in 1992, removing restrictions on routes across the continent.[11] Ryanair jumped first, relaunching itself as Europe's "first low-cost airline", followed by a whole spate of similar companies – Go, easyJet, Debonair, Zoom – all competing to offer fares which meant it often cost less to fly to Rome for the weekend than hop on the train from London to the seaside. "Ryanair marketed itself as the first, but actually Freddie Laker's Skytrain was the very first budget airline, back in the 1970s," says Sue Biggs. "He's often forgotten now, because the big boys squeezed him out, and he went bankrupt in the end. It often happens with whoever goes first with a new idea, they get attacked by everyone. Skytrain was long-haul, but it was exactly the same model as Ryanair and easyJet today."

Suddenly, a European holiday could mean anywhere from Paris to Prague, with cheap slots at Eastern European airports bringing tourists to relatively undiscovered cities such as Warsaw, Budapest and Tallinn. New destinations came onto the mainstream: Croatia emerged from the vicious civil war of 1991 to 1995 to become a serious player within two or three years, while Turkey – which I first visited in 1994 – was starting to be popular with holidaymakers who had grown tired of Spain's crowded beaches and the high-rise towers that had come to dominate the sun-kissed beaches on Portugal's Algarve. That first holiday to Kalkan is etched on my memory so clearly; Turkey felt positively exotic, an adventure beyond familiar Mediterranean shores that proved so extraordinary, my sister and I decided to miss our flights home and stay on for another week (during which time I decided a career as a boat captain's girlfriend was far preferable to a summer of secretarial temping, and went back for the whole season).

That summer and the next, when I worked as a holiday rep in the small resort of Turunç, felt like an adventure in a way it simply wouldn't now; the world finally opening up to a much broader cross-section of holidaymakers, rather than just the privileged few. It might not have been as intrepid as backpacking around Asia, but it still gave me that same thrill of exploration, experienced again and again over the centuries, from original Grand Tourers to those hundreds of thousands of Victorians who had piled onto the trains, fascinated to discover the unknown world around them. They might have travelled just a few miles, rather than a few thousand, but I suspect the delight, the fascination, the mind-spinning shock of the new, felt exactly the same. "We're a species that has evolved by discovery," says executive coach Mark Brocklesby. "We're curious by nature, and there's something about the wonder of being somewhere different that brings a sense of freedom, of joy, that's much more difficult to access in your own environment."

As the millennium turned, the power of the internet, its tentacles reaching into every corner of the holiday industry, elevated travel, holidays or time off – whatever you chose to call it – into the new pastime *du jour*. Rock-bottom prices – both for the flight and when you arrived – heralded the arrival of the short break. I remember writing articles about which flights you could grab on a Friday night, straight out of the office, returning at the crack of dawn on Monday morning; three nights away without a day's leave taken. Climate change wasn't even a consideration: airports thronged with weekend-breakers, TV ad breaks were filled with commercials that encouraged you to jet off at the drop of a rattan trilby and unfamiliar destinations with small, local airports – Aarhus in Denmark, Krakow in Poland and Perugia in Italy – suddenly found themselves tourist hotspots, thanks to the budget flights that touched down at least once or twice a week.

"In a lot of ways, short breaks were the perfect response to the long-hours working culture of the 90s and 00s," says Brocklesby. "It's a much easier option in terms of the prep you need to do beforehand, and the amount of work to catch up on when you're back. There's less time to recharge physically, but research shows people still feel the benefits; that sense of having been somewhere different, somewhere warm, spending time with family or friends. I was always struck when someone would come into the office; even if they'd only been away three or four days, they'd have a completely different energy." Brocklesby believes short breaks were also an antidote to the "presenteeism" culture of the time. "It's well documented that most employees don't take all their holiday allocation: when it was a strict, five-days-a-week working culture, some people would be quite concerned about taking time out of the office and what they might find when they came back. Short breaks allayed a lot of those anxieties." It's hard not to wonder what all those who fought so hard for the Holidays with Pay Act – the Labour women handing out their pamphlets, the trade unions – and the millions who benefited would think of a world where thousands of days of paid leave go untaken – a "luxury" (of sorts) they could simply never have imagined.

Suddenly, a fortnight in the sun in August didn't seem quite so attractive, when you could have a weekend in Paris, a sunny few days in Mallorca *and* a cheeky Christmas market jaunt to Munich for roughly the same cost. And as we flooded out of Luton, Stansted, Bristol, Glasgow and all the other airports suddenly welcoming a flurry of low-cost flights, so the ripple effect started to be felt at home. "I've always thought having lots of people go abroad is positive, because rising consumer expectations help our businesses at home think about what direction they have to invest in," says Patricia Yates. "In the late 1990s and early 00s, so many people were going abroad, to so many different places, and they came back with the same expectations of holidays here. That meant standards went up, and things – finally – began to change."

And change *was* necessary. Overseas trips might have been evolving at a rapid rate, but holidays at home continued to be seen as a poor substitute for "properly getting away". Cheap packages, guaranteed sunshine and the glamour of foreign travel had left the UK in the doldrums for decades, with once-glittering beach resorts more likely to be featured in newspapers for their problems with homelessness and social deprivation. But as new hotel brands such as Hotel du Vin and Malmaison began to tap into the more informal, hedonistic vibe of the late 90s and 00s, there was the beginning of a realisation that "Cool Britannia" might just be able to offer some short-break pleasures of its own.

"I remember when Babington House [the country-house outpost of the Soho House members' club] opened in 1998, how different it seemed," says Cath Urquhart. "You could go to the bar in your dressing gown if you were coming from the spa, wear jeans to dinner, there was Marmite on the breakfast menu and you could have cocktails at three in the morning. The new breed of boutique hotels weren't cheap, but they had a completely different feel to the old guard."

If anything could revive – and reinvent – the British holiday, it was the internet and the vast societal changes it ushered in. These were the party decades, when holidays were something you came home and recovered from, whether slamming tequilas by the pool in Cancun, lurching along on a bar crawl in Marmaris or sinking several Super Tuscans in the dimly lit bar in the Hotel du Vin, before sneaking off to the humidor for a cheeky Cuban cigar. Holidays were about indulgence; champagne at the breakfast buffet, rosé-fuelled lunches. And if your hotel did have a spa, it was most likely used for some kind of restorative, pampering treatment to ease the hangover from the night before. Roughing it was out, B&Bs with faded curtains and chintzy bedspreads began to be replaced by urban guesthouses with a Farrow & Ball paint palette and statement wallpaper, and the caricature of the grim-faced landlady, chivvying guests into breakfast, was challenged by young couples and older homeowners, back from their travels and keen to set up a tourism business of their own.

"I do acknowledge we had quite a part in kicking UK tourism into a different place," says Alastair Sawday, who published *British Hotels, Inns and Other Places* in 1997, part of his *Special Places to Stay* series, which started with France in 1994. "At that time, it seemed to me that most accommodation was either uninspiring or completely without taste or character – nylon sheets, unspeakable food. We wanted places with real character, run by interested – and interesting – individuals." Sawday employed an unorthodox approach to finding B&Bs and guesthouses to include in the guide, tasking friends and family (and himself) with finding places that looked interesting and then simply knocking on doors to see if they took guests, or might be interested in doing so. "Several factors helped us," says Sawday, when we speak on the phone, "not least the collapse of Lloyd's insurance, which meant a lot of people with big houses were suddenly rather short of funds. We worked closely with *Country Living* magazine, and I'd say we found 20 to 30 per cent of our properties this way in the early days. Most people who gave running a B&B or guesthouse a try found they rather enjoyed it."

Alongside the internet and budget flights, there were other, less happy events that propelled holidays in the UK back to the forefront in a lot of people's minds. "9/11 had a huge effect on tourism for a good while," says Cath Urquhart. "It really knocked people's confidence about flying. A year later, you had the Bali bombings, which killed over 200, then the Iraq War kicked off in 2003, and the Boxing Day tsunami in 2004 decimated holiday resorts in Thailand, along with terrible devastation in Indonesia and Sri Lanka." Increased security checks at airports, the looming threat of global terrorism and a sudden realisation of how unprepared some of the new tourist regions were for natural disasters caused many travellers to look again at the UK for an anxiety-free break. "I remember we ran articles saying, if you're not comfortable going abroad, here are some ideas for home-based holidays."

And it wasn't just hotels and B&Bs that were sharpening up their act; across the UK, almost every aspect of holidaymaking was changing, influenced by the new wave of ideas and innovation that rolled in on the back of the internet and the era of quick-hit, super-chic short breaks it ushered in. Self-catering cottages – now far easier to find and book – were forced to dust off shabby furniture and smarten themselves up for the image-hungry internet, and even camping – which had quietly been undergoing something of a resurgence since the early 1990s, when the deep recession saw it become an increasingly popular choice for cash-strapped families – got in on the act, with farmers beginning to see the new trend for affordable "staycations" as a way to diversify and put fallow land to profit.

"Tourism is one of the most important sectors of the rural economy," says Andy Pietrasik, Head of Travel at the *Guardian*. "Today, it's worth over £29 billion a year and accounts for over 12 per cent of rural employment. The 1990s saw the government actively supporting farmers in promoting tourism through grant schemes, while the British Tourist Authority [now Visit Britain] got together with the Farm Holiday Bureau to integrate farmhouses into a central booking system. Farmers began to renovate barns, and a lot more self-catering properties were developed, along with opening up fields for camping." And as increasing numbers of holidaymakers returned from safari trips, where the new breed of luxury tented camps came with gleaming silverware, champagne dinners and four-poster beds, there was a dawning realisation that a British holiday under canvas didn't have to mean slow-puncture airbeds and lukewarm soup for dinner.

"A holiday outdoors with a pinch of Disney magic," says Josie Fowler of Feather Down Farms, which has 22 safari-style campsites set on farmland across the UK. "That's what Luite Moraal, the founder of Feather Down, wanted to create. He'd worked at Disneyland and Center Parcs and believed there was a market for a form of luxury camping that took people back to nature, without compromising on comfort." The first Feather Down Farm opened in the UK in 2007, with "canvas hideaways" rather than tents, complete with en suite toilets, six-person dining tables, wood-burning stoves and room for all the Green & Blacks chocolate, South American Sauvignon and hand-baked granola the well-heeled guests could carry. "It was a journalist staying on a Feather Down Farm who first used the word 'glamping,'" says Fowler. "We don't have Wi-Fi or electricity, but we make sure you have a super-warm, super-comfortable night's sleep, a piping hot shower and a well-equipped kitchen."

It didn't take long for the idea to catch on, with tipis, yurts and bell tents beginning to sprout like giant mushrooms in farmers' fields around the country, and the *Cool Camping* guidebook series affirming that a holiday under canvas was now considered seriously hip. I remember writing a piece about a trip to Norfolk with all the latest gear, where our Cath Kidston tipi – with a cowboy pattern that had a distinctly *Brokeback Mountain* tinge – had other campers stopping by to take photos and raise eyebrows. We slept on a state-of-the-art, battery-pumped airbed, made supper on a two-ring gas stove that felt considerably more responsive than my rusty cooker at home and almost forgot we were camping altogether.

Even the great British boozer began to undergo something of a revolution, kicked off by the reinvention of a faded pub in London's

Farringdon neighbourhood into one of the hottest foodie tickets in town. The Eagle, founded in 1991 by chef David Eyre and restaurant manager Michael Belben, opened on a shoestring, with the aim of offering restaurant-quality food at pub prices. "After The Eagle's success, there was a real flight to the countryside of ambitious young chefs who took on old pubs and transformed them into gastropubs," says Pietrasik. "Places like Wales and Shropshire quickly became popular because they offered cheaper rents, meaning pubs could afford to offer fine dining in an informal atmosphere. And it wasn't just food; pubs like the Felin Fach Griffin, which opened in 1999, were among the first to offer rooms too." Twenty-five years later, the "gastropub-with-rooms" trend continues to go from strength to strength, with many historic coaching inns across the country restored to their original purpose.

Whether a fortnight in Florida, an Asian gap year or a cheeky glamping weekend in deepest Cornwall, every aspect of holidaying evolved radically from the mid-90s onwards, powered forwards by the internet and social media, with the industry soaring as high and as fast as the easyJet flights that poured out of British airports. We hopped on them like they were buses, ignoring the increasing clamour of the serious risks posed by climate change, unassailably confident of our new right to rock up just about anywhere on the planet, with little thought to what impact it might have in the future. We backpacked, cruised, hiked, cycled and sailed our way around the world, waving our selfie sticks, posting to Instagram, writing food blogs, taking adult gap years, blissfully sure that this was now the unshakeable norm, that the world was indeed our oyster, and we could slurp it back as often as our holiday allowances would allow.

And no one, not for one second, could have imagined what would happen next.

14

Passports Down

Bournemouth and Eryri

*"I live a very dull life here ... indeed I am
more like a state prisoner than anything else."*[1]
Martha Washington

12 January, 2020. On BBC World News, the journalist Rich Preston takes one minute and 15 seconds to report on the death of a man in China, from a new strain of the pneumonia-like SARS virus, which killed 774 people worldwide during an outbreak from 2002 to 2004. "Officials say the 61-year-old man shopped regularly at this seafood market," says Preston, as the camera pans across the giant blue frontage, each of the individual stalls now sealed off and disinfected, "and that this was the source of the virus." Fortunately, a Chinese health official is on hand to reassure families of the other 40 people infected, the hundreds that had come into contact with them and millions of viewers around the world, that the situation is in hand. "It's largely under control," says Dr Wang Guangfa, of Peking University First Hospital, in what must be the grossest underestimation of a situation[2] since General Haig reported back that the Battle of the Somme hadn't gone quite as well as he'd hoped.

Five weeks later, on a research trip in Umbria, I take a call from my sister, checking in to see if I'm OK. "It's this Coronavirus thing," she says, slightly irritably, when I tell her I have no idea what she was talking about. "Don't you watch the news?" That night, I turn on the TV to discover the northern Italian regions of Lombardy and the

Veneto have become virus hotspots;[3] a day later, 21 February, two Italians become the first Europeans to die of the disease.[4] When I arrive in Rome, all the hotel staff can talk about is the flood of emails and phone calls from the US, Britain and almost everywhere else cancelling bookings for the coming months. Two days later, walking through Fiumicino airport to board my flight home, I notice several other travellers wearing paper facemasks. It feels discomforting, worrying, distinctly odd.

But even then, like millions of others, I had no idea that little more than a month later, Britain would go into lockdown; shops and schools closed, offices empty, streets, roads and motorways devoid of cars. Travel plans were shelved, flights cancelled, hotel bookings postponed and as countries began to close their borders, friends and family members became stranded in holiday destinations and workplace postings; couples separated, parents unable to see their children. What began as a kind of extended break in unseasonably warm spring weather gradually dissipated into a relentless, attritional slog, a global Groundhog Day, only made worse by the sense that those in power seemed to have little idea of how to manage the global threat.

If ever there was a time when people needed a holiday, this was it, but the very nature of the outbreak meant travelling *anywhere* was virtually impossible. Two months after the first lockdown began, Mark Tanzer – then Chief Executive of ABTA (the Association of British Travel Agents) – called it the "deepest crisis" the travel industry had ever faced.[5] Even then, no one was prepared for the tsunami of restrictions, cancellations, vouchers, vaccination certificates and screenings that came to mean that even when international travel did begin to open up in late June, it was a vexed and stressful process. Over that year, the number of people passing through British airports dropped by 75 per cent,[6] while those who did opt for a holiday overseas arrived to find bars and restaurants imposing strict social distancing, hotels operating with reduced facilities and the constant threat of a country moving from green to the restricted amber status at a moment's notice, bringing with it the need to quarantine for two weeks once home.

"Covid-19 didn't just take our holidays from us," says chartered psychologist Audrey Tang. "It also took away the joy of planning one. Just the thought of time away, the chance to 'look forward to something' can be hugely positive for our mental health. We need things to move towards, to have treats and pleasures to aim for. Life should be a positive trajectory forwards. But the pandemic put us in a holding pattern, cooping us up, adding to the pressure of what was already a pretty terrifying situation." As someone who travelled for a living, it was more than holiday plans that folded in on themselves; suddenly my job simply didn't exist, with travel sections scrabbling to fill pages with non-destinational stories, including such gems as "My Favourite Souvenir" and how to recreate a beach holiday in your garden with little more than a paddling pool and a packet of cocktail umbrellas.

Suddenly, the UK was all we had to write about: that first summer, I found myself in Kent, Shropshire and the Brecon Beacons – although we had to come hurtling back after one night, having been identified as having been in contact with someone with Covid, summarily "pinged" on our phones, and sent back to Sussex. And we weren't alone; for most, escape in the summer of 2020 meant one thing (if it meant anything at all): holidaying at home, at the glamping sites, boutique B&Bs, gastropubs with rooms and every other spangly new iteration of staycationing that had evolved in the last two decades. As soon as restrictions were lifted, everywhere – from the Cornish coast to Northumberland's national parks – became flooded with visitors, with even the most rural corners of Britain seeing a huge upsurge in visitors. "People were just desperate to get away," says Victoria Rose, who worked for Harbour Hotels, which has 15 properties dotted across the UK. "When we turned the bookings line on it went crazy – like, record-breaking crazy – across the full sweep of hotels."

Across the country, people – myself included – were booking holidays almost before Boris Johnson had finished announcing when Britain would be able to open up again. I was lucky to snap up a holiday house in Croyde, Devon, for a gang of extended family, beginning on the first day the lockdown ended. We were incredibly fortunate to be slightly ahead of the crowd, spending a euphoric week on our favourite beach which was still slowly waking up from its pandemic-enforced slumber. Weeks later, I heard reports of long queues of traffic between Braunton – the nearest town – and Croyde; the 15-minute journey taking anything up to an hour and a half, pub gardens crammed with people, barely space to swing a surfboard on the vast sandy beach.

Those scenes were replayed in beach resorts across the country, as faded beachfront towns were suddenly catapulted back into their glory days, when every hotel room was taken and fish and chips shops were down to their last pickled egg by the end of each night. On 25 June 2020, the police declared a major incident in Bournemouth, with half a million visitors gridlocking the roads, desperate to escape towns and cities, gently frying in a 33°C heatwave.[7] Tempers frayed, with fights breaking out on the beach, 558 parking fines issued and 33 tonnes of litter removed from the sands on just one day.[8] "It was chaos for a while," says Victoria Rose, who lives in Bournemouth, and who I meet for coffee at the town's glamorous Miami-style hotel, The Nici. "People were allowed to travel, so there was this huge influx – but none of the infrastructure was open to support it. All the public toilets were closed, the car parks were overflowing – people were just leaving their cars anywhere. For residents, it was horrible; we avoided the beach at all costs."

The pictures on the news added to the sense of surreality; thousands and thousands of people squeezed in next to each other on the country's beaches, after weeks of being told to keep apart. "The more we suppress ourselves, the more we need to escape," says Audrey Tang. "It's partly why we Brits love holidays so much – we still live in a world with very set ways of behaving and rules to follow – getting away gives us the chance to shed all that. The pandemic suppressed us in a more intense way than most of us have ever experienced, and what happened when restrictions were lifted is a perfect demonstration of that."

On the day I visit, it's hard to imagine the chaos that engulfed Bournemouth in the summer of 2020. It's a quiet, blustery Monday and the leafy Lower Gardens – still ablaze with late-season chrysanthemums and powder-blue asters – are filled with picnicking pensioners and office workers nibbling sandwiches, soaking up the unexpectedly warm autumn sunshine. On a previous visit, not long after the pandemic was finally over, I was struck by how down-at-heel the town centre was; half the high street shops shuttered and closed down, giving the centre a mournful, slightly dystopian feel. Two years later, the whole place feels much brighter – the town's grande dame department store, Bobby's, reinvented as a mixed-use building, with different floors given over to shopping, a cafe and shared freelance workspace, while the gilded Royal Arcade is buzzing with shoppers.

"I think there's definitely been a positive legacy from the pandemic," says Victoria Rose. "Bournemouth has always had a reputation as a bit stuffy and old-fashioned, but what was good about Covid was the sense of discovery – people visiting places they never would have done normally, even if they were right on the doorstep. People would come and say, *Wow! It's really beautiful!* I know people who have decided to move here from London – and as a local, I'd say the town feels busier, we've definitely seen an increase in visitors."

But while for some the lure of traditional beachy pleasures was too strong to resist – even if it was Margate rather than Mallorca – for others, the need for a holiday was tempered by continued anxiety about the threat of Covid-19 and a desire to avoid crowded spaces and destinations. "Off-grid holidays and out of way places became hugely popular," says Emily Enright of Canopy & Stars, which specialises in rural glamping accommodation. "People wanted to be able to walk from their house to the car and drive to somewhere relatively close by, but away from big crowds." For those people shielding, or those who – like me – found themselves going stir crazy during the second or third lockdown period, "virtual holidays" briefly became a new craze, with websites and newspaper articles offering ways to create that "holiday feel" in the same four walls you'd been imprisoned in for months.

One particularly damp February weekend, when lockdown had been going on for at least four-and-a-half years, we decided to head off on a "ski weekend" to "Austria", packing our bags with salopettes and goggles, driving around the block and unpacking in a different room to our own. We gave ourselves a strudel-making class, listened to Radio Tyrol – with its fabulously predictable playlist of 80s power ballads (with "Rock Me Amadeus" on a once-hourly loop) – and ate schnitzel and *Kaiserschmarrn* (hot sugary pancakes, laced with jam) washed down with gallons of *glühwein*. On some level, it worked; the impenetrable German DJ, the softly spiced strudel and the deeply uncomfortable salopettes all a welcome reminder that the rest of the world was still out there somewhere, however out of reach it seemed.

Ironically, after years of struggling to find ways to attract a broader range of visitors, Britain's 15 national parks suddenly found themselves embodying the very things – space, peace and the chance of spending hours stomping across the countryside without encountering another living thing – that suddenly topped many people's holiday wish list. Record numbers swarmed into the Cairngorms, Exmoor and the Peak District, where 25 per cent of visitors said they'd never been to the National Park before.[9] Meanwhile, up in the north-west corner of Wales, the quiet roads that thread together the tranquil communities of the Eryri National Park (formerly Snowdonia) suddenly thronged with cars, motorbikes, cyclists and walkers. Some were long-term visitors to the region, returned for their annual hiking or biking holiday, but many were first-timers, apparently ready to tackle the treacherous mountain passes in little more than flip-flops and shorts.

"Summer 2020 was busy, but for us it was the summer of 2021 that was the major challenge," says Ioan Gwilym, Head of Communications for Eryri National Park. "We had a massive spike in visitor numbers – we're close to the big northern cities and people were desperate for a change, to get some space." According to Gwilym, the difference in restrictions between England and Wales – and the fact many of those who came were unprepared for Eryri's rough, challenging terrain – saw the park's infrastructure and support services stretched to the absolute maximum. "Over 600,000 people climbed Yr Wyddfa [formerly Mount Snowdon] in 2021 – at times it was just a slow-moving queue to the top. We were at the gate to the main route all summer, giving advice to people who thought they'd just stroll up in trainers, or without proper coats. Sometimes the temperature at the peak can be ten degrees lower than at sea level. People see Yr Wyddfa as a tourist attraction rather than a mountain, but climbing it is a serious undertaking."

There's little reminder of those extraordinary scenes when I arrive in the region on a damp November day. After my chat with Ioan at the National Park office, located in the entirely unpronounceable village of Penrhyndeudraeth, I set off to drive to Llanberis, which became the epicentre of the Covid crowds. The winding road from Beddgelert rises steadily in a series of hairpin bends and switchback turns, the slim ribbon of road flanked by dry stone walls and wild, unkempt grassland in faded yellow and bottle green. Beyond, the mountains are covered in a patchwork of rust-coloured soil, khaki moss and great slabs of volcanic rock; the scenery so dramatic that it's only after I almost swerve into a hedgerow for the third time that I decide it might be sensible to actually pull up and take in the view, rather than continue to drive with my head on a constant swivel.

A handful of other cars are already parked at the viewpoint: couples in fleeces and rain jackets taking photos, turning slowly, phones outstretched. I was lucky enough to be living in the countryside during lockdown; long solo walks a major factor in retaining my sanity. Looking at the vast scale of the mountains, the blue-grey waters of Llyn Dinas lake shimmering in the distance, I can't imagine how it must have felt to stand here after months of being cooped up in the strangely silent cities. "The actual periods of lockdown were amazing for those of us who live in the park – the first time since World War II there were no visitors around," says Gwilym. "But you did think a lot about people in high-rise flats in big cities, how they must have struggled. No wonder they all came here."

In a way, it reminds me of those Romantic Age travellers, whose plans for a Grand Tour were brought to an abrupt end by the French Revolution or the Napoleonic Wars, and who had to settle instead for exploring the wilds of the Wye Valley or the Cumbrian Lakes. It seems ironic that it would take something as drastic as the world shutting down for us to rediscover the beauty and drama of our own landscapes, but in spite of all the innovative, new holiday trends that had sprung up across Britain in the first two decades of the new millennium, for many, a holiday wasn't *really* a holiday unless it involved getting on a plane.

"We had lots of people come and stay with us that we wouldn't normally see," says Katie Valentine, who manages the Royal Oak Hotel in Betws-y-Coed. "Families from Manchester and Liverpool and the other big cities – and what's lovely is that now guests come and they say, *We came the first time because it was Covid and there was nowhere else to go. Now we come back because we love it.*" It's my first visit to Betws – a picturesque village that feels almost Alpine, with the peaks of the dense Gwydir Forest encircling the neat village green, flanked by cafes, shops and restaurants, along with the Royal Oak, which first opened its doors as a coaching inn in the late 18th century. The village quickly became an artist's colony, growing swiftly once the train line arrived in 1869,[10] so much so that by the 1880s it was arguably the first place in Wales to suffer from overtourism, with many painters and writers moving further up the valley to avoid the regular influx of summer crowds.[11]

It's busy when I visit, tables outside Hangin' Pizzeria and the Betws-y-Coed cafe packed with ice-cream scoffing toddlers and slightly weary-looking parents taking a half-term break. I wonder how many of them, before the pandemic, might have opted for a last hit of Mediterranean sunshine rather than a week in the Welsh hills.

While many holiday businesses struggled to keep afloat during – and after – the pandemic, there were those that took advantage of the fact that, particularly in 2021, a holiday cottage in Newquay was as desirable as a free week in the Seychelles. International flights were down 94 per cent in the first quarter of the year,[12] with cruise passengers falling from over 2 million in 2019 to just over 107,000[13] a year later, with websites offering holiday cottages and accommodation in the UK almost unable to cope with demand. "Staycation Inflation!" blazed the newspapers, with the *Daily Mail* reporting that the average cost of a night's stay in August 2021 was £176, a 32 per cent hike on 2019 prices.[14] Some holiday parks were quoting over £3,500 for a family of four (more than 50 per cent above their usual rate).[15] Center Parcs in particular came in for criticism, with some holidaymakers accusing them of charging more for a family week than a similar holiday in the Caribbean.[16]

Although plenty of people I chat to on my travels talk about a positive legacy from Covid – perhaps discovering a newfound appreciation for Llandudno's beaches, say, or the picture-book villages of the Yorkshire Dales – the figures don't bear it out. "We saw a big rise in domestic bookings when people could first go away again," says Patricia Yates, Chief Executive of Visit Britain, "but that's gone down by about 10 per cent year on year." Perhaps unsurprisingly, not everyone was satisfied with an overpriced and overcrowded week on the Cornish Riviera.

When Boris Johnson announced his "Road Map to Freedom" in February 2021, holiday websites such as easyJet and TUI almost spontaneously combusted, as the pent-up desire for some fun in the sun sent bookings through the roof – despite government ministers suggesting people should wait until the situation was a little clearer. easyJet recorded a 630 per cent increase in bookings, with TUI selling holidays to Greece, Spain and Turkey at six times the rate they would normally have anticipated[17] – in spite of the fact Turkey remained on the "red" list until October. "From my years in travel, I would say the British are very resilient about going overseas," says Patricia Yates. "If you were sitting there during Covid, watching what was happening on cruise ships – vessels quarantined, passengers stranded on board for weeks – would you ever want to go again? But now the sector is booming more than any other."

Even those countries that could be visited without the threat of being imprisoned in a hotel room for two weeks still came with an array of hoops to jump through. Locator forms had to be filled out, Covid passports arranged, swab tests taken – along with the risk of any country suddenly being switched back from green to amber or red, in which case all returning holidaymakers faced two weeks of quarantine. One of my most surreal memories of that time is sitting in a hotel room in Spain while my husband took a Zoom call with a very polite woman in India, just so she could watch him stick a swab up his nose and confirm the test showed no infection. There was something almost Python-esque about their awkwardly polite conversation: "Have you had a nice holiday?" "Lovely, thanks." "Perhaps that just needs to go a little further up your nose." "Right-ho."

That summer, most holidaymakers were delighted simply to get away from the same four walls they had been staring at for the last 18 months. "It was like Christmas," says Claire Smith, who ran two B&Bs in Blackpool at the time, but has since had to close one due to the financial implications of the pandemic. "Everyone was happy to be away. Not everyone had had a terrible time – you had to figure out how to handle people, and find out what each person's story was, but what united everyone was that they were sick of being stuck in the same place." But as the first waves of relief began to ebb away, the experience of the pandemic left many of us wanting – and expecting – more from our precious time away. "Because people had been boxed in for so long, when they finally got a break, senses were heightened – everything was heightened," says Mike Bevens, Group Managing Director of Sawdays and Canopy & Stars. "Before the pandemic, guests were happy to stay in a simple cabin; afterwards, they began to want all kinds of add-ons – an outdoor hot tub, sauna, wild swimming, an honesty bar, a swing to sit on while you're reading a book. People want more from a domestic holiday now, they're looking for a deeper, richer experience. That's definitely been the biggest change – the movement to wanting more from whatever people are doing in their daily life."

In a way, it's not surprising that we want more from our time away than ever before; having something that you love forcibly taken away is inevitably going to make you prize it even more highly. The pandemic brought our passion for holidays to a shuddering halt, but the hiatus only reinforced how integral they have become to our lives; the sense of release and respite needed ever more acutely in the troubled years that have followed on from the end of the pandemic. "People have definitely reprioritised holidays since Covid," says Patricia Yates. "One of the great lessons that came out of it was the importance of – and how much we missed – spending time with family and friends. People want holidays with their parents, their grandparents, old uni friends, and there's a real opportunity for businesses in this country to make something of that."

Four years on from the official end of the pandemic, it seems that very few of us are willing to compromise on an overseas holiday, unless pretty much every aeroplane is lashed to the floor and borders are closed so tightly even a Klingon cloaking device couldn't get through. Yates believes that unreliable weather and our island geography also play a part in our seemingly unshakeable yearning for foreign climes. "It's always going to be a challenge to get people to travel domestically, which is why we need to offer the highest quality across the board. But after Covid, that was more difficult than ever; tourism closed first and opened last, and most businesses had chewed through whatever cash reserves they had left."

But although foreign travel came back with a vengeance, there are some positive legacies from the pandemic; anecdotally, at least, it seems that 18 months of heavily restricted foreign travel has developed a new appreciation for the gorgeous landscapes, spectacular coastline and slick B&Bs, hotels, guesthouses and gastropubs that dot the country. "We definitely still have visitors to Eryri who would never have come if it wasn't for the pandemic," says Ioan Gwilym. "That period definitely created a greater understanding of the links between nature, walking and mental health and that has to be a good thing. I can't pretend that everyone who comes abides by the park rules – we do have problems with litter, some people take stones out of the dry stone walls, or let their dogs run free and scare the local livestock – but a lot of people have developed a greater understanding of our landscapes."

For some, discovering the unexpected beauty right on their doorstep meant holiday plans changed forever. "Even now there's an audience who are still very cautious," says Nathan Cousins, General Manager of St George's Hotel in Llandudno. "We have guests who don't want to go to an airport, who just aren't keen on foreign travel any more. They discovered us in the pandemic – our little sun-trap part of Wales, and now this is where they come." In a way, I suspect it's the uniquely special nature of our lockdown holidays – shining like a beacon in a great, grey sea of monotony, anxiety and not enough loo roll – that has made us more demanding; we want every break to deliver that same sense of giddy release and pin-sharp memories, shared with those we love.

"We get a lot of feedback from guests about the joy and relief of being in nature," says Mike Bevens. "There's quite an intense sense of the need for escapism – even if they've just gone an hour down the road."

The difficult truth – for holiday providers at least – is that however many hot tubs, firepits or treehouse suites with diamond chandeliers they create, nothing will ever quite match our Covid holidays. I still have the video on my phone of our first night in Croyde: sisters, husbands, nieces, nephews, best friend and goddaughter, all lined up together jigging about to some mad PlayStation dance-along game. And I remember the next morning, stumbling blearily from room to room, collecting up empty wine bottles and crumb-strewn plates, after finally falling into bed about 3 a.m. None of us had a hangover. None of us even felt tired. Instead, we all clambered into our wetsuits and jumped in the sea, fuelled by a great sense of release and relief – that we had made it through, come out the other side and, best of all, we were finally together.

15
Where Next?

London and Sussex

"You cannot escape the responsibility of tomorrow by evading it today."[1]
Abraham Lincoln

A crisp, blue-skied Thursday and I'm on a bus with an army of silver- and white-haired couples, mostly clad in sensible anoraks and comfortable shoes, backpacks jostling together as they embark. Aboard the C1 from Earls Court station, I am the youngest by at least a decade, but the air of anticipation is akin to teenagers going to a pop concert, albeit with fewer selfies and cans of cheap cider. Instead, we are all heading to Destinations, an annual travel show that brings together 600 different travel brands and 90 tourist boards, along with talks, workshops and the chance to build up the travel bucket list to end all bucket lists. The vast exhibition space of Kensington Olympia is filled with banners, hoardings and giant photographs depicting everything from Antarctic cruising to Zambian safaris. In a world where climate change and global unrest are supposedly curtailing our travelling habits, visitors to Destinations – around 80,000 in 2024 (London and Manchester)[2] – clearly haven't got the memo.

If the pandemic was supposed to have changed the way we holidayed, there's certainly little evidence to prove it now. In 2024, we took over 90 million trips abroad; still slightly down on 2019 (just over 93 million)[3], but considering the world is grappling with multiple wars, climate change and a profiteering[4], xenophobic[5], narcissistic[6] ego-maniac in the White House, frankly, it's surprising anyone fancies getting on a plane at all. "Travel momentum remains robust," says Natalia Lechmanova, Mastercard's Chief Economist for Europe, when I log on to Mastercard Economic Institute's Travel Report webinar. "Despite all the shocks we've had – high interest rates, the invasion of Ukraine – travel remains the bright spot, outperforming the broader economy globally." I *think* what she's saying is that – apart from a global pandemic – pretty much nothing will stop us from bagging our precious time away, and that we're taking holidays more frequently than ever – an average of 3.9 per person (including jaunts in the UK).[7]

It certainly looks that way in the jam-packed hall at Olympia. All life is here: from the jovial chap on the Sailing Holidays stand, resplendent in cream shorts, navy deck shoes and a stiff-peaked sailor's hat, to the Virgin team in their trademark scarlet suits, clashing noisily with the maroon-skirted Emirates crew next door. Everywhere, enticing taglines blaze into the melee: "Holidays for the Mature Solo Traveller", "Small Group Adventures", "Amazing Road Journeys", and my personal favourite, "Escorted Tours for the Discerning Traveller". I hope to find a stand offering "Unescorted Tours for Immature Group Travellers", which basically describes every holiday I've ever been on with my uni friends, but sadly, it fails to materialise. Destinations is not for your two-week holiday to the Costa del Sol; instead, there are hoardings for Discover Romania, Travel Carpathia and Nepalese Journeys. At the food demonstration stand, alongside Singaporean curry and *ossobuco* from Lombardy there is something called *Nap Naang* from Nagaland, which I Google on both counts (turns out to be a sticky rice pudding from northern India).

I've arrived just in time to hear Simon Calder – the BBC's man in travel and travel editor of the *Independent* – give a talk on his "Travel Bucket List and Q&A". He is upbeat but realistic about the travel industry and the current issues that surround it. "Tourism has a huge impact on the world," he says to the assembled group of star-struck travellers, "but overall, I believe it's good. My advice is simple: ensure you spend more with people who will benefit from your money, and do it in an environmentally friendly way." It's a neat soundbite, skating across the myriad issues that have begun to cloud our holiday horizons; climate change, overtourism, the environmental impact of multinational hotel chains chewing up the world's most beautiful stretches of coastline, gargantuan cruise ships rendering the ports they visit almost unliveable for local residents.

"Things are going to have to change," says Sue Biggs, former Managing Director of Kuoni. "While people are not prepared to compromise now, I do think we're going to have to learn to control ourselves and holiday in a more sustainable way – less Airbnb, fewer cruise ships. Destination countries will have to start controlling numbers, otherwise they'll kill the goose that laid the golden egg."

So how will our holidays change in the future? Already, climate change is affecting how, when and where we travel – from overtourism protests to oven-temperature summer heat and climatic weather events, such as the flooding in Valencia in 2024, which claimed over 220 lives[8]. To fly or not to fly has become an important debate; holidaying in Europe by rail is now increasingly offered by tour operators, aware that air travel contributes around 3 per cent of global emissions.[9] "Some people think, *Oh, that's a tiny percentage, flying can't be that bad*," says Anna Hughes, Director of Flight Free UK. "But only 5 per cent of the global population will fly internationally each year, rising to 10 per cent if you include domestic flights. So it's actually a massive impact for something that is basically a luxury of Western lifestyles."

Hughes – who set up Flight Free UK, which has had charity status for three years, in 2019 – believes taking flying out of the equation doesn't mean having to compromise on holidays. "People get very defensive about not flying because it's seen as the norm; we're pushed into it by advertising, the government is talking about expanding airports, and right now it's so cheap. But flying is also highly stressful, prone to delays – once people take a holiday by train, they often become quite evangelical about how much easier it is. Last year I went to Lake Como from London – it took nine hours and five different trains. That sounds a lot, but it was actually really relaxing – just sitting down, taking in the views."

While I'm not entirely convinced that taking five different trains would be the *most* relaxing way to start a holiday, train travel is certainly becoming an alternative for those who have the time and money to spare. New Nightjet services are opening up Europe, and Eurostar connections mean that cities such as Amsterdam, Cologne and Lyon (the gateway to the Alps in ski season) are just as quick and easy to reach by train as plane, particularly for those who live near to London. What doesn't add up, for now, at least, is the difference in cost. A recent trip to Lucca in Italy set me back around £70 for a return flight, considerably less than it costs to get to Wales on the train to visit my sister. But if the industry's aim of achieving net-zero carbon emissions by 2050 is to be achieved[10], flight prices will have to rise. Debate still rages about how – and if – this is even possible, with everything on the table from sustainable fuels to next-generation electric or hydrogen-powered aircraft, zero-emission ground vehicles and on- and off-site renewable energy generation.

All of which is going to cost millions – a percentage of which will inevitably find its way into ticket prices for travellers. And while flying less may be good for the environment, cutting back on flights will inevitably hurt destinations and communities that rely on tourism and are unreachable by any other method than long-haul flights. "I have a best- and worst-case scenario for future travel," says Tom Robbins, travel editor of the *Financial Times*. "At worst, it's thoughtful travellers who stop flying; people more likely to visit smaller destinations and community-based tourism. So, suddenly, a company that, say, sustains Himalayan villages with walking tours, can no longer stay in business. Meanwhile, those who don't care about the climate, or are climate-change deniers, keep on travelling to big, mass-market destinations, holidaying on cruise ships, etc."

And the best? "Online contact and social media increasingly permits direct connections with local guides, accommodation owners and small, independent businesses, allowing money to go directly to the communities hosting tourism and ending the current system where a big chunk of your cash goes to a tech company in the US, i.e., Airbnb."

Ah, Airbnb. What began as an innovative way for individuals to offer up spare rooms as an easy side hustle has become – according to some – a destroyer of worlds[11]. Gobbling up any and all available properties for short-term rentals, Airbnb has left many towns, villages and cities with a dearth of housing stock for locals and ushered in unprecedented numbers of visitors to places that simply don't have the infrastructure to cope.[12] "We're seeing super-high volumes of tourists at concentrated periods of time, which means car parks are overflowing, there's more litter and all public services are under pressure," says Mike Bevens, Group Managing Director of Sawdays and Canopy & Stars. "Governments need to start acting – limiting visas, restricting flights, imposing levies – but it's all difficult, and deeply unpopular. Instead, I think we'll see a trend for holidays that offer an escape from the crowds, to be on your own. In the future, it's all going to be about space."

This chimes with one of the things I've realised over recent years, that moving away from the most popular options – whether a city break to Venice, or a beach week in Mallorca – doesn't mean compromising on your holiday. I genuinely believe you'll eat better in Bologna, have a more authentic experience in Zaragoza and a much better chance of some tranquil Greek beach time on Patmos than in Rome, Barcelona or Santorini – albeit without being able to tick off those iconic sites, or snap yourself at Insta's most recent bar of choice. While people will always want to go up the Eiffel Tower, visit the Colosseum or stroll around the Parthenon, there is an element of box-ticking: these might be the places we supposedly *should* see, but would it really matter if we *didn't*? Might those two or three hours of overheated, overcrowded jostling be spent more enjoyably elsewhere? And if you choose to visit a different gallery in Florence from the Uffizi, but are actually able to see the paintings, rather than just the back of people's heads clustered around them, isn't that a better experience?

Of course, there's nothing new about travellers following the recommendations of others; from John Egerton's guide to the Wye, through Grand Tour adventurers recommending which bars and restaurants to frequent in Rome and Venice, right through to the 20th-century proliferation of guidebooks by companies such as Lonely Planet, Dorling Kindersley and Rough Guides, travellers have always relied on those who have gone before for tips on what to see and where to eat, drink and party. What has changed, thanks to the global reach of YouTube, Instagram and TikTok – now the leading sources of information on where and how to holiday – is the sheer number of people all descending on the same spot, sometimes with tragic results.

"The 'Instagram' effect started during the pandemic, and is still a real issue, with hundreds – sometimes thousands – of people flooding to one particular spot," says Ioan Gywlym, of the Eryri National Park. "The Watkin Path – where there are beautiful pools and waterfalls – have become massively popular, but it's not safe to swim." A week before I write this chapter, two young women were found drowned in the Watkin Pools, with local councillor June Jones telling BBC Radio Cymru: "We don't know what has happened ... social media encourages people to go to these beautiful places, and of course the water can be extremely cold."

The impact of social media recommendations can be seen everywhere; on a recent trip to Madrid, I was struck by the queues outside one historic *churreria* (cafes that specialise in *churros* – the city's artery-clogging treat of deep-fried doughnut sticks and gooey, unctuous hot chocolate), while another – that looked equally appealing – stood empty. Last time I stayed near Florence, the hotel staff actually advised me not to visit the city for an afternoon, telling me that the traffic and crowds would be so bad, I'd have to come back before I'd actually set foot in the Duomo.

We say "Oh, Spain has been ruined" or "There's no unspoiled Greek islands left" but in part this is because we don't explore beyond the same resorts that everyone else goes to. And while moving on to new destinations or countries does risk the same big hotel companies coming in and gobbling up the best bits – as with the fledgling destination of Montenegro – trying somewhere different does offer the chance both to escape the crowds and put some money into different local economies. "Albania is definitely the big one right now," says Sean Tipton of ABTA. "Hotel chains are investing and more flights are going in – once you get that, the infrastructure starts to be improved, decent roads from the airport, better-kept beaches. It might not have the cachet of the Amalfi coast or Ibiza, but it also doesn't have hordes of other tourists."

And if overtourism might start to change where we holiday, will climate change do the same? Last summer, I spent five languid days on Zakynthos, where the mercury topped 40 degrees every day. While it made for a super-relaxing break, after about 11 a.m., it was impossible to do anything but lie around pathetically like a consumptive heroine. I can't imagine what it must be like to holiday as a family in that temperature. At the beginning of the 2024 summer season, Spain had restricted water use to such an extent that villa owners on the Costa del Sol were not allowed to fill their pools. By June, it had reversed the decision, aware that – as temperatures rise – a pool is a non-negotiable for most visitors.[13] But do the soaring summer temperatures mean that soon we'll all be swapping Benidorm for Blokhus, on Denmark's white-sand coast? Will Gotland, Sweden's beach-fringed island, become the new Mallorca?

"I don't think so," says Tipton. "Every time there's a heatwave around the Med, people start talking about Scandinavia, but it goes back to sheer affordability. Not many people are going to spend the money on two weeks on the Danish coast. But what we are seeing is a switch in *when* people holiday, particularly for those without children. People have begun to realise that holidaying in July and August might be tradition, but actually, the Med is really pleasant from March to November. We did some research recently that showed increasing numbers of people are travelling in early spring, or September/October. One of the issues is whether hotels are open, but if tour operators feel there's a market for it then there's every chance we'll see what's known as the 'shoulder seasons' become an increasingly popular time to travel."

Elongating the tourist season makes sense not just for holidaymakers in search of a more peaceful experience, but also for those who work in the hotels, restaurants, bars and tourism-related businesses that depend on making the majority of their profits in a three-month window. In 2024, the Greek Prime Minister Kyriakos Mitsotakis spoke at the EU Tourism Summit about his desire to see a 12-month holiday season, which would spread the country's tourism – and the 30 million visitors that fly in annually – across the year.[14] When I stayed on the Athens Riviera last autumn, one of the waiters, Niko, told me that November was the absolute best time to be in the region. "The days are shorter, but the sea is so warm and almost all days are sunny," he said. "Best of all, it's quiet." I would have re-booked on the spot, but the hotel I was staying at – like most on the peninsula – closed at the end of October, although if Mitsotakis has his way, this may change before long.

This challenging combination of higher prices, soaring temperatures and global instability inevitably means staycations are becoming an increasingly popular option. "I think we will see a change," says Carl Castledine, Managing Director of Away Resorts. "I genuinely believe the sheen has come off air travel – where's the glamour now? It's stressful, there are queues everywhere, you're just wedged onto planes – and I think people are more worried about the sun, about skin cancer, constantly slathering on sun cream."

Of course, there may well come a time when we can travel anywhere in the world without actually leaving the country. The pandemic sped up the interest in virtual travel; sites like Flyover

Zone offer virtual tours of cultural heritage sites, while Google Arts & Culture partnered with over 2,000 museums and archives to allow viewers to see some of the world's most famous art and artefacts, with high-resolution imagery and augmented reality. Post-pandemic, tourist boards and attractions are using VR to bring history to life, from simple QR codes to full, augmented reality tours of ancient sites and historic buildings. Personally, I'm quite keen for a *Star Trek* "holodeck" in the basement, where I can step into whichever destination I fancy at the flick of a button. I suspect virtual holidays are closer than we think; recently, hospitality brand Leven has opened a hotel and a tropical resort in Decentraland, a browser-based, 3D, virtual-world platform in the Metaverse (nope, no idea either), where plots of land can be bought and developed using cryptocurrency, and nights away can be purchased at the Levenverse resort.[15]

But while technology may be the way some of us holiday in the future, many hoteliers believe that going "off-grid" – escaping our screens, leaving phones behind – will become one of the biggest trends in future holidays. "I do think I can see a world leaning into more of an analogue experience in travel," says Daniel Bayrenreuther, General Manager of Gleneagles. "In the winter, we build a pop-up ski lodge, we put board games in it – you wouldn't believe the joy it brings people to just sit, have a drink and play a board game. I see families doing falconry – nothing but the birds and some chatting. Things that are unplugged – the privilege of not being surrounded by all the blinking lights and technology – I can see a section of people saying, *This is what I'd like.*" It's a sentiment echoed by many of those I talk to across the industry: "It's definitely a trend we'll see in the future," says Mike Bevens of Sawdays. "In the past, holidays have all been about getting away and relaxing, in future, I think it will be about getting away from other people. To be on your own, away from the crowds – I think space is the future."

Perhaps. Although, from my privileged viewing point as a travel writer, my fear is that, once again, it is increasingly only the wealthiest travellers who will have access to the world's most beautiful, tranquil places, as luxury hotel groups and moneyed entrepreneurs buy up isolated stretches of coastline to create exclusive retreats, often on land and beaches no longer accessible to locals. It's why organisations like the Youth Hostel Association, and its overseas equivalents, are so valuable; ensuring that restorative natural landscapes are available to everyone, whatever their holiday budget. And while space might be the future for luxury travellers, for the rest of us, it seems that ease and straightforwardness are increasingly top of the wish list. The overwhelming nature of our constantly plugged-in lifestyles means that what we want more than anything is someone else to sort our holidays out for us. Cruising is booming, package holidays and all-inclusives are seeing a resurgence in popularity with everyone from Gen Z-ers to pensioners, and the lure of a Butlin's-style holiday camp, where everything is laid on, all in one place, is fast becoming as popular with families as it was in the 1950s.

But as the social structure of life changes, with many jobs no longer location specific and AI set to make many traditional careers redundant, will we still need holidays in the same way? The trend for "global nomads" and "workcations" has only grown since the pandemic, with millennials and Gen Z prioritising a work–life balance and mental wellbeing more highly than generations before them. And if you can swap a faded office space in the back end of Slough for a table in the bar on a Maldivian island, why wouldn't you do exactly that?

"I think WFA [working from anywhere] is a trend that's only going to grow," says Mark Hodson, ex-travel writer and co-owner of 101 Holidays, who now spends four or five months a year living and working in Chiang Mai in Thailand. "I think it's still just starting to dawn on a lot of people that this is something they can actually do – and it's only going to get easier. More countries are keen to issue digital nomad visas and are positively encouraging long-stay remote workers. They bring advantages – they tend to contribute good revenue to the host country and don't put a lot of strain on tourism infrastructure."

Among millennials and Gen Z, the "van life" trend (first espoused by everyone's favourite hipster and early adopter, Cliff Richard) is a more off-grid form of global nomadism; touring, living and working from a van, often for months at a time. "We wanted to enjoy the perks of travelling without having an end date," says Charlotte Osborn, who has done several stints of van life with her partner, James, including seven months in Europe. "The benefits are huge – you get to enjoy local culture while you work. In Bansko, we'd get a few snowboard runs in; in Croatia, we'd have a pre-work swim in the Adriatic and local food meant lunchbreaks were far more exciting than, say, a Tesco Meal Deal. Any time not working was spent exploring, and evenings wandering around the local city or countryside felt far more fulfilling than slumped in front of the TV."

While van life offers plenty of adventure, Osborn believes it's very different from an actual holiday. "Travelling can be tiring, and being frequently on the move left us exhausted at times. We missed friends and family – sometimes we'd feel we were letting them down during catch-ups; the reality was we wouldn't always have exciting updates. Sometimes it would just be, 'We've been working all week and it's been raining. How about you?' Living as a global nomad does blur the boundaries between work and rest – and it can be pretty demanding. We still needed a holiday afterwards – I think a break is always essential, no matter the style of life you're living."

While living and working out of the back of a converted Caddy isn't for everyone, the van life trend is proof that how we holiday will continue to evolve and change, sometimes in new and surprising ways. "One of the newest trends in the UK is wine tourism," says Patricia Yates of Visit Britain. "As our climate has changed, so our vineyards are able to compete in the global market – and winemakers are starting to realise that tourism can be a big part of their product." I know this to be true because I live in the heart of England's wine country, with vineyards rolling out across the fields just a few minutes' walk from my door. Twenty years ago – perhaps even ten – English wine was little more than a joke; now there are over 200 vineyards in Kent and Sussex,[16] many of them offering tours, tastings and slick overnight accommodation that is straight out of the Loire Valley playbook.

Before I finish writing this chapter, I take an early evening stroll out across the fields, as the sun is just starting to drift towards the low ridge of the Downs and the leafy rows of the Everflyht vineyard are flooded with warm, summer light. My route takes me south; if I'd headed north, I would have passed Court Garden and Ridgeview, east would have taken me to Artellium, with its sunlit wine terrace and glorious vineyard views. In another ten years, this beautiful corner of Sussex will be the new Tuscany[17], and maybe Spanish and Italian holidaymakers will flock to the beaches that lie just over the ridge of the hills, chased away from their own by temperatures that just keep on rising. Whatever happens, we will keep seeking out the new, the extraordinary and the beautiful, because at heart we're all explorers, all curious to know what lies around the corner, none of us willing to forego the pleasures of a holiday that have been knitted into ourselves since childhood.

But perhaps the time has come when we all need to think a little more about the holidays we take and the impact they make. Of course it's up to governments and holiday companies and tech billionaires to take some responsibility and start addressing the problems faced by many destinations, but isn't it down to us too? We ask ourselves where, when, but never *if*. Four hundred years of holidays has forged them in our collective psyche as an inalienable right, but it's a "right" that only exists for a minute percentage of the global population, and while tourism does bring benefits, income and positive development to many countries and communities, it can also have a massively detrimental impact.

Tracing the evolution of holidays – from their earliest incarnation in Bath and Buxton, through the great freedom brought by the trains, and the explosion of love for the Med – has made me realise how incredibly fortunate we are to be able to experience the world in more ways than ever before. Finances permitting, our holidays can be anything we wish for; at the beach, in the city, on a cruise ship, in a villa with friends, a holiday camp with the family or a chic hotel with a lover. We can travel solo, take the dog, walk, cycle, fly, drive, charter a yacht, rent a yurt or sleep in a glass igloo while the Northern Lights ripple across the skies. But somewhere along the line, it's as if we've forgotten the very thing that facilitates our travels; blithely determined to ignore the fact that the holidays we so treasure are seriously impacting the very places we love to visit most.

And we do *love* to visit them. Perhaps it's the rain, perhaps it's our island psyche, perhaps we're just a nation of explorers, built on the shoulders of Inigo Jones, Sir John Soane, Dorothy Wordsworth and Frances Burney; the legacy of Grand Tours and railway excursions and those first forays to unfamiliar continents written into our DNA. That "paid holiday" finally became a right, that turnpike roads, railways and air travel gradually opened up the world, that the internet brought the furthest corners of the world into our homes – these massive societal changes all helped to create our extraordinary era of travel and exploration. But that is not the end of the story.

Instead, change is happening again: to cities and landscapes, to the climate, to the planet itself – and right now, at least, it seems no one has any definitive answers to how we can begin to repair the damage. Tourist taxes, cruise ship embargos, carbon-neutral flights, virtual trips – can anything stop the holiday juggernaut that has evolved over the last 400 years? And should it be stopped? In our vexed world, isn't time out more essential than ever before? And if the answer is yes, then surely we need to be part of the next change, to think about where we holiday, *how* we holiday, what impact it has, what impact *we have*. However much "time off" may be an inalienable right, a "holiday" remains a privilege: a chance to experience somewhere different, exciting, invigorating – but somewhere that other people simply call home. Changing how we holiday isn't easy, but it is necessary. The next chapter, really, is up to us all.

Acknowledgements

I've always believed it takes a village to write a book; with *The Great Escape*, it's pretty much taken an entire town. Four hundred years is a lot of holidays to cover, and it would have been impossible without so many people taking time to chat and reminisce, to offer opinions and – most precious of all – share their memories of holidays across seven decades.

One of the biggest lessons from *The Great Escape* is the number of custodians of local history we have, working in libraries, museums and archives, writing books, forming societies – all deeply passionate about keeping our heritage alive. Huge thanks to Keren Guthrie at Blair Castle, who showed me original letters from Queen Victoria, the inimitable and dapper Richard Croisdale at the Blackburn Museum, Sue Palmer at Sir John Soane's House, Jane Birtles at A La Ronde, the delightful staff at the Armitt Library, Louise Peskett at Brighton Museums, Marie Batty and the staff at Wordsworth Grasmere, Judith Phillips at the Llandudno Museum, Mary Painter at Blackburn Library, Simon Wenham, Duncan Simpson and Dave Richardson.

It was wonderful, too, to talk so many who work in our holiday industry now, from CEOs to B&B owners, guides and tourist board staff. Claire & Mark Smith, Carl Castledine, Jon Hendry Pickup, Jeremy Pardey, Fay Donegan, Theresa Jenkins, Ruth Waycott, Gordon Lightburn, Patricia Yates, Simon Kershaw and Christiane from Bike & Boot, Kevin Dixon, Sarah Stacey, Emmanouela Tabois-Kastouli, Daniel Bayrenreuther, Mike Bevens, Andrew Robson, Emma Gray, Sergio Frau, Leila Bilbao, Wendy Akin-Smith, Josie Fowler, Ioan Gwilym, Katie Valentine, Alvin Delanghe, James Allen, Michael Duxbury – thank you for all your insights, stories and unshakeable belief in the strength of UK tourism.

And if I didn't know already, writing *The Great Escape* reminded me how fortunate I am to have worked in the travel industry for a quarter of a century. Colleagues and contacts were so generous with their time; thank you to Cath Urquhart, Jane Knight, Andy Pietrasik, Tom Robbins, Tom Chesshyre, Noel Josephides, Sue Bryant, Alastair Sawday, Graham Simpson, Stella Photi, Robin Hutson, Sean Tipton, Gary Buchanan, Mark Hodson, Peter Hughes, Carmen Roberts, Sue Biggs, Anna Hughes and Victoria Rose.

The Great Escape would have been incomplete without personal memories and insights; thank you to Paul O'Brien, Lily Allenden, Katie Nesling, Justine Campbell, Chris Bulpitt, Steve & Glynis Gatenby, Charlotte Osborn, Anne Jones, Camille Hobby-Limon. Also to Dr Shona Goodall, Mark Brocklesby and Audrey Tang for giving valuable insights and psychological perspective.

But none of this would have come to be if it wasn't for the hard work of my agent, Elly James, and the fantastic team at DK Red, particularly the lovely Zoë Rutland, who endlessly championed and believed in the book from the start. Thanks, too, to Gemma Doyle and Katie Cavanagh for the beautiful cover, Geetam Biswas for her hard work on sourcing the perfect images to accompany the text and Hannah Boursnell, for her thorough and thoughtful editing.

Finally, to my gorgeous friends and family – you are, as always, my greatest support, and none more so than my husband, Mark. Neither of us had any idea what an adventure this would turn out to be; more complex, overwhelming, uplifting and rewarding than I had ever imagined. Thank you, my love, for always keeping hold of my hand along the way. It means more than you know.

Notes

Chapter 1: Waddling to the Waters

1. Jane Austen, *Northanger Abbey* (Herts, Wordsworth Classics, 1992).
2. William Turner, *A Booke of the natures & properties as well of the Bathes in England* (Arnold Birckman, 1562).
3. Geoffrey Moorcroft, *The Last Divine Office: Henry VIII and the Dissolution of the Monasteries* (New York, BlueBridge, 2012).
4. Phyllis Hembry, *The English Spa 1560–1815* (London, The Athlone Press, 1990).
5. Ibid.
6. Romola Davenport and Jim Oeppen, "Three score and ten?" The Cambridge Group for the History of Population and Social Structure, University of Cambridge, n.d., available at www.campop.geog.cam.ac.uk/blog/2024/08/15/three-score-and-ten/ (accessed December 2024).
7. J. A. R. Pimlott, *The Englishman's Holiday: A social history* (Brighton, The Harvester Press Ltd, 1976).
8. Brigitte Mitchell, "English Spas", available at www.historyofbath.org/images/BathHistory/Vol%2001%20-%2008.%20Mitchell%20-%20English%20Spas.pdf (accessed November 2024).
9. "History of British newspapers", n.d., available at https://newsmediauk.org/history-of-british-newspapers/ (accessed December 2024).
10. J. A. R. Pimlott (1976), see note 7.
11. Ibid.
12. Ibid.
13. Jane Austen, *Northanger Abbey* (London, Penguin Classics, 2003).
14. "The Roman Baths & Pump Room welcomes 1 million visitors", available at www.romanbaths.co.uk/news/roman-baths-pump-room-welcomes-1-million-visitors (accessed December 2024).
15. Katie Birkwood, "Rules for gouty people; eighteenth-century advice", Royal College of Physicians, available at https://history.rcp.ac.uk/blog/rules-gouty-people-eighteenth-century-advice (accessed December 24).
16. Ibid.
17. George Cheyne, *An Essay on the Gout, With an Account of the Nature and Qualities of the Bath Waters* (Edinburgh, George Strahan, 1722).
18. J. A. R. Pimlott (1976), see note 7.
19. Thorstein Veblen, *The Theory of the Leisure Class* (Oxford, Oxford University Press, 2009).
20. Daniel Defoe, *A Tour thro' the Whole Island of Great Britan* (London, Penguin Classics, 2005).
21. Steven Morris, "After 30 years and £40m, is Bath finally ready to turn on the taps?", *Guardian*, 2 May 2006, available at www.theguardian.com/artanddesign/2006/may/02/architecture.communities (accessed November 2024).

22. Lucy Tegg, "Call to introduce tourist tax in 'heritage cities'", BBC News, 16 July 2025, available at www.bbc.co.uk/news/articles/cy7n3yxrmm4o (accessed August 2025).
23. R. Grundy Heape, *Buxton under the Dukes of Devonshire* (London, Robert Hale Ltd, 1948).
24. Ibid.
25. Peter Collinge, "'I swim like a frog that has lost the use of its hind legs': The pursuit of health and leisure in Buxton, 1781–90", *Journal for Eighteenth-Century Studies*, Volume 40, No. 3 (2017).
26. Kate Leahy, "Buxton Crescent review: the grand old spa and hotel comes back to life", *Guardian*, 12 October 2020, available at www.theguardian.com/travel/2020/oct/12/buxton-crescent-health-spa-hotel-review-peak-district (accessed November 2024).
27. Melanie King, *The Secret History of English Spas* (Oxford, Bodleian Library, 2021).
28. Phyllis Hembry, *British Spas from 1815 to the Present* (New York, Fairleigh Dickinson University Press, 1995).
29. Ibid.
30. J. A. R. Pimlott (1976), see note 7.
31. Richard Warner, *A New Guide through Bath and Its Environs* (Charleston, Nabu Press, 2010).
32. P. Hembry (1990), see note 4.
33. William and Richard Arthur Austen-Leigh, *Life and Letters of Jane Austen* (London, Smith, Elder & Co., 1913).
34. Anna Seward, *The Letters of Anna Seward: Written Between the Years 1784 and 1807* (Cambridge, Cambridge University Press, 2013).
35. W. & R. A. Austen-Leigh (1913), see note 33.
36. P. Hembry (1990), see note 4.
37. Frances Burney, *The Diary and Letters of Madame D'Arblay Vol. II* (London, Vizetelly & Co, 1891).

Chapter 2: A Grand Adventure

1. Henry Matthews, *Diary of an Invalid, the Journal of a Tour in Portugal, Italy, Switzerland and France* (Miami, Hardpress Ltd, 2019).
2. Jeremy Black, *The British Abroad: The Grand Tour in the Eighteen Century* (Stroud, Sutton Publishing, 1992).
3. "What was the Grand Tour?" Royal Museums Greenwich, n.d., available at www.rmg.co.uk/stories/art-culture/what-was-grand-tour (accessed December 2024).
4. Ibid.
5. Ibid.
6. Nicholas A. Barr, Peter Kellner, "British society by the mid 18th century", Britannica, n.d., available at www.britannica.com/place/United-Kingdom/British-society-by-the-mid-18th-century (accessed June 2024).
7. Ibid.
8. Ibid.
9. Black (1992), see note 2.

10. Ibid.
11. George Cecil White, *A Versatile Professor: Reminiscences of the Rev. Edward Nares, D.D., Regius Professor of Modern History in the University of Oxford 1813–1841* (London, Forgotten Books, 2018).
12. Jeremy Black, *The British and the Grand Tour* (Kent, Crook Helm Ltd, 1985).
13. John Lee, "Voltaire and the myth of England", Cambridge University Press, 28 May 2009, available at www.cambridge.org/core/books/abs/cambridge-companion-to-voltaire/voltaire-and-the-myth-of-england/00D5B6D836E8299A9F85FE573A902952 (accessed June 2025).
14. W. S. Lewis (Ed.), *Horace Walpole's Correspondence, Sir Horace Mann VI, 29 Jan 1762–8 March 1768* (London, Oxford University Press, 1960).
15. Black (1992), see note 2.
16. Ibid.
17. Ibid.
18. Christopher Hibbert, *The Grand Tour* (London, Thames Methuen, 1987).
19. Emily Snow, "Who was Rosalba Carriera?", *The Collector*, 9 January 2024, available at www.thecollector.com/who-was-rosalba-carriera/ (accessed December 2024).
20. Hugh Belsey, "Cameos from the Grand Tour: The paintings of Pompeo Batoni", *History Today*, 8 August 1982, available at www.historytoday.com/archive/cameos-grand-tour-paintings-pompeo-batoni (accessed December 2024).
21. Black (1985), see note 12.
22. *Sir John Soane's Museum: A Complete Description* (London, Sir John Soane's Museum, 2018).
23. Ibid.
24. Charlotte Haslam, "26 Piazza di Spagna history album", The Landmark Trust, 2015, available at www.landmarktrust.org.uk/globalassets/3.-images-and-documents-to-keep/history-albums/piazza-di-spagna-history-album.pdf (accessed December 2024).
25. Ibid.
26. Feargus O'Sullivan, "How the 2025 jubilee is reshaping Rome", Bloomberg, 30 January 2025, available at www.bloomberg.com/news/articles/2025-01-30/rome-s-jubilee-brings-a-wave-of-public-space-and-traffic-projects (accessed June 2025).
27. Brian Dolan, *Ladies of the Grand Tour* (London, Harper Collins, 2002).
28. Lady Mary Wortley Montagu, *The Letters and Works of Lady Mary Wortley Montagu Volume One* (London, Forgotten Books, 2018).
29. *The Parminter Ladies' Grand Tour*, National Trust, n.d., available at www.nationaltrust.org.uk/visit/devon/a-la-ronde/the-parminter-ladies-grand-tour (accessed May 2025).
30. Ibid.
31. Ibid.
32. Brian Dolan (2002), see note 27.
33. Ibid.
34. Jeremy Black (1992), see note 2.

Chapter 3: The Search for the Picturesque

1. Dorothy Wordsworth, *Recollections of a Tour Made in Scotland A.D. 1803* (Miami, Hardpress Ltd, 2018).
2. "Truman Quotes", Truman State University, n.d., available at: www.truman.edu/about/history/our-namesake__trashed/truman-quotes/ (accessed February 2025).
3. Malcolm Andrews, *The Search for the Picturesque: Landscape, Aesthetics and Tourism in Britain, 1760–1800* (Aldershot, Scolar Press, 1989).
4. Brian Duignan, "Enlightenment", Britannica, 19 August 2025, available at www.britannica.com/event/Enlightenment-European-history (accessed August 2025).
5. John Locke, *An Essay Concerning Human Understanding* (London, Penguin Classics, 1997).
6. Brian Dugnan, "Inventors and inventions of the industrial revolution", Britannica, n.d., available at www.britannica.com/list/inventors-and-inventions-of-the-industrial-revolution (accessed August 2025).
7. William Dalrymple, *The Anarchy: The Relentless Rise of the East India Company* (London, Bloomsbury, 2020).
8. Andrews (1989), see note 3.
9. Christopher Lloyd (Ed.), *The Diary of Fanny Burney* (London, Roger Ingram, 1948).
10. "The Wye tour", Wye Valley National Landscape, n.d., available at www.wyevalley-nl.org.uk/exploring-wye-valley-aonb/heritage/the-wye-tour/ (accessed February 2025).
11. Ibid.
12. "The Wye tour", Forest of Dean and Wye Valley, n.d., available at www.visitdeanwye.co.uk/blog/the-wye-tour (accessed February 2025).
13. "The Picturesque Wye tour", Wye Valley AONB, n.d., available at https://dean-wye.files.svdcdn.com/production/business-directory/The-Wye-Tour-by-The-Wye-Valley-AONB.pdf?v=1743802451&dm=1743802451 (accessed February 2025).
14. Andrews (1989), see note 3.
15. Ibid.
16. William Gilpin, *Observations on the River Wye* (Surrey, The Richmond Publishing Co. Ltd, 1973).
17. Hilary Clash, "The History of the George Inn, Chepstow", *The Journal of Gwent Local History*, Vol. 64, 1 April 1998.
18. Gilpin (1973), see note 16.
19. Daniel Defoe, *A Tour thro' the Whole Island of Great Britain* (London, Penguin Classics, 2005).
20. Thomas West, *A Guide to the Lakes* (London, Richardson and Urquhart, 1780).
21. Stephen Gill, *William Wordsworth: A Life* (Oxford, Oxford University Press, 2020).
22. William Wordsworth and Antonia Till, *The Collected Poems of William Wordsworth* (Towcester, Wordsworth Editions, 1994).
23. Dorothy Wordsworth, *Grasmere Journals* (Oxford, Oxford Paperbacks, 1993).

24. Ibid.
25. William Hutchinson, *An Excursion to the Lakes in Westmorland and Cumberland; With a Tour through Part of the Northern Counties in the Years 1773 and 1774, 2 vols* (London, J. Wilkie, 1776).
26. "Tourism", Lake District National Park, n.d., available at https://www.lakedistrict.gov.uk/learning/facts_and_figures/factstourism (accessed February 2025).
27. "Visitor travel in the Lake District: A 2040 vision", Lake District National Park, n.d., available at www.lakedistrict.gov.uk/caringfor/smarter-travel (accessed February 2024).
28. Dorothy Wordsworth, *Recollections of a Tour Made in Scotland AD 1803* (Edinburgh, David Douglas, 1984).
29. Ibid.
30. Samuel Johnson and James Boswell, *A Journey to the Western Isles of Scotland and The Journal of a Tour to the Hebrides* (London, Penguin Classics, 1984).
31. Wordsworth (1984), see note 28.
32. Angie Brown, 'How the King's visit saw kilts become Scotland's national dress', BBC Alba, 13 August 2022, available at www.bbc.co.uk/news/uk-scotland-edinburgh-east-fife-62464709 (accessed February 2025).
33. Ibid.
34. Ibid.
35. D. Duff (Ed.), *Victoria in the Highlands: The personal journal of Her Majesty Queen Victoria* (Zurich, Muller, 1968).

Chapter 4: Beside the Seaside

1. Euripides, *Iphigenia in Taurus* (London, Penguin Classics, 1974).
2. A. R. Pimlott, *The Englishman's Holiday: A social history* (Brighton, The Harvester Press Ltd, 1976).
3. Ibid.
4. Phyllis Hembry, *The English Spa 1560–1815* (London, The Athlone Press, 1990).
5. Sarah Howell, *The Seaside* (London, Cassell & Collier Macmillan, 1974).
6. John Floyer, *Psychrolousia: Or, the History of Cold Bathing, Both Ancient and Modern* (Charleston, Legare Street Press, 2018).
7. Louise Allen, *The Georgian Seaside* (Louise Allen, 2016).
8. Anonymous, *A Journey from London to Scarborough, In Several Letters From a Gentleman There, to His Friend in London*, (Charleston, Legare Street Press, 2023).
9. John Rushton, "The Yorkshire smuggler – the smuggling of contraband", *Scarborough Maritime Heritage Centre*, n.d., available at www.scarboroughsmaritimeheritage.org.uk/article.php?article=259 (accessed December 2024).
10. Hembry (1990), see note 4.
11. Ibid.
12. Pimlott (1976), see note 2.
13. John K. Walton, *The English Seaside Resort: A Social History 1750–1914* (Leicester, Leicester University Press, 1983).
14. Howell (1974), see note 5.

15. Richard Russell, *A Dissertation on the Use of Sea Water in the Glands* (1760), (Montana, Kessinger Publishing, 2009).
16. "Old Steine, Old Steine Gardens, Brighton", Brighton & Hove City Council, n.d., available at www.brighton-hove.gov.uk/planning/heritage/local-list-heritage-assets-directory/old-steine-old-steine-gardens-brighton (accessed December 2024).
17. Howell (1974), see note 5.
18. Ibid.
19. Pimlott (1976), see note 2.
20. Sue Berry, *Georgian Brighton* (Bognor Regis, Phillimore & Co., 2008).
21. Frances Burney, *The Diary of Fanny Burney* (London, Everyman's Library, 1961).
22. Howell (1974), see note 5.
23. Ibid.
24. *Morning Post*, July 1785, quoted in Yvonne Cloud, *Beside the Seaside* (London, The Bodley Head, 1934).
25. George Saville Carey, *The Balnea: Or, an Impartial Description of all the Popular Watering Places in England* (Michigan, Gale Ecco, 2018).
26. John Feltham, *A Guide to all the Watering and Seabathing Places*, (Charleston, Legare Street Press, 2022).
27. Caroline Roope, "All of the fun of the fair", The Genealogist, September 2019, available at www.thegenealogist.co.uk/featuredarticles/discover-your-ancestors/periodical/77/all-the-fun-at-the-fair-6644/?#:~:text=By%20the%2018th%20century%2C%20fairs,the%20Lord%20Mayor%20of%20London (accessed December 2024).
28. "The history of the Grand Scarborough", Britannia Hotels, n.d., available at www.britanniahotels.com/hotels/the-grand-scarborough-hotel/history (accessed December 2024).

Chapter 5: The Wings of the Wind

1. Samuel Smiles, *The Life of George Stephenson, Railway Engineer* (Charleston, Legare Street Press, 2023).
2. "Stockton: Where passenger railways began", Stockton-on-Tees Borough Council, n.d., available at https://heritage.stockton.gov.uk/articles/stories/stockton-where-passenger-railways-began/ (accessed March 2025).
3. Anon., "Opening of the Stockton & Darlington railway", *Durham County Advertiser*, 1 October 1825.
4. "First in the world: The making of the Liverpool and Manchester railway", Science + Industry Museum, 20 December 2018, available at www.scienceandindustrymuseum.org.uk/objects-and-stories/making-the-liverpool-and-manchester-railway (accessed March 2025).
5. Jeremy Black, *Nineteenth-Century Britain* (London, Macmillan Foundations, 2003).
6. Ibid.
7. J. A. R. Pimlott, *The Englishman's Holiday: A social history* (Brighton, The Harvester Press Ltd, 1976).

Notes

8. Susan Major, *Early Victorian Railway Excursions* (Barnsley, Pen & Sword Books, 2015).
9. Sharon Brown, "The opening of the Liverpool and Manchester railway", National Museums Liverpool, n.d., available at www.liverpoolmuseums.org.uk/stories/opening-of-liverpool-and-manchester-railway (accessed March 2025).
10. Major (2015), see note 8.
11. Pimlott (1976), see note 7.
12. Karla Cripps, "Thomas Cook: A history of one of the world's oldest travel firms", CNN, 23 September 2019, available at www.edition.cnn.com/travel/article/thomas-cook-history-timeline (accessed March 2025).
13. Simon Calder, "Thomas Cook: A timeline of the world's oldest tour operator", *Independent*, 5 July 2020, available at www.independent.co.uk/travel/news-and-advice/thomas-cook-bankrupt-timeline-tour-operator-travel-package-holiday-a9116836.html (accessed February 2025).
14. Pimlott (1976), see note 7.
15. Charles Dickens, *Dombey and Son* (London, Oxford University Press, 1950).
16. "From humble beginnings to the world's busiest train station: The history of Blackpool Central", *The Gazette*, 10 December 2018, available at www.blackpoolgazette.co.uk/news/from-humble-beginnings-to-worlds-busiest-train-station-the-history-of-blackpool-central-192035 (accessed February 2025).
17. John K. Walton, *Blackpool* (Edinburgh, Edinburgh University Press, 1998).
18. John Hannavy, *The English Seaside in Victorian and Edwardian Times* (London, Shire Library, 2003).
19. Ibid.
20. Charles Dickens, *Short Stories Volume V* (Munich, Grin Verlag, 2009).
21. John K. Walton, *The English Seaside Resort: A Social History 1750–1914* (Leicester, Leicester University Press, 1983).
22. Ibid.
23. Pimlott (1976), see note 7.
24. Samuel Solly, "The influence of railway travelling on public health", *The Lancet*, 15 February 1862, available at www.thelancet.com/journals/lancet/article/PIIS0140-6736(02)58591-3/fulltext (accessed February 2025).
25. Anon., *The Railway Traveller's Handy Book: Hints, Suggestions and Advice, Before the Journey, On the Journey and After the Journey* (Moretonhampstead, Old House Books, 2012).
26. Ibid.
27. "What is the prime meridian – and why is it in Greenwich?", Royal Museums Greenwich, n.d., available at www.rmg.co.uk/stories/time/what-prime-meridian-why-it-greenwich (accessed February 2025).
28. Pimlott (1976), see note 7.
29. Kevin Dixon, *Torquay: A Social History* (Kevin Dixon, 2022).
30. Ibid.
31. Ibid.
32. David Mason and Alan Heather, *Torquay: A century of change* (Cheltenham, The History Press, 2006).

33. Phyllis Hembry, *British Spas from 1815 to the Present* (New York, Fairleigh Dickinson University Press, 1995).
34. Pimlott (1976), see note 7.
35. Ibid.
36. Ibid.

Chapter 6: A Place to Stay

1. George Bernard Shaw, *You Never Can Tell* in *Plays Pleasant* (London, Penguin Books, 1981).
2. J. A. R. Pimlott, *The Englishman's Holiday: A social history* (Brighton, The Harvester Press Limited, 1976).
3. Ibid.
4. Angel and Royal, www.angelandroyal.co.uk/about-us (accessed January 2025).
5. The Old Bell Hotel, www.oldbellhotel.co.uk/about-us/ (accessed January 2025).
6. The Star at Alfriston, www.thepolizzicollection.com/the-star/hotel/ (accessed January 2025).
7. The Spread Eagle Hotel & Spa, www.hshotels.co.uk/spread-eagle (accessed January 2025).
8. "History of the Post", Great North Road, n.d., available at www.greatnorthroad.co.uk/post-history (accessed January 2025).
9. Daniel Maudlin, "The urban inn: Gathering space, hierarchy and material culture in the eighteenth-century British town", *Urban History*, Volume 46, Issue 4, November 2019, available at www.cambridge.org/core/journals/urban-history/article/abs/urban-inn-gathering-space-hierarchy-and-material-culture-in-the-eighteenthcentury-british-town/4FE2AED8D73A3526AE5FF161DB7CA5AD (accessed January 2025).
10. Daniel Maudlin, "Inns and elite mobility in late-Georgian Britain", *Past & Present*, Volume 247, Issue 1, May 2020, available at www.academic.oup.com/past/article/247/1/37/5715969 (accessed January 2025).
11. Peter Tydesley, "Royal Clarence may not be the oldest in England", *Guardian*, 30 October 2016, available at www.theguardian.com/travel/2016/oct/30/royal-clarence-hotel-may-not-be-the-oldest-in-england, (accessed January 2025).
12. "London's first hotelier", *Look and Learn History Picture Archive*, 14 May 2012, available at www.lookandlearn.com/blog/18150/david-low-was-londons-first-hotelier/ (accessed January 2025).
13. Annie Lewis, "Claridge's Mayfair: The history and heritage of London's last word in luxury hospitality", *Luxury London*, 26 July 2004, available at www.luxurylondon.co.uk/travel/london/claridges-mayfair-hotel-history/ (accessed January 2025).
14. "History & Heritage", The Connaught, n.d., available at www.the-connaught.co.uk/about-the-hotel/history/ (accessed January 2025).
15. "Historical Insider: Brown's Hotel", Rocco Forte Hotels, n.d., available at www.roccofortehotels.com/blog-repository/articles/historical-insider-brown-s-hotel/ (accessed January 2025).
16. Lewis (2004), see note 13.

17. The Connaught, see note 14.
18. Christian Wolmar, *Fire and Steam: How the railways transformed Britain* (London, Atlantic Books, 2008).
19. Jack Simmons, "Railways, hotels and tourism in Great Britain, 1839–1914", *Journal of Contemporary History*, Volume 19, No. 2, April 1984, available at www.jstor.org/stable/260593?read-now=1&seq=3#page_scan_tab_contents (accessed January 2025).
20. Ibid.
21. Ibid.
22. Michael Patterson, *Railway Hotels* (Stroud, Amberley Publishing, 2016).
23. "The Good Organisation – York's Railway Heritage", York Museums Trust, n.d., available at www.yorkmuseumstrust.org.uk/blog/the-good-organisation-yorks-railway-heritage/ (accessed January 2025).
24. "History of the Milner York", The Milner York, n.d., available at www.themilneryork.com/history-of-the-hotel (accessed January 2025).
25. Karen Averby, *Seaside Hotels* (Britain's Heritage) (Stroud, Amberley Publishing, 2018).
26. "Our Story", The Langham, n.d., available at www.langhamhotels.com/en/the-langham/london/our-story/ (accessed January 2025).
27. "1865, The Langham, London", Historic Hotels of the World, Then and Now, n.d., available at www.historichotelsthenandnow.com/langhamlondon.html (accessed January 2025).
28. "History and Heritage", The Savoy, n.d., available at www.thesavoylondon.com/information/history-heritage/ (accessed January 2025).
29. Arnold Bennett, *The Grand Babylon Hotel* (London, Chatto & Windus, 1971).
30. James Collard and Justine Picardie, *Gleneagles: The glorious playground* (New York, Rizzoli, 2024).
31. Ibid.
32. Pimlott (1976), see note 2.
33. Ibid.
34. Ibid.
35. Sir Billy Butlin, *The Billy Butlin Story* (London, Robson Books Ltd, 1998).
36. Adam Raphael, "Sharrow Bay: A great hotel reborn", Good Hotel Guide, 4 April 2024, available at www.goodhotelguide.com/sharrow-bay-a-great-hotel-reborn/ (accessed January 2025).

Chapter 7: The Great Outdoors

1. Anne Frank, *The Diary of a Young Girl* (London, Penguin, 2007).
2. Robert McCrum, "The 100 best novels: No. 25 – *Three Men in a Boat* by Jerome K. Jerome (1889')", *Guardian*, 10 March 2014, available at www.theguardian.com/books/2014/mar/10/100-best-novels-three-men-boat-jerome (accessed January 2025).
3. Jerome K. Jerome, *Three Men in a Boat* (London, Collins Classics, 2012 ed.).
4. Michael Paterson, *A Brief History of Life in Victorian Britain* (London, Robinson, 2008).

5. Ibid.
6. Smitha Mundasad, "Victorian keep-fit exercises and gym regimes revealed", BBC News, 27 September 2014, available at www.bbc.co.uk/news/health-28858090 (accessed January 2025).
7. "The Safety Bicycle", National Cycle Museum, n.d., available at www.cyclemuseum.org.uk/TypesOfBicycleListing.aspx?ID=4 (accessed January 2025).
8. Frank J. Berto, "Bicycle", Britannica, n.d., available at www.britannica.com/technology/bicycle (accessed January 2025).
9. Ibid.
10. Sheila Hanlon "Happy Birthday Cycling UK: Celebrating 139 years of cycling history", Cycling UK, n.d., available at www.cyclinguk.org/article/campaigns-guide/happy-birthday-cycling-uk-celebrating-139-years-cycling-history (accessed January 2025).
11. Charles G. Harper, *Cyle Rides Round London* (London, Chapman & Hall Ltd, 1902).
12. Sheila Hanlon, "Women's cycling fashion from the 1870s onwards", Cycling UK, n.d., available at www.cyclinguk.org/womensfashion1870s (accessed January 2025).
13. Ibid.
14. Simon Wenham, *Pleasure Boating on the Thames: A history of Salter Bros, 1858–present* (Cheltenham, The History Press, 2014).
15. Jerome (2012), see note 3.
16. David Cretney, "The Man who built an Isle of Man holiday camp that housed thousands", *Isle of Man Today*, 8 September 2004, available at www.iomtoday.co.im/news/the-man-who-built-an-isle-of-man-holiday-camp-that-housed-thousands-719543 (accessed January 2025).
17. Hazel Constance, *First in the Field: A century of the Camping and Caravanning Club* (Coventry, The Camping and Caravanning Club, 2001).
18. Ibid.
19. Thomas Hiram Holding, *Cycle and Camp* (London, De Vere & Co., 1898).
20. Constance (2001), see note 17.
21. Thomas Hiram Holding, *The Camper's Handbook* (Charleston, Legare Street Press, 2022).
22. Rose Staveley-Wadham, "The birth of the camping holiday", The British Newspaper Archive, 9 June 2021, available at https://blog.britishnewspaperarchive.co.uk/2021/06/09/the-birth-of-the-camping-holiday/ (accessed January 2025).
23. "Hops in Kent", Kent Country Council, n.d., available at www.kentarchives.org.uk/hops-in-kent/ (accessed January 2025).
24. Tim Adams, "Hopsters meet hipsters as East End families relive the exodus to Kent", *Guardian*, 13 September 2014, available at www.theguardian.com/science/2014/sep/13/hopsters-hipsters-london-kent-hop-picking-beer (accessed January 2025).
25. John Marsh, *Hops and Hopping* (London, Simpkin, Marshall, Hamilton, Kent, 1892).

26. Ibid.
27. "Memories of the Kent hop fields", National Trust, n.d., available at www.nationaltrust.org.uk/visit/kent/scotney-castle/memories-of-the-kent-hop-fields# (accessed January 2025).
28. "Forgotten Stories: hop-picking in the fields of Kent", London's Royal Docks, n.d., available at www.londonsroyaldocks.com/forgotten-stories-hop-picking-fields-kent/ (accessed January 2025).
29. Hilary Hefferman, *Voices of Kent and East Sussex Hop Pickers: Tempus oral history series* (Cheltenham, The History Press, 2004).
30. Constance (2001), see note 17.
31. Ibid.
32. Rose Staveley-Wadham, "Hiking in the 1930s – Exploring the Phenomenon of Post-War Youth", The British Newspaper Archive, 1 June 2021, available at www.blog.britishnewspaperarchive.co.uk/2021/06/01/hiking-in-the-1930s/ (accessed January 2025).
33. Ibid.
34. Duncan M. Simpson, *Open to All – how youth hostels changed the world* (feedaread.com, 2016).
35. Ibid.
36. Ibid.
37. Rose Staveley-Wadham (2021), see note 32.
38. Ibid.
39. Jennifer Harby, "Kinder Scout Trespass: How mass action 90 years ago won ramblers roaming rights", BBC News, 24 April 2022, available at www.bbc.co.uk/news/uk-england-derbyshire-61008955 (accessed January 2025).

Chapter 8: Wakes Weeks

1. *The Football League Show*, BBC1, 26 September 2009.
2. Allan Brodie & Matthew Whitfield, *Blackpool's Seaside Heritage* (London, Historic England, 2014).
3. Ibid.
4. Ibid.
5. Hugh Hollinghurst, *Southport History Tour* (Stroud, Amberley Publishing, 2018).
6. Tom Stringfellow, "Don't all rush at once", BBC, September 2005, available at www.bbc.co.uk/bradford/going_out/2005/sowerby_rushbearing_festival_preview.shtml (accessed November 2024).
7. Charles Booth, *Life and Labour of the People in London* (Charleston, Legare Street Press, 2022).
8. J. A. R. Pimlott *The Englishman's Holiday: A social history* (Brighton, The Harvester Press Ltd, 1976).
9. "Illuminating history", Visit Blackpool, n.d., available at www.visitblackpool.com/things-to-do/blackpool-illuminations-and-lightpool/illuminating-history-(1)/ (accessed November 2024).
10. "History & heritage", The Blackpool Tower, n.d., available at www.theblackpooltower.com/history/ (accessed November 2024).

11. "From Wakes Week to working class holidays: the 20th-century holiday", Lancashire Museums, n.d., available at www.lancashiremuseumsstories.wordpress.com/2021/07/30/from-wakes-week-to-working-class-holidays-the-20th-century-holiday/ (accessed November 2024).
12. Pat Mancini, *Queen of Blackpool* (Worcestershire, Polperro Heritage Press, 2008)
13. Pimlott (1976), see note 7.
14. Kathryn Ferry, "Summer holiday revolution: when were Britons first allowed to take paid holiday?" BBC History Extra, 22 June 2020, available at www.historyextra.com/period/20th-century/holiday-revolution-were-all-going-on-a-summer-holiday/ (accessed November 2024).
15. Pimlott (1976), see note 8.
16. Ibid.
17. Ibid.
18. Ferry (2020), see note 14.
19. Pimlott (1976), see note 8.
20. Ferry (2020), see note 14.
21. John Hudson, *Wakes Week: Memories of Mill Town Holidays* (Stroud, Alan Sutton Publishing, 1992).
22. Ibid.
23. Ibid.
24. Ibid.
25. "Boom to bust – the decline of the cotton industry", BBC Online, n.d., available at www.bbc.co.uk/nationonfilm/topics/textiles/background_decline.shtml (accessed November 2024).
26. Neal Keeling, "Manchester libraries, Salford and Bury Museums to get boost to funding", *Manchester Evening News*, 20 March 2023, available at www.manchestereveningnews.co.uk/whats-on/arts-culture-news/manchester-libraries-salford-bury-museums-26508994 (accessed November 2024).

Chapter 9: Good Morning Campers!

1. Billy Butlin, Butlin's slogan.
2. "Pitching the value: 2024 economic benefit report: Holiday parks and campsites", UK Caravan & Camping Alliance, n.d., available at www.ukcca.org.uk/report-2024/#pdfFindings (accessed February 2025).
3. J.A.R. Pimlott, *The Englishman's Holiday: A social history* (Brighton, The Harvester Press Ltd, 1976).
4. Sir Billy Butlin, *The Billy Butlin Story* (London, Robson Books Ltd, 1998).
5. Jill Drower, *Good Clean Fun: A social history of Britain's first holiday camp* (London, Scrudge Books, 2018).
6. "Seaside camp marks its centenary", BBC News, 5 April 2006, available at http://news.bbc.co.uk/1/hi/england/norfolk/4825238.stm (accessed February 2025).
7. Rose Staveley-Wadham, "'The most remarkable, invigorating and enjoyable holiday you will ever have' – the holiday camp phenomenon", The British Newspaper Archive, 30 July 2019, available at www.blog.britishnewspaperarchive.co.uk/2019/07/30/the-holiday-camp-phenomenon/ (accessed February 2025).

Notes

8. "A Potted History; the story of Potters resorts and the Potter family", Potters Resorts, n.d., available at www.pottersresorts.com/the-potter-family/ (accessed March 2025).
9. Staveley-Wadham (2019), see note 7.
10. Butlin (1998), see note 4.
11. "Dovercourt Camp: Extract from a report by Women's Voluntary Services, 12 January 1939", National Archives, n.d., ref MH 55/689, available at www.nationalarchives.gov.uk/education/resources/kindertransport/dovercourt-camp/ (accessed August 2025).
12. Staveley-Wadham (2019), see note 7.
13. Kathryn Ferry, *The Nation's Host: Butlin's and the story of the British seaside* (London, Viking, 2016).
14. Ibid.
15. Staveley-Wadham (2019), see note 7.
16. Ferry (2016), see note 13.
17. Jack Grey & Matthew Richards, "Pontins: What happened to the former UK holiday park giant?" BBC News, 1 December 2023, available at www.bbc.co.uk/news/uk-wales-67589538 (accessed February 2025).
18. "About Haven", Haven, n.d., available at https://news.haven.com/about/haven (accessed February 2025).
19. Ferry (2016), see note 13.
20. "Bobby Butlin: Chairman of Butlins from 1968 to 1984", *The Times*, 10 February 2009, available at www.thetimes.com/travel/destinations/uk-travel/bobby-butlin-chairman-of-butlins-from-1968-to-1984-3f66pgl8jqg (accessed February 2025).
21. "Our history", Center Parcs, n.d., available at https://corporate.centerparcs.co.uk/about-us/history.html (accessed March 2025).
22. Ibid.
23. Gill Martin, "Inside out, it's a real tropical paradise", *Daily Express*, 8 August 1987.
24. Ibid.
25. Ibid.
26. Lauren Bell, "The best UK holiday parks for your summer getaway", *Which?*, 16 July 2025, available at https://www.which.co.uk/reviews/holiday-lets/article/uk-holiday-parks-and-resorts-aFkHw2W8X7x8 (accessed July 2025).

Chapter 10: The Rush to the Med

1. Leo Roozenstraten & Leo Caerts, "Y Viva España", 1971.
2. "Travel Trends 2024", Office for National Statistics, 26 August 2025, available at www.ons.gov.uk/peoplepopulationandcommunity/leisureandtourism/articles/traveltrends/2024#:~:text=1.,Italy%20(4.8%20million%20visits)(accessed August 2025).
3. Ibid.
4. Robin Searle "Turkey hails 16.6% increase in UK visitor numbers in 2024", *Travel Weekly*, 3 February 2025, available at www.travelweekly.co.uk/in-depth/turkey-hails-16-6-increase-in-uk-visitor-numbers-in-2024#:~:text=Tour%20OperatorsFeb%203%2C%202025,Tour%20Operators (accessed March 2025).

5. Jonathan Miles, *Once Upon a Time World: The dark and sparkling story of the French Riviera* (London, Atlantic Books, 2024).
6. Ibid.
7. Ibid.
8. "Le Train Bleu: Paris to Menton", Pure France, 4 March 2021, available at www.purefrance.com/en/blog/le-train-bleu-paris-to-menton (accessed March 2025).
9. Zelda Fitzgerald, *Save Me the Waltz* (London, Penguin, 2022).
10. Rose Staveley-Wadham, "Travelling Abroad: The astonishing rise of the British holidaymaker", *The British Newspaper Archive*, 13 August 2024, available at www.britishnewspaperarchive.co.uk/2024/08/13/history-of-travelling-abroad/ (accessed April 2025).
11. Roger Bray & Vladimir Raitz, *Flight to the Sun: The story of the holiday revolution* (London, Continuum, 2001).
12. Ibid.
13. "Explore Our Past", British Airways, n.d., available at www.britishairways.com/content/information/about-ba/history-and-heritage/explore-our-past (accessed March 2025).
14. Karla Cripps, "Thomas Cook: A history of one of the world's oldest travel firms", CNN, 23 September 2019, available at www.edition.cnn.com/travel/article/thomas-cook-history-timeline (accessed March 2025).
15. Bray & Raitz (2001), see note 11.
16. "Benidorm – an unlikely sustainability hub in the Mediterranean", European Commission, 27 March 2025, available at www.smart-tourism-capital.ec.europa.eu/press-1/news/benidorm-unlikely-sustainability-hub-mediterranean-2025-03-27_en (accessed March 2025).
17. Stephen Burgen, "Tallest apartment building in EU finally completed in Benidorm", *Guardian*, 20 July 2021, available at www.theguardian.com/world/2021/jul/20/tallest-apartment-building-in-eu-finally-completed-in-benidorm (accessed March 2025).
18. "Our History", Hotel Pez Espada, n.d., available at www.hotelpezespada.com/en/our-history (accessed March 2025).
19. Stephen Emms, "Torremelinos: Where Spain's gay rights movement began", BBC Travel, 6 June 2003, available at www.bbc.co.uk/travel/article/20230605-torremolinos-where-spains-gay-rights-movement-began (accessed April 2025).
20. Bray & Raitz (2001), see note 11.
21. Rose Stavley-Wadham (2024), see note 10.
22. Dave Richardson, *Let's Go: A History of Package Holidays and Escorted Tours* (Stroud, Amberley Publishing, 2016).
23. Juliet Dennis, "Yugotours staff reunion more than 20 years after operator closed", *Travel Weekly*, 1 May 2019, available at www.travelweekly.co.uk/news/yugotours-staff-reunion-more-than-20-years-after-operator-closed (accessed August 2025).
24. Alison Adams, "How many tourists visit Mallorca each year?" Hotelagio, 15 September 2025, available at www.hotelagio.com/mallorca-tourism-statistics/ (accessed September 2025).

25. Ashifa Kassam, "Spain proposes 100% tax on homes bought by non-EU residents", *Guardian*, 13 January 2025, available at www.theguardian.com/world/2025/jan/13/spain-proposes-100-tax-on-homes-bought-by-non-eu-residents (accessed March 2025).
26. Greg Dickinson, "Venice doubles controversial entry fee for 2025 season", *Telegraph*, 17 February 2025, available at www.telegraph.co.uk/travel/destinations/europe/italy/veneto/venice/venice-tourist-tax-entry-fee-how-pay/ (accessed March 2025).
27. "Spanish Tourism Satellite Account", Instituto Nacional de Estadística, 26 December 2024, available at www.ine.es/dyngs/INEbase/en/operacion.htm?c=Estadistica_C&cid=1254736169169&menu=ultiDatos&idp=1254735576863 (accessed March 2025).

Chapter 11: Cruise Control

1. Jacques Cousteau, *Life and Death in a Coral Sea* (London, Cassell, 1971).
2. Alessandro Scotto di Santolo, "Europe's rainiest city is stunningly beautiful but gets terrible weather", *Express*, 7 October 2023, available at www.express.co.uk/news/world/1818932/europe-rainiest-city-bergen-norway (accessed February 2025).
3. "Viking Ocean Viking Saturn ship information", *Travel Weekly*, n.d., available at www.travelweekly.com/Cruise/Viking-Ocean/Viking-Saturn (accessed February 2025).
4. Chris Leadbeater, "A first look at Icon of the Seas, the world's biggest cruise ship", *Telegraph*, 22 January 2024, available at www.telegraph.co.uk/travel/cruises/articles/biggest-cruise-ship-icon-of-the-seas-maiden-voyage-miami/ (accessed February 2025).
5. "2024 Global source passenger market report", CLIA, n.d., available at www.cruising.org/resources/2024-global-source-passenger-market-report (accessed March 2025).
6. "State of the cruise industry report 2025", CLIA, n.d., available at www.cruising.org/sites/default/files/2025-05/State%20of%20the%20Cruise%20Industry%20Report%202025.pdf (accessed March 2025).
7. Max Woolf, "45+ Cruise industry statistics for 2025 [Ships, passengers, capacity, revenue and more]", photoAID, 31 March 2025, available at www.photoaid.com/blog/cruise-industry-statistics/#:~:text=Top%20Cruise%20Industry%20Statistics,-In%202024%2C%20approximately&text=A%20total%20of%20323%20cruise,from%20North%20America%20in%202022 (accessed April 2025).
8. Danny Birchall, "Flying the flag: A history of the P&O brand", P&O Heritage, 26 September 2024, available at www.poheritage.com/story/brand-history/#event-posabrandahistory (accessed March 2025).
9. Ibid.
10. "The history of a transatlantic cruise", *Cunard*, n.d., available at www.cunard.com/en-gb/cruise-destinations/transatlantic-cruises/history-of-a-transatlantic-cruise (accessed May 2025).

11. Ibid.
12. Charles Dickens, *American Notes* (London, Penguin Classics, 2000).
13. Rose Staveley-Wadham, "The culture of the cruise – A look at the history of the cruise holiday", The British Newspaper Archive, 3 August 2020, available at https://blog.britishnewspaperarchive.co.uk/2020/08/03/the-history-of-the-cruise-holiday/ (accessed March 2025).
14. Ibid.
15. Ibid.
16. Jacob Lyngsoe, "The lost origin", The Cruise Insider, 12 May 2020, available at www.cruiseinsider.dk/post/the-lost-origin-of-cruising, (accessed March 2025).
17. William Makepeace Thackeray, *Notes on a journey from Cornhill to Grand Cairo* (California, Createspace Independent Publishing Platform, 2014).
18. Ibid.
19. Ibid.
20. Darko Manevski, "Journal from first commercial cruise around the world goes on sale" *Newsweek*, 15 July 2022, available at www.newsweek.com/journal-first-commercial-cruise-around-world-sale-1724910 (accessed March 2025).
21. Darryl Austin, "The history of the world's first cruise ship built solely for luxurious travel", *Smithsonian Magazine*, 22 July 2021, available at www.smithsonianmag.com/history/history-worlds-first-cruise-ship-built-solely-luxurious-travel-180978254/ (accessed March 2025).
22. Ibid.
23. Chris Frame, Rachelle Cross and Stephen M. Payne, *180 Years of Cunard* (Cheltenham, The History Press, 2020).
24. Ibid.
25. Rumeana Jahangir, "WW1 sinking of Lusitania recalled", BBC News, 27 March 2015, available at www.bbc.co.uk/news/uk-england-merseyside-32020234 (accessed March 2025).
26. "The history of a transatlantic cruise", Cunard, n.d., available at www.cunard.com/en-gb/cruise-destinations/transatlantic-cruises/history-of-a-transatlantic-cruise (accessed May 2025).
27. "Cruising in the 1970s and 1980s! A fascinating look at how it was", Ritzy Travel Guide, n.d., available at www.youtube.com/watch?v=rdjt1veVOdk&t=170s (accessed April 2025).
28. "Gangway to paradise", P&O Heritage, n.d., available at www.youtube.com/watch?v=XevYJDKq65Y (accessed April 2025).
29. Emily Wright, "Majorca tourist chaos as seaside city invaded by 23 cruise ships in one week", *Express*, 5 May 2025, available at www.express.co.uk/news/world/2051007/majorca-tourist-chaos-cruise-ships-docked (accessed May 2025).
30. Ella Sagar, "Clia UK and Ireland hails record passenger numbers for 2024", *Travel Weekly*, 8 May 2025, available at: www.travelweekly.co.uk/news/clia-uk-and-ireland-surpasses-record-passenger-numbers-for-2024 (accessed May 2025).
31. "Historic 7-ship day at Nassau Cruise Port", Nassau Cruise Port, 12 March 2024, available at www.nassaucruiseport.com/content/news/historic-7-ship-day-at-nassau-cruise-port/ (accessed April 2025).

32. Rosie Frost, "Which European cities are trying to cut back the number of cruise ship visits?", Euronews, 13 May 2025, available at www.euronews.com/travel/2024/05/13/cruise-ships-erosion-air-pollution-and-overtourism-are-driving-cities-towards-bans (accessed May 2025).
33. Michael Smith and Jim Wyss, "Luxury Cruises Pours $1.5 billion into private islands, beaches", Bloomberg, 8 May 2024, available at www.bloomberg.com/news/features/2024-05-08/royal-caribbean-norwegian-cruises-buy-caribbean-islands-beaches?embedded-checkout=true (accessed March 2025).

Chapter 12: Holidays on Screen

1. *Fawlty Towers*, "Communication Problems", Season 2, Episode 1, 1979, BBC.
2. Rose Staveley-Wadham, "Travelling abroad: The astonishing rise of the British holidaymaker", The British Newspaper Archive, 13 August 2024, available at https://blog.britishnewspaperarchive.co.uk/2024/08/13/history-of-travelling-abroad/ (accessed March 2025).
3. Lottie Gross, "How Britain fell out of love with the caravan", *Telegraph*, 17 July 2025 www.telegraph.co.uk/travel/comment/how-britain-fell-out-of-love-with-caravan/ (accessed July 2025).
4. Mary-Jo Murphy, "Rudolf Valentino in 'The Sheik'", *New York Times*, 7 July 2014, available at www.nytimes.com/2014/11/07/nyregion/weekend-entertainments-from-the-archives-of-the-new-york-times.html (accessed March 2025).
5. Ibid.
6. Ibid.
7. Guy Lodge, "From steamy summertime romances to spring-break chaos: The 20 best films about holidays", *Guardian*, 20 July 2024, available at www.theguardian.com/film/article/2024/jul/20/from-steamy-summertime-romances-to-spring-break-chaos-the-20-best-films-about-holidays (accessed March 2025).
8. Frances Mayes, *Under the Tuscan Sun* (London, Transworld, 2004).
9. Elizabeth Gilbert, *Eat, Pray, Love: One woman's search for everything across Italy, India and Indonesia* (London, Bloomsbury, 2007).
10. "Summer Holiday (1963 film)", Wikipedia, n.d., https://en.wikipedia.org/wiki/Summer_Holiday_(1963_film) accessed (March 2025).
11. "Alan Whicker interview", *Wanderlust*, 1 October 2004, available at www.wanderlustmagazine.com/inspiration/alan-whicker-interview/ (accessed December 2024).
12. Alan Whicker, *Within Whicker's World: An autobiography* (London, Elm Tree Books, 1982).
13. Ibid.
14. "'Holiday' programme axed after 37 years", *The Standard*, 13 April 2012, available at www.standard.co.uk/hp/front/holiday-programme-axed-after-37-years-7207867.html (accessed March 2025).
15. Steven Morris, "Hotel that inspired John Cleese's classic Fawlty Towers is demolished", *Guardian*, 16 March 2016, available at www.theguardian.com/tv-and-radio/2016/mar/16/hotel-inspired-john-cleese-classic-comedy-fawlty-towers-demolished (accessed March 2024).

16. Jodie Halford, "Morning campers! The inside story of 80s sitcom Hi-de-Hi!", *BBC News*, 30 January 2018, available at www.bbc.co.uk/news/uk-england-essex-42772378 (accessed March 2024).
17. Ibid.
18. Sam Wollaston, "Benidorm review – it's like an embarrassing uncle who's stuck in the 1970s", *Guardian*, 26 Jan 2016, available at www.theguardian.com/tv-and-radio/2016/jan/26/benidorm-review-silent-witness (accessed December 2024).
19. Jason Deans, "More than 7 million jet in for Benidorm", *Guardian*, 28 February 2011, available at www.theguardian.com/media/2011/feb/28/benidorm-itv1-tv-ratings (accessed March 2025).
20. Gemma Daubeney, "How has Bergerac's island changed since the 1980s?" *BBC News*, 16 March 2025, available at www.bbc.co.uk/news/articles/cg5dzqe9z2no (accessed March 2025).
21. Andrew Ffrench, "Inspector Morse ITV series raised millions of tourism cash for city", *Oxford Mail*, 11 March 2023, available at www.oxfordmail.co.uk/news/23378344.inspector-morse-itv-series-raised-millions-tourism-cash-city/ (accessed December 2024).
22. Sam Wollaston, "Sun, sea and subtitles – how Eldorado became TV's biggest flop", *Guardian*, 9 July 2018, available at www.theguardian.com/tv-and-radio/2018/jul/09/eldorado-bbc-one-soap-opera (accessed March 2024).
23. Holly Fleet, "Michael Palin: Around the World in 80 Days star talks 'worst' moment 'In a very bad mood'" *Express*, 29 September 2020, available at www.express.co.uk/celebrity-news/1341070/Michael-Palin-travels-of-a-lifetime-around-the-world-in-80-days-worst-day-filming-news (accessed March 2025).
24. Ibid.
25. Alex Garland, *The Beach* (London, Viking, 1996).
26. Philip Sherwell, "Leonardo DiCaprio's beach, Maya Bay, closed to tourists", *The Times*, 27 May 2018, available at www.thetimes.com/uk/science/article/dicaprio-s-beach-closed-to-tourists-in-bid-to-rescue-ruined-coral-from-the-brink-wv3djxl6p (accessed March 2025).
27. Agence France-Presse, "Thai court orders repair of The Beach location 22 years after filming", *Guardian*, 13 September 2022, available at www.theguardian.com/world/2022/sep/13/thai-court-orders-repair-of-the-beach-location-maya-bay-ko-phi-phi-leh-22-years-after-filming (accessed December 2024).
28. Chris Leadbeater, "The fascinating story behind 'hobbit tourism' in New Zealand", *Telegraph*, 19 December 2021, available at www.telegraph.co.uk/travel/destinations/oceania/new-zealand/fascinating-story-behind-hobbit-tourism-new-zealand/ (accessed December 2024).
29. Jade Bremner, "Game of Thrones filming boosts Dubrovnik tourism numbers", *Radio Times*, 9 January 2015, available at www.radiotimes.com/tv/drama/game-of-thrones-filming-boosts-dubrovnik-tourism-numbers/ (accessed December 2024).
30. Katelyn Mensah, "Sir Michael Palin spills on next TV series amid travel host competition", *Radio Times*, 25 September 2023, available at www.radiotimes.com/tv/entertainment/michael-palin-new-tv-series-newsupdate/ (accessed March 2024).

31. David Craig, "Michael Palin says his next travel documentary could be his last", *Radio Times*, 11 November 2024, available at www.radiotimes.com/tv/documentaries/michael-palin-travel-documentary-possibly-last-newsupdate/ (accessed March 2024).

Chapter 13: The New Wave

1. *Newsnight*, 3 December 1999, BBC.
2. Rory Cellan-Jones, "Amazon's profitless path", BBC News, 15 July 2015, available at www.bbc.co.uk/news/technology-33534256 (accessed April 2025).
3. Hayley Spencer, "eBay at 25: How the online marketplace paved the way for the circular shopping revolution", *Independent*, 4 September 2020, available at www.independent.co.uk/life-style/fashion/ebay-25-years-circular-shopping-depop-auction-sites-a9705336.html (accessed April 2025).
4. Kevin May, "How 25 years of the Web inspired the travel revolution", *Guardian*, 12 March 2014, available at www.theguardian.com/travel/2014/mar/12/how-25-years-of-the-web-inspired-travel-revolution (accessed April 2025).
5. Cath Urquhart, *The Times Holiday Handbook* (Norfolk, Navigator Guides, 2006).
6. May (2014), see note 4.
7. Lee Glendinning, "Row over dirty tricks led to decade of hostilities", *Guardian*, 2 August 2007, available at www.theguardian.com/business/2007/aug/02/theairlineindustry.britishairways (accessed April 2025).
8. Chris Leadbeater, "How we went from an annual two-week holiday to six trips a year", *Telegraph*, 2 September 2023, available at www.telegraph.co.uk/travel/travel-truths/multi-break-britain-death-of-two-week-holiday-cheap-flights/ (accessed March 2025).
9. Luke Peters, "From small-scale startup to low-cost leviathan – marking 40 years of Ryanair", Aerotime, 17 February 2024, available at www.aerotime.aero/articles/40-year-ryanair-history (accessed April 2025).
10. Ibid.
11. Louise Butcher, "Aviation: European liberalisation, 1986–2002", UK Parliament Online, 13 May 2010, available at https://researchbriefings.files.parliament.uk/documents/SN00182/SN00182.pdf (accessed May 2025).
12. Amanda Morison, "Camping for yummy mummies", *Guardian*, 2 September 2006, available at www.theguardian.com/travel/2006/sep/02/camping.shortbreaks.unitedkingdom (accessed June 2025).
13. Susie Mesure, "The Eagle: Britain's first gastropub celebrates its 25th birthday", *Independent*, 10 January 2016, available at www.independent.co.uk/news/uk/home-news/the-eagle-britain-s-first-gastropub-celebrates-its-25th-birthday-a6804221.html (accessed April 2025).

Chapter 14: Passports Down

1. Patricia Brady, *Martha Washington: An American Life* (New York, Penguin USA, 2006).
2. Li Yuan, 'China silences critics over deadly virus outbreak, *New York Times*, 22 January 2020, available at www.nytimes.com/2020/01/22/health/virus-corona.

html#:~:text=The%20central%20government%20backed%20Wuhan's,during%20an%20inspection%20in%20Wuhan (accessed November 2024).
3. Associated Press, "Coronavirus: Northern Italian towns close schools and businesses", *Guardian*, 23 February 2020, available at www.theguardian.com/world/2020/feb/23/coronavirus-northern-italian-towns-close-schools-and-businesses (accessed November 2024).
4. Ibid.
5. Rob Gill, "Industry going through it's 'deepest crisis', says ABTA boss", TTG, 7 May 2020, available at www.ttgmedia.com/news/industry-going-through-its-deepest-crisis-says-abta-boss-22827#:~:text=Covid%2D19%20has%20caused%20the,Abta's%20chief%20executive%20Mark%20Tanzer (accessed November 2024).
6. Julia Kollewe, "UK airport passenger numbers drop 75% to 74m in 2020", *Guardian*, 13 June 2021, available at www.theguardian.com/business/2021/jun/13/uk-airport-passenger-numbers-drop-75-to-74-million-in-2020 (accessed December 2024).
7. Imogen Braddick, "Major incident declared as thousands flock to beaches on England's south coast", *The Standard*, 25 June 2020, available at www.standard.co.uk/news/uk/major-incident-declared-beaches-england-south-coast-hot-weather-a4480221.html (accessed December 2024).
8. Ibid.
9. Helen Pidd, "'The litter was a shock': 2020's Covid-driven rush on UK national parks", *Guardian*, 1 January 2021, available at www.theguardian.com/environment/2021/jan/01/the-litter-was-a-shock-2020-covid-rush-on-uk-national-parks (accessed November 2024).
10. Peter Lord, *Clarence Waite and the Welsh Art World – the Betws-y-coed Artists' Colony 1844-1914* (Llandudno, Coast & Country Productions, 2009).
11. Ibid.
12. Anya Chapman, "How the pandemic has changed holidaymaking in Britain", The Conversation, 28 September 2021, available at www.theconversation.com/how-the-pandemic-has-changed-holidaymaking-in-britain-168409 (accessed December 2024).
13. "Sea Passenger Statistics, All Routes", gov.uk, 17 November 2021, available at: www.gov.uk/government/statistics/sea-passenger-statistics-all-routes-2020 (accessed December 2024).
14. Jack Wright, "Is the Pandemic staycation boom OVER", *Daily Mail*, 14 November 2022, available at www.dailymail.co.uk/news/article-11425325/Is-pandemic-staycation-boom-Average-price-UK-holiday-bookings-plunges.html (accessed December 2024).
15. Miles Brignall, "'Prices are ridiculous': UK holiday costs more than Europe as demand grows", *Guardian*, 19 June 2021, available at www.theguardian.com/business/2021/jun/19/prices-are-ridiculous-uk-holiday-costs-more-than-europe-as-demand-grows (accessed November 2024).
16. Emma Munbodh, "Center Parcs accused of exploiting lockdown with 'holidays pricier than the Caribbean'", *Mirror*, 6 April 2021, available at www.mirror.

co.uk/money/center-parcs-accused-exploiting-lockdown-23861329 (accessed November 2024).
17. Julia Kollewe, "Holiday bookings surge in UK after lockdown exit plans revealed", *Guardian*, 23 February 2021, available at www.theguardian.com/business/2021/feb/23/holiday-bookings-uk-lockdown-exit-plans-easyjet-tui (accessed November 2024).

Chapter 15: Where Next?

1. James Bryce, *Speeches and Letters of Abraham Lincoln 1832-65* (Charleston, Legare Street Press, 2022).
2. "Destinations: The Holiday and Travel Show", Destinations Show, n.d., available at www.destinationsshow.com/london/benefits-exhibiting (accessed May 2025).
3. Georgina Hutton, "Research Briefing: Tourism: Statistics and Policy", House of Commons Library, 18 March 2025, available at https://researchbriefings.files.parliament.uk/documents/SN06022/SN06022.pdf (accessed May 2025).
4. Alastair Dawber, "How Presidency saved Trump from ruin and made him a fortune," *The Times*, May 13 2025, available at www.thetimes.com/us/american-politics/article/how-trump-got-rich-president-worth-7qqr8csg9 (accessed May 2025).
5. Jesse Hassenger, "Trump's attack on the film industry is a sign of xenophobic contempt," *Guardian*, 5 May 2025, available at www.theguardian.com/global/2025/may/05/hollywood-trump-tariffs-international (accessed May 2025).
6. Jeffrey Kluger, "The truth about Donald Trump's narcissism," *Time*, 11 Aug 2015, available at https://time.com/3992363/trump-narcissism/ (accessed May 2025).
7. "Number of holidays taken per person reaches new high as people seek a getaway to get together", ABTA, 8 October 2024, available at www.abta.com/news/number-holidays-taken-person-reaches-new-high-people-seek-getaway-get-together (accessed May 2025).
8. Nick Beake, "Valencia floods: Spain clings to fragments of hope in time of disaster", BBC News, 14 November 2024, available at www.bbc.co.uk/news/articles/c3vl11511gvo (accessed May 2025).
9. "Air Travel and Sustainability", IATA, n.d., available at www.iata.org/en/youandiata/travelers/environment/ (accessed May 2025).
10. Ibid.
11. Sirin Kale, "How Airbnb is ruining local communities in North Wales," *Guardian*, 10 August 2022, available at www.theguardian.com/technology/2022/aug/10/i-wanted-my-children-to-grow-up-here-how-airbnb-is-ruining-local-communities-in-north-wales (accessed May 2025).
12. Rob Perkins, "How AirBnB went wrong and how to fix it," *Responsible Travel*, n.d., available at https://www.responsibletravel.com/copy/how-airbnb-went-wrong#:~:text=How%20does%20Airbnb%20cause%20overtourism,recruit%20new%20hosts%2C%20fuelling%20growth (accessed May 2025).
13. María Ramírez, "What will Spain look like when it runs out of water?" *Guardian*, 15 February 2024, available at www.theguardian.com/commentisfree/2024/feb/15/spain-water-barcelona-farmers-tourism-catalonia-drought (accessed May 2025).

14. Sotiras Nikitas, "Greek PM Mitsotakis says climate change can benefit from climate shift", Bloomberg, 22 September 2023, available at www.bloomberg.com/news/articles/2023-09-22/mitsotakis-says-greek-tourism-can-benefit-from-climate-change (accessed May 2025).
15. "LEVEN wants you to vacation in the Metaverse", The Spaces, 21 June 2023, available at www,thespaces.com/leven-wants-you-to-vacation-in-the-metaverse/ (accessed May 2025).
16. "Vineyards in Kent", Visit Kent, n.d., available at www.visitkent.co.uk/stay-and-eat/food-and-drink/vineyards-in-kent/ (accessed May 2025).
17. Rebecca Pitcairn, "Welcome to Sussex wine country and its 138 vineyards", *The Argus*, 6 October 2024, available at www.theargus.co.uk/news/24631180.wines-put-sussex-literally-map/ (accessed May 2025).

Image credits

The publisher would like to thank the following for their kind permission to reproduce their photographs:

(Key: b-below/bottom; t-top)

Colour plate 1: Getty Images: Sepia Times / Universal Images Group (b). **The Metropolitan Museum of Art:** The Elisha Whittelsey Collection, The Elisha Whittelsey Fund, 1959 (t). **Colour plate 2: Bridgeman Images:** From the British Library archive (b). **Rijksmuseum, Amsterdam:** Legacy of Mr. JG de Groot Jamin, Amsterdam (t). **Colour plate 3: Getty Images:** Central Press / Hulton Archive (b). **Mary Evans Picture Library:** Francis Frith (t). **Colour plate 4: Getty Images:** Daily Herald Archive / SSPL (b); Chris Ware / Archive Photos (t). **Colour plate 5: Bridgeman Images:** © The Advertising Archives. **Colour plate 6: Alamy Stock Photo:** Pictorial Press Ltd (b). **Getty Images:** Felix Man / Picture Post (t). **Colour plate 7: Alamy Stock Photo:** MAD / Associated Press (b). © **P&O Heritage Collection:** (t). **Colour plate 8: Alamy Stock Photo:** Jasmine Bryan (t); Emilio Morenatti / Associated Press (b).

Bibliography

Allen, Louise, *The Georgian Seaside* (Louise Allen, 2016).
Andrews, Malcolm, *The Search for the Picturesque: Landscape Aesthetics and Tourism in Britain, 1760–1800* (Aldershot, Scolar Press, 1989).
Austen, Jane, *Northanger Abbey* (London, Penguin Classics 2003).
Austen-Leigh, William and Richard Arthur, *Life and Letters of Jane Austen* (London, Smith Elder & Co, 1913).
Averby, Karen, *Seaside Hotels* (Britain's Heritage) (Stroud, Amberley Publishing, 2018).
Bennett, Arnold, *The Grand Babylon Hotel* (London, Chatto & Windus, 1971).
Berry, Sue, *Georgian Brighton* (Bognor Regis, Phillimore & Co, 2008).
Black, Jeremy, *Nineteenth-Century Britain* (London, Macmillan Foundations, 2003).
Black, Jeremy, *The British Abroad: The Grand Tour in the Eighteenth Century* (Stroud, Sutton Publishing, 1992).
Booth, Charles, *Life and Labour of the People in London* (Charleston, Legare Street Press, 2022).
Brady, Patricia, *Martha Washington: An American Life* (New York, Penguin USA, 2006).
Bray, Roger and Raitz, Vladmimir, *Flight to the Sun: The Story of the Holiday Revolution* (London, Continuum, 2001).
Bryce, James, *Speeches and Letters of Abraham Lincoln 1832–65* (Charleston, Legare Street Press, 2022).
Burney, Frances, *The Diary and letters of Madame D'Arblay, Vol II* (London, Vizetelly & Co, 1891).
Butlin, Sir Billy, *The Billy Butlin Story* (London, Robson Books Ltd, 1998).
Collard, James and Picardie, Justine, *Gleneagles: The Glorious Playground* (New York, Rizzoli, 2024).
Constance, Hazel, *First in the Field: A Century of the Camping and Caravanning Club* (Coventry, CCC, 2001).
Cousteau, Jacques, *Life and Death in a Coral Sea* (London, Cassell, 1971).
Dalrymple, William, *The Anarchy: The Relentless Rise of the East India Company* (London, Bloomsbury, 2020).
Defoe, Daniel, *A Tour through the Whole Island of Great Britain* (London, J. M. Dent & Sons Ltd, 1962).
Dickens, Charles, *Dombey & Son* (London, Oxford University Press, 1950).
Dickens, Charles, *Short Stories Volume V* (Munich, Grin Verlag, 2009).
Dixon, Kevin, *Torquay: A Social History* (Kevin Dixon, 2022).
Dolan, Brian, *Ladies of the Grand Tour* (London, Flamingo, 2002).
Drower, Jill, *Good Clean Fun: A Social History of Britain's first holiday camp* (London, Scrudge Books, 2018).
Euripides, *Iphigenia in Taurus* (London, Penguin Classics, 1974).
Ferry, Kathryn *The Nation's Host: Butlin's and the story of the British Seaside* (London, Viking, 2016).
Fitzgerald, Zelda, *Save Me the Waltz* (London, Penguin, 2022).

Floyer, John, *Psychrolousia: Or, the History of Cold Bathing, Both Ancient and Modern* (Charleston, Legare Street Press, 2018).
Frank, Anne, *The Diary of a Young Girl* (London, Penguin, 2007).
Garland, Alex, *The Beach*, (London, Viking, 1996).
Gilbert, Elizabeth, *Eat, Pray, Love: One Woman's Search for Everything across Italy, India and Indonesia* (London, Bloomsbury, 2007).
Gill, Stephen, *William Wordsworth: A Life* (London, Oxford University Press).
Gilpin, William, *Observations on the River Wye* (Surrey, Richmond Publishing Co Ltd, 1973).
Grundy Heape, R., *Buxton Under the Dukes of Devonshire* (Robert Hale Limited, 1948).
Hannavy, John, *The English Seaside in Victorian and Edwardian Times* (London, Shire Library, 2003).
Harper, Charles. G., *Cycle Rides Around London* (London, Chapman & Hall Ltd, 1902).
Havins, P. J. N., *The Spas of England* (Robert Hale & Co, 1976).
Hefferman, Hilary, *Voices of Kent and East Sussex Hop Pickers: Tempus Oral History Series* (Cheltenham, The History Press, 2004).
Hembry, Phyllis, *The English Spa, 1560–1815: A Social History* (Associated University Press, 1990).
Hembry, Phyllis, *British Spas from 1815 to the Present: A Social History* (Fairleigh Dickinson Univ Press, 1997).
Hern, A., *The Seaside Holiday* (The Cresset Press, 1967).
Hibbert, Christopher, *The Grand Tour* (London, Thames Methuen, 1987).
Hiram Holding, Thomas, *Cycle and Camp* (London, De Vere & Co, 1898).
Hiram Holding, Thomas, *The Camper's Handbook* (Charleston, Legare Street Press, 2022).
Hollinghurst, Hugh, *Southport History Tour* (Stroud, Amberley Publishing, 2018).
Howell, Sarah, *The Seaside* (London, Cassell and Collier Macmillian, 1974).
Hudson, John, *Wakes Weeks: Memories of Mill Town Holidays* (Stroud, Alan Sutton Publishing, 1992).
Hussey, Christopher, *The Picturesque* (London, Frank Cass & Co, 1967).
Hutchinson, William, *An Excursion to the Lakes in Westmorland and Cumberland: With a Tour through Part of the Northern Counties in the Years 1773 and 1774, 2 vols* (London, J Wilkie, 1776).
Jerome, Jerome K., *Three Men in a Boat* (London, Collins Classics, 2012).
Johnson, Samuel, *A Journey to the Western Isles of Scotland AND The Journal of a Tour to the Hebrides* (London, Penguin Classics, 1984).
King, Melanie, *The Secret History of English Spas* (Bodleian Library, 2021).
Langrish Warner, Valerie, *A Warner Story – Seasons in the Sun 1931–2010* (2010).
Lewis, W. S. (Ed), *Horace Walpole's Correspondence, Sir Horace Mann VI, 29 Jan 1762–8 March 1768* (London, Oxford University Press, 1960).
Lord, Peter, *Clarence Waite and the Welsh Art World – the Betws-y-Coed Artists Colony 1844–1914* (Llandudno, Coast & Country Productions, 2009).
Lloyd, Christopher (Ed.), *The Diary of Fanny Burney* (London, Roger Ingram, 1948).

Bibliography

Mancini, Pat, *Queen of Blackpool* (Worcs, Polperro Heritage Press, 2008).
Major, Susan, *Early Victorian Railway Excursions* (Sussex, The Harvester Press, 1976).
Marsh, John, *Hops and Hopping* (London, Simpkin Marshall Hamilton Ken, 1892).
Mason, David and Heather, Alan, *Torquay: A Century of Change* (Cheltenham, The History Press, 2006).
Matthews, Henry, *Diary of an Invalid, the Journal of a Tour in Portugal, Italy, Switzerland and France* (Miami, Hardpress Ltd, 2019).
Mayes, Frances, *Under the Tuscan Sun* (London, Transworld, 2004).
Moorcroft, Geoffrey *The Last Divine Office: Henry VIII and the Dissolution of the Monasteries* (New York, Bluebridge, 2012).
Patterson, Michael, *A Brief History of Life in Victorian Britain* (London, Robinson, 2008).
Patterson, Michael, *Railway Hotels* (Stroud, Amberley Publishing, 2018).
Pimlott, J. A. R., *The Englishman's Holiday: A Social History* (London, Faber & Faber Ltd, 1947).
Richardson, Dave, *Let's Go: A History of Package Holidays and Escorted Tours* (Stroud, Amberley Publishing, 2016).
Seward, Anna, *The Letters of Anna Seward: written between the years 1784 and 1807* (London, Forgotten Books, 2019).
Smiles, Samuel, *The Life of George Stephenson, Railway Engineer* (Charleston, Legare Street Press, 2023).
Shaw, George Bernard, *Plays Pleasant* (London, Penguin Books, 1981).
Thackray, William Makepeace, *Notes on a journey from Cornhill to Grand Cairo* (California, Createspace Independent Publishing Platform, 2014).
Turner, William *A Booke of the nature & properties as well of the Bathes in England* (Arnold Birckman, 1652).
Urquhart, Cath, *The Times Holiday Handbook* (Norfolk, Navigator Guides, 2006).
Veblen, Thorstein, *The Theory of the Leisure Class* (Oxford University Press, 2009).
Victoria, Queen of Great Britain and D, Duff, *Victoria in the Highlands: the personal journal of HM Queen Victoria* (Zurich, Muller, 1968).
Walton, J. K., *The English Seaside Resort: A Social History 1750–1914* (Leicester University Press, 1983).
Wenham, Simon, *Pleasure Boating on the Thames: A History of Salter Bros 1858–present* (Simon Wenham, 2014).
West, Thomas *A Guide to the Lakes* (London, Richardson and Urquhart, 1780).
Wolmar, Christian, *Fire and Steam: How the Railways Transformed Britain* (London, Atlantic Books, 2008).
Wordsworth, Dorothy, *Grasmere Journals* (Oxford, Oxford Paperbacks, 1993).
Wordsworth, Dorothy, *Recollections of a tour made in Scotland AD 1803* (Edinburgh, David Douglas, 1984).
Wortley Montagu, Lady Mary, *The Letters and Works of Lady Mary Montagu Volume One* (Forgotten Books, 2018).

Index

Advertisements 19, 99, 140, 170, 199
Airbnb 148, 229
Airlines 163, 199–200, 202
Albania 231
Alps, the 38, 45–6, 228
Angel Inn, Grantham, Lincolnshire 97
Around the World in 80 Days (TV series) 191, 193
Austen, Jane 20–21, 29
Australia 200–201
Away Resorts 137, 147–8, 232

Ballin, Albert 172
B&Bs 96, 105, 131–3, 206
Bank Holidays 104
Bath, Somerset 17, 18, 20–30, 39, 69
Beach, The (film) 192–3
Beaches *see* Seaside towns
Benidorm, Spain 157–9
Benidorm (TV series) 190
Bergen, Norway 167, 181
Blackburn, Lancashire 125, 130
Blackpool, Lancashire 77, 85, 86
 in Wakes Weeks 123–4, 126–7, 129–30, 132, 134–5
Boating 52–5, 109–10, 112–13
Bognor Regis, West Sussex 75, 142–3
Bournemouth, Dorset 91, 214–15
Boutique hotels 106, 205
Boys' clubs 114
Branson, Richard 199–200
Brighton (Brighthelmstone), East Sussex 70, 71–5, 77, 87, 102
British Airways (BA) 155, 199–200, 202

Brougham and Vaux, Henry Brougham, Baron 152–3
Brown's, Mayfair, London 99
Bulgaria 161
Burney, Fanny 30, 51, 73
Butlins 104, 137–46, 147, 149–50, 190
Buxton, Derbyshire 17, 18, 25–8, 67, 91

Caister-on-Sea, Norfolk 138–9, 147
Calais, France 36–7
Camping 112–16, 118–19, 121, 138, 207–8
Canals 79, 80, 124
Cannes, France 152–3
Caribbean, the 175, 179, 199, 200
Cenis, Mont, France 38, 46
Center Parcs 137, 145–7, 219
Charles II, King 19, 34
Cheltenham, Gloucestershire 30
Claridge's, Mayfair, London 99
Claude Glasses 53–4
Climate change 227–8, 231, 236, 237
Connaught, the, Mayfair, London 99
Cook, Thomas 83–4, 141–2, 155, 177, 198
COVID-19 pandemic 211–23, 226
Crete, Greece 161–2
Croatia 161, 164, 179, 193, 203
Croyde, Devon 214, 222
Cruise ships 167–81, 219, 220, 227
Cumbria 55–9, 89, 105
Cunard, Samuel 169–70, 173, 174, 176–7
Cunningham, Joseph 114, 138
Cycling 111–12, 115, 116, 118, 145

Defoe, Daniel 23, 55
Destinations Travel Show 225–6
Devonshire, Dukes of 26, 28, 87, 99
Dickens, Charles 84, 87, 169–70
Dippers 71, 72–4
Diseases 22, 67, 70–71, 89, 212
Dorset 51–2
Douglas, Isle of Man 133
Dover, Kent 36–7, 153
Dovercourt Camp, Essex 140
Dubrovnik, Croatia 161, 164, 179, 193
Duty Free (TV series) 189–90

Eastbourne, East Sussex 87, 90, 142
East India Company 51
EasyJet 202, 219
Echo tourism 58
Edward VII, King 91
Egerton, John 52, 53
Egypt 141, 169
Eldorado (TV series) 191
Elizabeth I, Queen 17–18, 97, 98
Elizabeth II, Queen 62
English Civil War 19, 34
Epsom, Surrey 19, 20, 91
Eryri National Park (Snowdonia) 216–19, 222, 230
Euston, the (hotel), London 100
Excursion trains 82–4
Expedia 148, 198
Factory Acts 92, 104
Fairs 76, 81, 130
Fawlty Towers (TV series) 189, 190–91
Filey, North Yorkshire 140
Films 183–6, 193, 195
Fitzgerald, F. Scott and Zelda 153–4

Florence, Italy 38, 39, 43, 44, 230–31
France 19, 96, 152, 175
French Revolution 47, 54, 74
see also Paris, France
Franco, Francisco 157–8
Friendly Societies 81, 92

Gap years 36, 43, 200
Gastropubs 96, 108, 209
Gatwick Airport 152, 155
George IV, King 63, 72, 74–5
Germany 19, 119, 172–3
Glamping 146–7, 208
Glencoe, Scotland 60–61
Gleneagles Hotel, the, Perth and Kinross 103–4, 233
Global nomads 234–5
Grand Hotel, Covent Garden, London 99
Grand Tour 33–47, 84, 90
Greece 161–2, 163–4, 179, 184–5, 232
Greenwich Mean Time 89
Gunn, Martha 73–4

Haiti 180
Harberton, Florence Wallace Pomeroy, Viscountess 111–12
Harrogate, North Yorkshire 19, 29, 30
Hastings, East Sussex 75, 87
Health clubs 27
Henry VIII, King 17
Hi-di-Hi! (TV series) 137, 189, 190
Highlands, Scotland 60–63, 89, 103–4
Holding, Thomas Hiram 114–15
Holiday (TV series) 187–9, 192
Holiday, The (film) 195
Holiday camps / parks 104, 114, 137–50
Holydays 16, 34, 75, 81, 104
Hop farms 116–18
Horizon Holidays 154–5

Horses 84, 98
Hotels 95–108, 121, 153–4, 205–6
Hove, East Sussex 71, 72

Icon of the Seas (cruise ship) 168, 173–4
Industrial Revolution 50–51
see also Railways
Inns 97–9, 108
Instagram 43, 49, 230
Internet 148, 163, 192, 198–209
social media 43, 229, 263
Isle of Man 133, 138
Isle of Wight 147
Italy 156
see also Rome, Italy; Venice, Italy

James Bond (film series) 185
Jerome, Jermone K. 109–10, 113–14
Johnson, Samuel 61
Jones, Inigo 34

Kent 70, 116–17, 236

Lake District, Cumbria 55–9, 89, 105
Lancashire 124, 125, 127, 135–6
see also Blackpool, Lancashire
Langham, the, London 102
Levante, Spain 158–9
Llandudno, Conwy 82, 85–6, 133, 142, 222
Lloret de Mar, Spain 160
Lodging houses 21, 99, 131
Lomond, Loch, Scotland 60, 61
London 19, 36, 40–41, 90, 208–9
hotels 99–100, 106–7
Lusitania (cruise ship) 174

Madeira 22
Mallorca, Spain 162–3, 165
Mamma Mia! (film) 195
Margate, Kent 70–71, 75, 77, 142

Mary I, Queen of Scotland 18
Mauretania (cruise ship) 173
Mediterranean, the 91, 151–65, 171–2, 179, 232
Melba, Nellie 102
Menorca, Spain 162–3
Milan, Italy 44
Milner York, the, North Yorkshire 101
Monasteries 96–7
Morecambe, Lancashire 130, 134–5
Mostyn family 82, 85

Napoleon III, Emperor 91
Napoleonic Wars 41, 47
Nash, Beau (Richard) 20, 22, 29
National Parks 59, 158–9, 216–17, 230
Nice, France 153, 154

Old Bell, Malmesbury, Wiltshire 97
Overtourism 25, 59, 153, 192–3, 227
in Europe 42–3, 164–5, 179, 231

P&O 169, 170–72
Package holidays 52, 154–6, 159–61, 200, 205
Paid holiday 92, 104, 127–9, 139, 204
Palin, Michael 191, 193
Pandemics 211–23, 226
Paris, France 37–8, 46, 47, 153, 155
Parminter, Jane and Mary 45–6, 47
Peninsula, the, London 106–7
Picturesque tours 55
Pontins 114, 138, 142, 144–5, 147
Portland, William Cavendish-Bentinck, Duke of 58
Portugal 22, 164, 169, 203

Index

Potters Resorts 139, 147
Prince Regent (George VI) 63, 72, 74–5
Prinzessin Victoria Luise (cruise ship) 172–3
Pubs 96, 108, 209

Railways 80–90, 99–104, 110, 112, 228
Raitz, Vladimir 154–6
Rambling 120
Rhyl, Denbighshire 85, 127
Ripley, Surrey 111
Romances 24, 185
Roman Holiday (film) 184
Romanov, House of 90, 153
Rome, ancient 15, 17, 34
Rome, Italy 34, 38, 40, 41–2, 46
Rough Guides to the World (TV series) 191–2
Royal Caribbean 167–8, 175
Russia 175–6
Ryanair 202

Sandy Balls Holiday Village, Hampshire 148
Savoy, the, London 102
Sawday, Alistair 206
Scandinavia 167, 281, 231
Scarborough, North Yorkshire 19, 66–70, 76–7, 102, 107
Scotland 60–63, 89, 103–4, 233
Scott, Walter 61–2
Seaside towns 65–78, 85–91, 104–5
  see also Wakes Weeks
Seasonal employment 116–18
Self-catering holidays 207
Sheik, The (film) 183–4
Sherwood Forest, Nottinghamshire 145
Ships, cruise 167–81, 219, 220, 227
Shirley Valentine (film) 184–5
Sidmouth, Devon 89
Skegness, Lincolnshire 143

Slave Trade 59
Soane, John 40–41
Social media 43, 229, 230
Southport, Merseyside 87, 91, 124, 126, 131
Spain 152, 157–64, 169, 179, 231
Spa towns 17–30, 66, 91
Spread Eagle, the, Midhurst, West Sussex 97–8, 106
Star, the, Alfriston, East Sussex 97
Staycations 207, 219, 232
Stephenson, George 79–80
St Leonards, East Sussex 87
Streatley, Berkshire 113
Summer Holiday (musical) 185–6
Summertime (film) 184
Sustainability 227–8
Swimming 66, 72–3, 86

Tagus (passenger ship) 170–71
Temperance groups 83, 92
Terrorism 206–7
Thackeray, William Makepeace 54, 171–2
Thailand 192–3, 201, 207, 234
Thames Valley 109, 112–13
Timetables 89
Titanic (passenger ship) 173, 174
Torquay, Devon 89–91, 189, 190–91
Torremolinos, Spain 159, 187
Travel Agents 83–4, 159–60, 163, 198
TUI 163, 219–20
Tunbridge Wells, Kent 19, 20, 23, 30, 91
Turkey 152, 203, 220
Turner, William 16, 17
Turnpikes 35, 36, 67, 71, 98
TV programmes 145, 186–95

USA 169, 199–200

Valentino, Rudolf 153, 184

Van life 186, 235
Venice, Italy 34, 36, 38–40, 164, 179
Victoria, Queen 62–3, 110, 153
Viking Saturn (cruise ship) 167, 177
Virgin Holidays 199–200
Virtual holidays 216, 232–3

Wakes weeks 16, 125–35
Wales 19, 89, 119
  see also Eryri National Park (Snowdonia); Llandudno, Conwy
Walpole, Horace 28, 38
Warner's 138, 139, 140, 142
Webster, Elizabeth 46, 47
Westmorland 55
Weymouth, Dorset 72
Whicker, Alan 186–7
Wine tourism 235–6
Wish You Were Here.? (TV series) 187, 188–9, 192
Wittie, Dr 66–7, 72, 76
Wordsworth, Dorothy 56–8, 60–61
Wordsworth, William 54, 56–8, 60, 61
Workcations 234
World War I 118, 174
World War II 105, 131, 140, 154–5, 174
Wortley Montagu, Mary 44
Wye Valley 52–5

York, North Yorkshire 88, 100–101
Youth hostels 104, 119–20, 121, 234
Yugoslavia 161

Zaragoza, Pedro 157–8